Terrorism and the
Politics of Fear

Terrorism and the Politics of Fear

David L. Altheide

ALTAMIRA
PRESS

A Division of
ROWMAN & LITTLEFIELD PUBLISHERS, INC.
Lanham • New York • Toronto • Oxford

AltaMira Press

A Division of Rowman & Littlefield Publishers, Inc.
A wholly owned subsidary of The Rowman & Littlefield Publishing Group, Inc.
4501 Forbes Boulevard, Suite 200
Lanham, MD 20706
www.altamirapress.com

PO Box 317, Oxford, OX2 9RU, UK

British Library Cataloguing in Publication Information Available

Library of Congress Cataloging-in-Publication Data

Altheide, David L.
  Terrorism and the politics of fear / David L. Altheide.
    p. cm.
  Includes bibliographical references and index.
  ISBN-13: 978-0-7591-0918-6 (cloth : alk. paper)
  ISBN-10: 0-7591-0918-4 (cloth : alk. paper)
  ISBN-13: 978-0-7591-0919-3 (pbk. : alk. paper)
  ISBN-10: 0-7591-0919-2 (pbk. : alk. paper)
  1. Mass media—Social aspects—United States. 2. Mass media and public
opinion—United States. 3. Terrorism in mass media—United States. 4. Fear—
United States. 5. Propaganda—United States. 6. Social control—United States.
I. Title.

  HN90.M3A47 2006
  302.230973'090511—dc22

                                                                  2005028887

Printed in the United States of America

For our grandchildren and
their friends everywhere

Contents

Preface and Acknowledgments   ix

1   Introduction   1

2   The Social Reality of Fear   15

3   The Mass Media as a Social Institution   47

4   Crime and Terrorism   73

5   Consuming Terrorism   87

6   Terrorism and the Politics of Fear   113

7   The Control Narrative of the Internet   133

8   The Propaganda Project and the Iraq War   157

9   Constructing Pat Tillman   185

10 Conclusion: Beyond the Politics of Fear   207

References   223

Index   241

About the Author   247

Preface and Acknowledgments

This book is about social power and the role that the mass media play in constructing social life. Fear is a scary topic. Most people have experienced fear, but few really understand it. I know it firsthand, and after fifteen years of research on the topic, I also know how others use and exploit fear for their own agendas. That is my topic: the origin, use, and consequences of fear and propaganda for social life. This is very important for me because I have grandchildren, who deserve a future that is free from the politics of fear. By the politics of fear, I mean decision makers' promotion and use of audience beliefs and assumptions about danger, risk, and fear in order to achieve certain goals.

This is my second book about fear. The first one, *Creating Fear: News and the Construction of Crisis* (2002), was in the final stages of production when hijacked aircraft carried death and destruction to New York and Washington, D.C. That work demonstrated that use of the word "fear" is widespread in American life and, increasingly, throughout much of Europe as well. This pervasive use of fear is part of the social construction of reality in the modern age. By this I mean that the meanings and frameworks that are used to make sense out of events are created. I was able to add the following to the preface of that book as it went to press: "The entertainment format, use of visuals, emerging icons of fear, slogans, and especially the emphasis on the fear frame and 'evil' provide many examples of how these attacks contributed to the expansion of the discourse of fear into more attempts at social control."

That sentence set my research agenda for the next four years; this book reports what I discovered during a journey across thousands of documents, including television news reports, documentaries, movies, novels, Internet URLs, several hundred scholarly books and articles, many conversations and much e-mail correspondence with scholars throughout the world, and extensive conversations with colleagues and graduate students working on similar issues. It is not a happy story, but it needs to be told; the following pages give an account of how fear is socially constructed, packaged, and presented through the mass media by politicians and decision makers to protect us by offering more control over our lives and culture. Fear entertains us and helps others control us. But the politics continue even when the specific fears subside; programs that are enacted to protect us at one point in time endure to influence other social action. This process has expanded and accelerated with our entertainment-oriented popular culture as we are constantly given more things to fear, which tend to accumulate, socially hibernate for a time, but then are reawakened by the next crisis and provide audiences with a context and interpretative frameworks for believing that "here we go again" and that this crisis is merely an extension of the fear stuff that gave us the others. And so on.

My approach to this project is informed by symbolic interactionism and the social construction of reality. Power can be defined as the ability to define a situation for self and others. The mass media are a major source of audience's definitions of fear and issues. This book illustrates how symbolic meanings about safety, danger, and fear can lead to major institutional changes and even war. The following chapters illustrate how media representations inform audience's and decision makers' perspectives and understandings. The politics of fear is built on audience perceptions and beliefs about the nature and source of fear. Fears associated with beliefs and statements by powerful claims makers can be tracked over time using qualitative content analysis. This approach has been set forth in several publications and is now widely used throughout social science (cf. Altheide 1996).

This has been a long-term project. Graduate seminars, work and assistance from graduate assistants, and helpful suggestions from colleagues inform the materials in this book. In particular, students in the seminar "Justice and the Mass Media (JUS 588)" collaborated on course projects that provided insights and information that were particularly relevant for the material in chapter 4. Drafts of several of the chapters appeared elsewhere:

Chapter 3: "The Mass Media." In *Handbook of Symbolic Interactionism*, edited by Larry T. Reynolds and Nancy J. Herman-Kinney, 657–84. Walnut Creek, Calif.: AltaMira Press, 2003. Courtesy of Rowman & Littlefield Publishers.

Chapter 4: "Mass Media, Crime and the Discourse of Fear." In *La Tele-visione del Crimine*, edited by Gabrio Forti and Marta Bertolino, 287–306. Milano, Italy: Vita e Pensiero, 2005. Courtesy of Vita e Pensiero.
Chapter 5: "Consuming Terrorism." *Symbolic Interaction* 27, no. 3 (2004): 289–308. Courtesy of the University of California Press.
Chapter 6: "Terrorism and the Politics of Fear." *Cultural Studies↔Critical Methodologies*, edited by Norman K. Denzin. Thousand Oaks, Calif.: Sage Publications, forthcoming. Courtesy of Sage Publications.
Chapter 7: "The Control Narrative of the Internet." *Symbolic Interaction* 27, no. 2 (2004): 223–45. Courtesy of the University of California Press.
Chapter 8: With Jennifer N. Grimes. "War Programming: The Propaganda Project and the Iraq War." *The Sociological Quarterly* 46 (2005): 617–43. Courtesy of the University of California Press.

Several of the projects reported in this book benefited from graduate student contributions, including Michael Coyle, Kimber Williams, and Jennifer Grimes (who coauthored a different draft of a paper that informed chapter 8). My undergraduate students also contributed by indulging my modest attempts to underscore data with meaningful interpretations. Virginia "Ginny" Hill, an exceptional instructor at The Evergreen State College, graciously permitted me to engage her creative students with early versions of many of these ideas. Unlike most journal editors in social science, Simon Gottschalk and Norman Denzin are among the most helpful and encouraging editors and inspire and promote new ideas. Many colleagues contributed valuable ideas, critiques, and suggestions during the past few years: Arthur Vidich, Gray Cavender, John Johnson, Richard Ericson, Aaron Doyle, Frank Furedi, Gary Marx, and Randel Hanson. I am also indebted to University of Missouri faculty members Jay Gubrium, Clarence Lo, Peter Hall, and Charles Davis for providing an intellectual forum to present some of my ideas, which were subsequently improved with comments from Joel Best, another speaker. I must also thank Professor Gabrio Forti (Professore ordinario di Diritto penale e Criminologia nella Facoltà di Giurisprudenza dell'Università Cattolica del S.C. di Milano), who organized an exceptional seminar for scholars investigating crime and the mass media. Colleagues Annamarie Oliverio and Pat Lauderdale provided insights and perspectives through their conversations and work (Lauderdale and Oliverio 2005; Oliverio 1998). Steve Chermak, Martin Innes, Paul Mason, and Aaron Doyle were among the participants who provided helpful suggestions. My longtime colleague Robert Snow, who helped develop our original formulations about media logic and the power of communications formats, remains an inspiration even in retirement. Mitch Allen (AltaMira Press), widely regarded as one of the most knowledgeable and supportive editors in social science, was particularly helpful. My brother, Duane, provides many examples of power and resistance. My wife and love, Carla, still believes in my work, forgives my inattentiveness when I draft papers in my head, and provides more love and understanding than anyone deserves. I am most fortunate.

1

Introduction

It was the lightest tap on my door that I've ever heard in my life. . . . I opened the door and I seen the man in the dress greens and I knew. I immediately knew. But I thought that if, as long as I didn't let him in, he couldn't tell me. And then it—none of that would've happened. So he kept saying, "Ma'am, I need to come in." And I kept telling him, "I'm sorry, but you can't come in."

—Paula Zasadny when she learned that her nineteen-year-old daughter, Holly McGeogh, had been killed by a bomb in Kirkuk, Iraq; from HBO documentary "Last Letters Home" and Herbert (2004)

This is a book about power: Paula Zasadny felt like the loved ones of more than 2,200 dead American soldiers and an estimated 100,000 dead Iraqi civilians, although we never heard any of the Iraqi stories. Paula Zasadny had very little power. She and thousands of other parents who sent their loved ones off to war believed that their government told them the truth and was doing the right thing. While one is tempted to blame zealous politicians for the death and destruction that has occurred in Iraq, it is not that simple. Of course, politicians' decision making played a big part in the Iraq War, but they also depended on propaganda and a willing U.S. Congress and American public. This book is about the politics of fear and the war-making process that killed Holly McGeogh. The war in Iraq is part of an expanding politics of fear, or decision makers' promotion and use of audience beliefs and assumptions about danger, risk, and fear in order to achieve certain goals. Political leaders rely on fear to promote social control of citizens. The mass media are the most important source of information and social control because they have helped make fear a part of our life, our language, and our point of view. This book examines how entertaining news and popular culture meshed well with two decades of fear of crime and eventually terrorism. I argue that authorities promote fear among citizens because they know that concerns for personal safety will tempt even the most cynical observer to hand over their lives for protection. This chapter sets forth a basic argument and an overview of the rest of the book. My basic thesis is that fear as entertainment informs the production of popular culture and news, generates profits, and enables political decision makers to control audiences through propaganda. This process is referred to as the politics of fear.

PLAYING TO FEAR

This is a story about fear, dread, death, terror, and entertainment. One way to illustrate the connection between entertainment and fear is to liken it to a baseball game. There is the history of baseball that fans know and appreciate, the key players, the particular season and rivals, and the consequences of a particular game. As all fans realize, the outcome of a particular game is of interest, but it is always contextualized by the previous considerations. The context is what is important for baseball, fear, and war. All these are brought to us by the mass media and popular culture.

Let me locate myself in this story. I was at an Arizona Diamondbacks baseball game on May 1, 2003, watching batting practice just prior to the first pitch, while mindless advertisements played on the JumboTron to entertain early arrivals, who were not really baseball fans but had become accustomed to visual action and entertainment. As I enjoyed a beer and followed the flight of big-league smashes landing in the outfield seats, a hurried voice interrupted the promo about an upcoming concert and urged the fans to watch live coverage of the president of the United States, who was about to make an important announcement. Field activity stopped. Sluggers took off their batting gloves and averted their eyes to the massive screen in Bank One Ballpark, named after a bank but built and planned by Jerry Colangelo, the man in charge of the Diamondbacks.

Jerry Colangelo, a local politician, who took pride in escaping "Hell's Kitchen," parlayed some street smarts and good breaks in landing the Phoenix Suns basketball team—and eventually the Arizona Diamondbacks—into a fortune. He hobnobbed with local politicians and, like most people with wealth, voted Republican and supported the most recent U.S. war in Iraq. Colangelo and many other powerful people in the United States thought that it was perfectly appropriate to invade Afghanistan and then Iraq as part of the war on terrorism after the attacks of September 11, 2001. It did not matter that there was no evidence that Iraq was involved in the attacks on the United States or that it had any weapons that could harm us. He and the owners of other major league baseball teams went along with the political propagandists to have fans sing "God Bless America" during the seventh-inning stretch, prior to "Take Me Out to the Ball Game." He saw nothing at all wrong with interrupting America's pastime with a political stunt; after all, the difference between mass-media fantasy and political reality had long since disappeared. So we stared at the JumboTron as President George W. Bush, costumed like a fighter pilot, landed on an aircraft carrier, the *Abraham Lincoln*. He had his picture taken with sailors in front of a banner that read, "Mission Accomplished." He told the sailors and the media representatives, who had been assembled for this ultimate photo opportunity, that "major combat operations in Iraq have ended." The president grinned, the sailors cheered on cue, the fans cheered the JumboTron—but I booed—and soon the game began.

Packaged patriotism is cheap; authentic patriotism is priceless. The Iraq War gave us more of the former. In the seventh inning, some fans sang "God Bless America," but I did not. I never do. I only sing "Take Me Out to the Ball Game." Most major league baseball players follow their instructions and also pause during the seventh inning to participate in what an astute sports columnist referred to as "patriotic packaging." Not all players play the patriotic game. Carlos Delgado, a Toronto Blue Jays slugger from Puerto Rico, prefers to sit in the dugout and tries to avoid standing with hat in hand. He, along with some other Puerto Rican notables, has tried unsuccessfully for several years to stop the U.S. naval testing off the island of Vieques. Of course, Delgado has been chastised by some fans for his independence.

Delgado's protest, of course, is political rather than musical. The Puerto Rican slugger objects to America's Iraq policy—"the stupidest war ever," he calls it—and he has chosen "God Bless America" to register his dissent. Though he continues to stand for both the American and the Canadian national anthems, Delgado has declined to participate this season in the seventh-inning solemnity that baseball introduced after the terrorist attacks of September 11, 2001:

> "I'm not trying to get anyone mad," Delgado told The New York Times this week. "This is my personal feeling. I don't want to draw attention to myself or go out of my way to protest. If I make the last out of the seventh inning, I'll stand there. But I'd rather be in the dugout." (Sullivan 2004)

The war in Iraq raged for several more baseball seasons even though some Bush supporters and generals acknowledged that most goals of the war had not been met. Since the president played aviator, some 2,000 Americans have died and more than 10,000 injured, along with an estimated

100,000 Iraqis. Private Jess Givens did not see the presidential charade before he was killed that day in Iraq. This is how his wife reacted to the news of his death:

> Melissa Givens was told by a chaplain that her husband, Pfc. Jesse Givens, who was 34, had drowned when his tank fell into the Euphrates River. Distraught, she insisted that the chaplain was lying. But she said that was O.K., because she would never tell anyone that he had lied. She said he could walk away and she would just forget about the whole thing. (Herbert 2004)

The Middle East is more fragmented and alien from the Western world than at any time in the past fifty years, and the United States is hated throughout the First, Second, and Third worlds. Yet politicians would continue to play to fear as other crises would be contextualized and informed by the Iraqi experience.

Toughness plays well in a climate of fear. President Bush started the war with ample assistance from Congress, a compliant news media, and an embarrassingly uninformed American electorate. Chapter 8 explains how this war was actually planned in 1992 by a group called the Project for a New American Century, which included future Bush cabinet members (e.g., Dick Cheney, Colin Powell, and Paul Wolfowitz) and influential publishers like William Kristol, who had been former Vice President Dan Quayle's chief of staff. Most Americans never heard of this group because the compliant news media did not want to be critical of the Bush agenda after the infamous 9/11 attacks, and with a few exceptions, refrained from even mentioning it until after Bush played fighter pilot. Indeed, Bush was reelected despite incontrovertible evidence that he and his administration misled the American people about the reasons and necessity to go to war. His competition, Senator John Kerry, tried to sound tougher and more bellicose than the incumbent.

Kerry also believed in terror and fear. Kerry argued that Bush was wrong in the rationale for going to war, had done a miserable job of guiding the war effort, and had enacted draconian domestic surveillance programs (e.g., the USA Patriot Act) that threatened the civil liberties of all citizens. (In later chapters, it will be noted that journalists referred to people concerned about civil liberties, especially government surveillance, as "privacy advocates.") Kerry proclaimed that he would be tougher on terrorists, would "track down and kill Osama bin Laden," and would make America stronger—brutal words for a presidential candidate. He did not say that we would bring bin Laden to "justice" or that he would have bin Laden judged by the world; he simply said that he would kill him. Kerry also vowed to protect us more by patrolling our borders. Kerry knew that the mood of the country was following the tone of countless newspaper and television news reports about the horrendous bin Laden and his loose-knit organization, al Qaeda. Popular culture and network television news, particularly Fox (headed by Roger Ailes, former media consultant for Richard Nixon, Ronald Reagan, George Bush, and corporate giant Philip Morris), presented U.S. audiences with ample propaganda about the horrors of Afghanistan and Iraq. Congress was aware of the media and political mood about "taking it to the enemy," so at the start of the war, it did not pay much attention to how the nearly $4 billion a month being spent on these military ventures was distributed to a handful of contractors (e.g., Halliburton, whose previous chief executive officer [CEO] was Dick Cheney) without any bidding, even though a whistle-blower, Bunnatine Greenhouse, had complained a month before the start of the war that Halliburton inappropriately received a five-year contract instead of a one-year deal (Zagorin and Burger 2004). The corruption eventually became so blatant that the FBI, Congress, and the Pentagon opened investigations. Vice President Cheney, former CEO of Halliburton, objected to being asked about some blatant improprieties and argued that these investigations into contractual improprieties were "political." Indeed, on June 22, 2004, he told Senator Patrick Leahy, who was involved in hearings about Halliburton's improprieties, "to fuck yourself." More tough talk.

Street-level discourse is permissible in a world of fear. It sounds tough, and within the discourse of fear, toughness trumps intelligence and sophistication. Recall that former President Reagan drew on his acting background, and when faced with possible plans for tax increases that he would oppose, he quoted the gun-toting character in the movie *Dirty Harry*, to "make my day." Part of the propaganda hype for the first Gulf War in 1991 starred President George H.W. Bush proclaiming to members of Congress that "Saddam Hussein was going to get his ass kicked" (*Los Angeles Times*, March 6, 1991, p. E1). Numerous T-shirts, bumper stickers, and street signs added to the lingo of fighter pilots about "kicking ass." One notable T-shirt read, "Hussein—I'll Kick Your Ass and Take Your Gas" (*Washington Post*, October 21, 1990, p. F2). The younger George Bush also knew a good street slogan and used it after sixty-five soldiers had died following his jet ride to the aircraft carrier. When told that Iraqi fighters would be attacking American troops, Bush replied, "Bring them on" (*USA Today*, July 2, 2003). This phrase became very popular throughout the campaign and was used by several Democratic challengers as well.

Fearful messages have strong effects on the political process partly because leaders can tap the emotional churning from audiences' basic concerns about safety for themselves and their families. Indeed, fear is such a basic emotion that humans probably could not survive without it. There is clearly a biological and psychological component of fear; there are physical responses to fear, including adrenaline charges that provide the bursts of energy and strength that become part of personal heroics and historical lore. The psychological dimension of fear may be tapped by propaganda about threat and death. These images and feelings can be generated not only by real, immediate threats, such as one's child being hurt, but also by skillful use of symbols and language, including photos. Psychologists who study this aspect of fear report profound changes in people who are confronted by scenes and images of death, including the following: (1) having more favorable evaluations of people with similar religious and political beliefs and more unfavorable evaluations of those who differ on these dimensions, (2) being more punitive toward moral transgressors and more benevolent to heroic individuals, (3) being more physically aggressive toward others with dissimilar political orientations, and (4) striving more vigorously to meet cultural standards of value (Pyszczynski, Greenberg, and Solomon 2003; Solomon, Greenberg, and Pyszczynski 2004).

Moreover, the researchers examined how people responded to different scenarios and types of leaders (Solomon et al. 2004). They found that when asked to think about the events of 9/11 and their own death, support for President Bush increased noticeably. The researchers argued that part of this can be explained by the associated images of the destruction of 9/11 plus the often-repeated slogans about combating an evil enemy. They conclude,

> We also do not mean to imply that all support for President Bush is necessarily a defensive reaction to concerns about death. And although it is a matter of public record that President Bush's re-election campaign has been carefully crafted to emphasize the war on terrorism and domestic security, the strategic use of fear to advance political agendas has a long history in American politics (all politics for that matter) and is by no means confined to the Republican Party.
>
> However, the fact that a subtle, brief manipulation of psychological conditions (asking people to think about their own death or the events of 9/11) produced such striking differences in political preferences (for charismatic leaders in general and President Bush in particular) suggests that close elections could be decided as a result of non-rational terror management concerns. We'd like to think that Americans across the political spectrum would agree that this is antithetical to the democratic ideal that voting behavior should be the result of rational choice based on an informed understanding of the relevant issues. National elections are no guarantee against totalitarian outcomes. (Solomon et al. 2004, p. 15)

The politics of fear, then, is central to the psychology of fear. Leaders learn to promote fear in their media messages. For example, the artful use of terrorist attacks was an explicit strategy during the presidential campaign of 2004:

Republican leaders said yesterday that they would repeatedly remind the nation of the Sept. 11 attacks as their convention opens in New York City today. (*New York Times*, August 30, 2004)

The Bush campaign followed the guidelines, especially three ads that ran in sixteen critical states:

All three ads are designed to highlight President Bush's leadership amid economic uncertainty and national security challenges. Two of the new spots show fleeting images of the World Trade twin towers' collapse, with an American flag flying over the debris and firemen working in the smoldering wreckage. Closing the images is the tagline: "President Bush: Steady Leadership in Times of Change." (On Line News Hour, March 5, 2004; www.pbs.org/newshour/updates/bushads_03-05-04.html)

So offensive were the ads to the families of those killed in the 9/11 attacks that one organization, Sept. 11 Families for Peaceful Tomorrows, asked candidates and political parties not to use the images. A few comments illustrate the depth of feeling:

"But to show the horror of 9/11 in the background, that's just some advertising agency's attempt to grab people by the throat."
    One of the ads, titled "Safer, Stronger," which also includes a Spanish version, features a one-second shot of firefighters removing the flag-draped remains of a victim from the twisted debris. Both ads showcase ground-zero imagery with shots of two firefighters.
    "It's as sick as people who stole things out of the place," said firefighter Tommy Fee of Queens Rescue Squad 270. "The image of firefighters at Ground Zero should not be used for this stuff, for politics."
    "It's a slap in the face of the murders of 3,000 people," Monica Gabrielle, whose husband died in the twin tower attacks, told the New York Daily News. "This is a president who has resisted the creation of the 9/11 Commission. . . . For anyone to use 9/11 for political gain is despicable." (On Line News Hour, March 5, 2004; www.pbs.org/newshour/updates/bushads_03-05-04.html)

Later, Vice President Cheney urged voters to support President Bush and be safe: "If we make the wrong choice, the danger is that we will get hit again, that we'll be hit in a way that is devastating." As one undecided voter said of Bush, "He has conviction. . . . He's taking the fight to the terrorists. . . . I love my kids. I want my kids to be safe" (ABC affiliate, Phoenix, Arizona, October 13, 2004). The message about fear carried the day for many Americans. A CNN analysis of why people voted found that Bush supporters were more likely to be worried about terrorism and also believed that the Iraq War made them more secure. Bush won the election of 2004, the war raged, more people died, parents wept, and fear reigned. It's getting late in the game, and we are losing.

My argument in this book is not that fear is bad but that it is promoted and exploited by leaders for their own survival and policies rather than that of their audiences. The challenge is to recognize how fear is being used politically. I take note of a recommendation by psychologists who show how focusing on one's own mortality and death can influence political decision making:

> As a culture, we should also work to teach our children and encourage our citizens to vote with their "heads" rather than their "hearts." And it may also be helpful to raise awareness of how concerns about mortality affect human behavior. Hopefully, such measures will encourage people to make choices based on the political qualifications and positions of the candidates rather than on defensive needs to preserve psychological equanimity in response to reminders of death. (Solomon et al. 2004, p. 15)

AN APPROACH TO THE POLITICS OF FEAR

My approach to the study of the politics of fear is well grounded in sociological theory, mass communications research, and qualitative research methods. First, I start with a basic assumption that the most important thing that one can know about another person is what he or she takes for granted. What do people assume to be the order of things, the rock-bottom reality of how the world operates, the source of problems, and likely threats? Fundamental changes in the mass-mediated world cannot be understood without careful consideration of culture and symbolic construction of meanings that are produced by a few and shared by many. Second, I assume that it is the meaning of things that drives people to action or nonaction, and these meanings are derived through a communication process that involves symbols (e.g., language) and images. Third, the mass media and popular culture are the major sources of information for most people about events with which they do not have direct experience. These media involve television, radio, newspapers, magazines, movies, videos, video games, and conversations with peers that are informed largely by these sources. Fourth, many of the experiences that we have with the mass media provide a language and perspective for viewing events in our daily lives. Fifth, many of the experiences that we have in everyday life tend to be consistent with our media messages.

These theoretical assumptions inform a basic methodological point: important symbolic messages can be studied by comparative systematic investigation of mass-media publications over a period of time. This qualitative media approach has been well documented and used rather extensively by scholars in several disciplines (Altheide 1996). Its specific application to the politics of fear involves "tracking discourse," or following certain issues, words, themes, and frames over a period of time, across different issues, and across different news media. Tracking discourse is a qualitative document analysis technique that applies an ethnographic approach to content analysis to new information bases, such as NEXIS, that are accessible through computer technology (Altheide 1996; cf. van Dijk 1988; Grimshaw and Burke 1994; Weiler and Pearce 1992; Wuthnow 1992). While there are many differences in some of the approaches, all share an assumption that symbolic representations are enmeshed in a context of other assumptions that are not stated as such. Our approach blends interpretive, ethnographic, and ethnomethodological approaches with media logic, particularly studies of news organizational culture, information technology, and communication formats. The capacity to examine numerous documents with specific conceptually informed search terms and logic provides a new way of "exploring" documents, applying "natural experimental" research designs to the materials, and retrieving and analyzing individual documents qualitatively. Moreover, because the technology permits immediate access to an enormous amount of material, comparative exploration, conceptual refinement, and data collection and analysis can cover a longer time period than other technologies can.

My basic argument is that the politics of fear trades on audience beliefs, expectations, and taken-for-granted meanings about social reality, threats, and the nature of those who pose the threats—namely, "outsiders," or "the other." We know from previous research that the entertainment media promote fear as a feature of entertainment, most commonly crime in the past thirty years (Surette 1998). But there is more to it than merely repeating news reports night after night that crime is rampant, dangerous, and threatening to us all. The numerous crime shows, movies, and video games are also not enough to explain the rise of the politics of fear, but they do add a lot to the entertainment mix of experience that Americans have about the nature, appearance, and threat of the "other."

PLAN OF THE BOOK

Much of this book's focus is on the war on terrorism that followed the death, destruction, and official government reactions to the September 11, 2001, crashing of hijacked airliners into the World Trade Center and the Pentagon and the downing of an aircraft that was reportedly destined for another target in Washington, D.C. Unlike some other good books on the 9/11 attacks, I try to place the position of the United States in a context of social control and change. I focus on how fear has become incorporated into political decisions, language, and much of everyday life. I wish to understand the reactions and definitions associated with these acts that gave special meaning to the deadly deeds by an outlaw organization and quickly came to mean an all-out war against "evil" that pitted the United States against most of the world, including numerous Middle Eastern countries, but also the United Nations and allies in Europe and beyond. My focus is on how this happened.

Much of the book examines how the mass media and popular culture contributed to the political use of fear. Chapter 2, "The Social Reality of Fear," provides some context, including an overview of the rise of the politics of fear, especially in the United States, and how this is experienced in everyday life. Following an examination of how fear relates to force and social control, brief analyses are given of the significance and consequences of the politics of fear in recent wars; crime legislation; the drug war; the complicity of business, universities, and religion in playing to fear; and the growing acceptance of uniforms and the look of control.

Chapter 3, "The Mass Media as a Social Institution," offers an analysis of social institutions transformed through media in order to illustrate how the logic and forms of media perspectives have transformed much of the social stock of knowledge we share. A major thesis in this book is that terrorism and the politics of fear are constructed by media logic and the growing impact of mass-media formats on our everyday lives and social institutions. The mass media are significant for our lives because they are both form and content of cultural categories and experience. As form, the mass media provide the criteria, shape, rhythm, and style of an expanding array of activities, many of which are outside the "communication" process. As content, the new ideas, fashions, vocabularies, and a myriad of types of information (e.g., politics) are acquired through the mass media. A discussion of media logic illustrates how news coverage from other wars is ideological and reflects entertainment formats that promote fear. Media logic is defined as a form of communication and the process through which media transmit and communicate information. Elements of this form include the distinctive features of each medium and the formats used by these media for the organization, the style in which the information is presented, the focus or emphasis on particular characteristics of behavior, and the grammar of media communication. This logic, or the rationale, emphasis, and orientation promoted by media production, processes, and messages, tends to be evocative, encapsulated, highly thematic, familiar to audiences, and easy to use. In a broad sense, media culture refers to the character of such institutions as religion, politics, or sports that develops through the use of media. Specifically, when media logic is employed to present and interpret institutional phenomena, the form and content of those institutions are altered.

Chapter 4, "Crime and Terrorism," discusses how news coverage of war reflects fear and closely resembles two decades of crime news. Crime in particular and fear in general have become a major part of the message as news media throughout the world have adapted "entertainment formats" to attract audiences. One consequence of this emphasis is to promote a discourse of fear, or the pervasive communication, symbolic awareness, and expectation that danger and risk are a central feature of everyday life. As this discourse becomes more common and taken for granted, it influences many aspects of everyday life, including the rapidly expanding popular culture. National and international priorities are influenced by this discourse, as in the United States, where "terrorism" reports are strongly influenced by a long history of crime reports.

Chapter 5, "Consuming Terrorism," describes the mass communications process that linked giving and spending to patriotism, domestic control, and a major foreign policy shift following the terrorist attacks on September 11, 2001. Analysis of news reports and advertisements suggests that popular-culture and mass-media depictions of fear, patriotism, consumption, and victimization contributed to the emergence of a "national identity" and collective action that was fostered by elite decision makers' propaganda and the military–media complex. Initial declarations about recovery and retaliation to promote patriotism became a "war on terrorism" with no end in sight. Global policing that would justify a "first strike" against sovereign governments was socially constructed as commensurate with personal caring and a national identity. These findings are organized around three points: (1) fear supported consumption as a meaningful way for audiences to sustain an identity of substance and character, (2) consumption and giving were joined symbolically as government and business propaganda emphasized common themes of spending/buying to "help the country get back on track," and (3) the absence of a clear target for reprisals contributed to the construction of broad symbolic enemies and goals.

Chapter 6, "Terrorism and the Politics of Fear," develops the argument that the terrorist attacks of 9/11 were socially constructed to have both a specific and a broad meaning. The analysis examines how news reports about terrorism in five nationally prominent U.S. newspapers reflect the terms and discourse associated with the politics of fear. Data were analyzed with a qualitative content analysis method, "tracking discourse," which tracks words, themes, and frames over a period of time, across different issues, and across different news media. While some qualitative materials are presented, the emphasis in this chapter is on the changes in the extent of coverage in news reports linking fear with terrorism and victimization that occurred after 9/11. Examining the prevalence and meaning of the words "fear," "victim," "terrorism," and "crime" eighteen months before and after the attacks of 9/11 shows that there was a dramatic increase in linking terrorism to fear, coverage of crime and fear persisted (but at a very low rate), and there was a large increase in news reports linking terrorism to victim.

Chapter 7, "The Control Narrative of the Internet," expands on how the politics of fear and the penchant for social control reaches well beyond a specific event to include some of the most basic communication processes in our culture. Fear is used as a form of social control; fear of terrorism reflects a politics of fear that cuts through basic communication practices and information technologies as part of everyday life. Internet use promotes social control. This chapter addresses how a control narrative is becoming the story of the Internet. The control narrative refers to the relevance for the communication process and social action of actors' awareness and expectation that symbolic meanings may be monitored and used by diverse audiences for various purposes. The expansion of surveillance, monitoring, and control informs how people use the Internet and suggests changes in private and public communication. Organizational contexts and structures inform individual use as part of a "technological seam," the uneasy fit between everyday life routines and technological formats. Electronic formats and the visual nature of the Internet exemplify a surveillance culture that is fueled by a discourse of fear. Efforts to police the Internet are confounded by the paradox of Internet security that it requires violation and surveillance. Discussion of the implications of this expanding surveillance is informed by an analysis of "Internet filters," surveillance by business and police agents, and "Internet stings."

Chapter 8, "The Propaganda Project and the Iraq War," addresses how the invasion of Iraq was justified to the American people by the most massive propaganda campaign since World War II. One objective of this chapter is to show how the members of the Project for a New American Century (PNAC) had been developing the rationale for the invasion as a "public conspiracy" for more than a decade. The second objective is to describe and clarify why the PNAC's plans for Iraq and for an imperialist foreign policy received very little news media coverage. The third aim of this chapter is to set forth a theoretical argument for analyzing modern propaganda campaigns as a feature of mass-mediated discourse crafted by media logic. Qualitative content analysis of news materials suggests that the news sources and news media shared a logic and perspective about "timely and entertaining news." The PNAC plan was not publicized by the major news media because it fell outside the focus of the Bush administration's propaganda campaign to demonize Iraq and its leader, Saddam Hussein, who was held to be responsible for attacks on the United States. We propose that the current structure of policy and critique is now institutionalized and formatted as "war programming," which connects criticism within a narrative sequence, including critiques and reflections about journalistic failings. The scope of the action is so immense that it precludes and preempts its critique. I suggest that a new approach is needed to offer critique before the event. The implications of such a well-organized propaganda campaign for future news coverage of war are discussed.

Chapter 9, "Constructing Pat Tillman," focuses on how popular culture and propaganda socially construct a hero fighting terrorism. Pat Tillman was a twenty-seven-year-old promising professional football player who walked away from a multi-million-dollar contract with the Arizona Cardinals to join the U.S. Army and serve as a Ranger in Afghanistan, where fellow Rangers killed him on April 22, 2004. Sports and nationalism are joined in popular culture through narratives, metaphors, language, and emotions. This is particularly true with wars. Audiences recognize and identify with individual athletes who are associated with familiar sports. Propagandists, such as government officials, seek to link athletes and others who are well known with values, causes, and justifications for a particular war. The positive link is forged through "heroism," as the dead individual(s) are deemed "heroes." The construction process provides a sociological glimpse into (1) organizations (e.g., the propaganda of the U.S. Army and the news media), (2) the political process in a mass-mediated age (e.g., how politicians link names and "faces" to international conflict as an emotional identifier for audiences—there is now a "face" to this war), (3) collective identity and symbolic commensuration (e.g., "he's still a hero" even if his own men shot him), (4) value-enriching morality plays ("be worthy of the sacrifice made on our behalf"), and (5) contemporary popular and political usage of "hero."

Chapter 10 summarizes the effect of terrorism coverage on the politics of fear and links these media reports with the social construction of the Iraq War. The relevance of war programming (discussed in chapter 8) for future coverage of social issues will be discussed, along with noting key questions and topics that should be investigated in the future. Finally, the theoretical contribution of viewing the politics of fear from a mass communications perspective will be set forth.

2

The Social Reality of Fear

DEFINING THE POLITICS OF FEAR

All social change and expansion of social control occurs through an act of power, which may be defined as the ability to define a situation for self and others. When social control changes are institutionalized, they become part of the fabric of social life. To the extent that formal social control efforts expand, we can see the growth in the politics of fear. To repeat, the politics of fear refers to decision makers' promotion and use of audience beliefs and assumptions about danger, risk, and fear in order to achieve certain goals. The politics of fear should correspond well with the amount of formal social control in any society. The source of fear may be an authority, God, or an internal or external enemy. Tracking the expanded control efforts over time can illustrate how the politics of fear has evolved in any social order. Moreover, behind most efforts to enact more control will be a series of events and accounts about "what should be done." Changes in public language and in the discourse of fear will also accompany social control changes. However, once such changes are enacted, they symbolically enshrine the politics of fear even when public perceptions about the specific source of that fear process may diminish.

The politics of fear is exercised during times of conflict, but it accumulates and gradually informs policy and everyday life behavior, even if there are occasional bouts of resistance. The politics of fear does not imply that citizens are constantly afraid of, say, a certain enemy, day in and day out. The object of fear might change, but fear of threats to one's security is fairly constant. The context of control promotes this, as do numerous messages about menaces that justify general social control measures. This chapter examines how fear has informed political decisions that resulted in social control and the enactment of policies and programs that had long-term effects on social life. This overview includes crime control, previous wars, the expansion of surveillance, the role of business and universities in promoting fear, organized religion's complicity in playing to the politics of fear, and the importance of uniforms in communicating control in everyday life.

FEAR IN CONTEXT

Fear has been part of the game plan to control populations for centuries. Previous work has shown that fear abounds in the United States and western Europe (Altheide 2002c; Furedi 1997; Glassner 1999). As argued throughout this chapter, the expanding use of fear in everyday life has produced a discourse of fear. When fear becomes a familiar experience and expectation, then the symbolic environment is ripe for the politics of fear. The war in Iraq, terrorism, and concerns about crime have promoted the politics of fear. I wish to trace some of these developments in order to set forth an argument that fear is perpetuated by entertaining media that rely on fear, which in turn encourages political actors to frame messages about fear in order to get the most public attention and gain support that they are looking out for the public's interest and well-being. There is a long history to the politics of fear in the United States, and I will touch on only part of it while paying the most attention to events in the United States since the 1970s. This history includes several decades of domestic crime hysteria (especially the "drug wars") as well as recent international wars, such as Grenada, Panama, and the first Gulf War, which were also occasionally justified as part of the drug war.

The politics of fear results when social control is perceived to have broken down and/or a higher level of control is called for by a situation or events, such as a "terrorist attack." But the politics of fear can key off other events as well. During the Cold War in the twentieth century, the United States was involved in numerous terrorist activities, but there were very few against us. Yet the politics of fear was rampant. As a child, I learned to get under my desk at school whenever we heard an air-raid siren. This was to protect us from a nuclear attack from the "Russians" and the "communists," but the real political purpose was to indoctrinate young children as well as our parents that we were threatened by a major enemy and that we had to rely on the U.S. government to protect us, even if the actions seemed reckless at the time. We were being taught a story about our lives, others, and trusting our leaders.

Like most official stories, it was partly true, partly invention, and partly omission. The nuclear nightmare narrative was fueled by an interior ideological drama—a dangerous invention—that perpetrated mass fear in public forums, schools, churches, and civic groups. Its rhetoric touched every person and every institution in America, and, when combined with the domestic persuasory campaigns of the USIA, it demonstrated the power of fear and heightened anxiety in gaining acceptance for the basic political message. As Parry-Giles puts it, "the narrative repetition of the Cold War message from 1945 to 1960 helped normalize the Cold War ideology that resonates in the U.S. collective memory of that battle." (Goodall 2004, p. 18)

Actions like the infamous McCarthy hearings on un-American activities in 1950 became a witch hunt against scores of Americans. Then, as during the enactments of the USA Patriot Act in 2002, individual civil liberties were suspended, spying was encouraged, and numerous lives were disrupted. Individuals were forced to testify and "name names" of communist sympathizers and collaborators. The chapters to follow devote some attention to new forms of social control (see chapter 7).

While a specific crisis might erupt suddenly, the politics of fear emerges gradually when there is a cumulative public definition of a crisis that will challenge political leadership, sovereignty, national identity, or ideology. Thus, not all international crises result in the politics of fear. Natural disasters can be a crisis but not one that evokes the politics of fear. For example, the devastating loss of life of more than 200,000 in India, Sri Lanka, and Indonesia from a massive tsunami in December 2004 shocked the world into mobilizing for aid; countries seemed to want to "outbid" each other for offering money and relief. One survey estimated that nearly half of U.S. families had made private contributions to go along with several hundred million dollars in aid. This crisis did not generate fear, or negative action, which is usually violent and destructive. Rather, it marked a time of human suffering and called on people to empathize with millions of homeless people.

The critical point is how an event is defined. It is the way in which this definition is shaped and engineered that also requires some attention. Thus, not all wars evoke the politics of fear, although most are justified in terms of the basic framework noted previously (e.g., challenge to political leadership, sovereignty, national identity, or ideology). The basic process of defining the situation and justifying the politics of fear involves propaganda, or the manipulation of information for a specific purpose. Several of the following chapters examine how propaganda has contributed to the politics of fear. Propaganda is very significant because the politics of fear is set in motion by appealing to audiences' emotions and stereotypes. Stated differently, part of the problem is that audiences are systematically misinformed about events and policies, yet the ways in which information is presented—often by credible newspeople and respected leaders—misleads audiences. The problem, then, is partly what audiences think they know about the relevant policy or events. For example, after the 9/11 attacks, several neighbors told me that many people in Muslim nations hated the United States because of our freedom and quality of life. They had been told this by a number of news commentators and government spokespersons. There was no understanding of how our foreign policy—and that of several western European nations—may have contributed to perceived injustices for more than fifty years. A blue-collar worker I know recently told me that his niece came home from Europe "when Muslims began exploding car bombs in France or Spain or somewhere. Those guys think that if they die they'll see Allah or someone. They're crazy." He added that there are 24,000 terrorists in the United States waiting for instruction. It is what this man "knows" that enables slick leaders to gain leverage over his perception, values, votes, and tax dollars for various policies.

Citizen beliefs often are constructed and then manipulated by those who seek to benefit. Fear does not just happen; it is socially constructed and managed by political actors to promote their own goals. The goal of such manipulators might be money, but more often than not it is political power and symbolic dominance: getting one's view of the world accepted opens the door to many other programs and activities to implement this view. This is where ideology comes to play a large part in the manipulation of fear. A key aspect of all ideology is the promotion of a mythology, a set of ideas or "stories" that explains things, organizes our view of the world, and puts people, places, and events in convenient categories (Davis 1986; Kappeler et al. 1999).

One of the most important myths that has been promoted by politicians is that of "good" versus "evil," with "your side" being good and the "other side" being evil. A documentary by the British Broadcasting Corporation (BBC), *The Power of Nightmares*, captured many of the key points about this myth for U.S. foreign and domestic policies, as well as the perspective of a small but very influential group of Islamists (Curtis 2004). This documentary argues that two absolutist perspectives—the Islamists and neoconservative Americans—contributed to the modern politics of fear. Both saw the importance of creating myths about good and evil. Both believed that individualism was the root of many social problems. Their only difference was that their side was good and the other evil. Ironically, they needed each other, especially in later years, and they played off their common views about evil, even though this meant that they would hate and fight each other. Both views were supported by intellectuals: Sayyed Qutb, originally in Egypt, developed some of the rationale for a radical Islamic stance, while Leo Strauss, a philosopher in the United States, set forth a rationale that would be used by followers to promote an imperial order against the "evil" opposition.

The BBC report states that in 1949, Sayyed Qutb attended school in Greeley, Colorado, and thought that the United States was decadent and promoted individualism and pleasure seeking over deeper religious values. He returned to Egypt and preached more fundamentalism, including anti-Americanism. He was not highly influential, although a student, Ayman Zawahiri, also taught that America was decadent and a threat to Islam. Zawahiri was executed for participating in the assassination of Anwar Sadat. Very importantly, he was the mentor of the alleged "mastermind" behind the 9/11 attacks: Osama bin Laden.

The American intellectual foundation to combat evil was buttressed by classical philosopher Leo Strauss. Strauss believed that modern philosophy's contribution to the Enlightenment had overstated the importance of individual freedom and expression at the expense of community and national values. He sought to remedy this intellectual mistake, arguing that the masses need to be led to do the right thing, and this would require leaders to adapt the classical Platonic notion that the masses needed to be deceived by simple myths, the "noble lie," promoted by elite leaders. Strauss, who became one of the leading intellectuals for neoconservatives, had several students who believed that America's stand against evil is a worthwhile myth that the masses would follow. He enjoyed the television western *Gunsmoke* as well as *Perry Mason*, about the defense attorney who pulled many surprises from his briefcase to defend clients. *Gunsmoke*'s hero, Marshall Matt Dillon, was admired because he wore a white hat and used force against clear evil: the bad guys in black hats. Mason defended people, but even if he suspected that they might be guilty, he would work behind the scenes to have things go the way he thought was just. Strauss was more influential politically than academically, although he spawned a cadre of followers known as the "Straussians." He strongly influenced several academic departments, mainly of philosophy and political science, at the University of Chicago, Boston College, the University of Ottawa, and a few others. Many of his students, like William Kristol, were not able to get jobs in universities but could gain influence in Washington, D.C. Kristol stated,

> Well, many of them couldn't get academic jobs, and the political science and philosophy faculties were not terribly friendly to those of a conservative or moderately conservative disposition. And the truth is that a lot of people who ended up in Washington started out as academics. I did; Paul Wolfowitz did; and decided they probably didn't have very good prospects in the academy. What we all had in common, I think, was a certain doubt about what once seemed a kind of great certainty and confidence in liberal progress. The philosophic grounds for liberal democracy had been weakened. (Curtis 2004)

Among their targets—and justifications that "liberal" policies had failed—were civil rights, feminism, and a general moral relativism. According to Irving Kristol, one of the founding members of what came to be known as "neoconservatism,"

> If you had asked any liberal in 1960, we are going to pass these laws, these laws, these laws, and these laws, mentioning all the laws that in fact were passed in the 1960s and '70s, would you say crime will go up, drug addiction will go up, illegitimacy will go up, or will they get down? Obviously, everyone would have said, they will get down. And everyone would have been wrong. Now, that's not something that the liberals have been able to face up to. They've had their reforms, and they have led to consequences that they did not expect and they don't know what to do about. (Curtis 2004)

Neoconservatives also found supporters among certain religious fundamentalist groups that opposed what were seen as tolerance for "sin," such as homosexuality, abortion, and the "women's movement." Many in this group, including William Kristol, argued that the founding fathers had made a mistake in separating church from state.

While most intellectuals were not persuaded by the arguments of Strauss and his students, several politicians welcomed an academic argument in support of policies against a number of social programs and took a stronger stance against the Soviet Union. Ronald Reagan would eventually champion their cause. These politicians could influence Reagan and others, and the mantra became that the Soviet Union was "the evil empire." The neoconservatives did not like Henry Kissinger; he was interested less in morality and more in practical politics. According to a Reagan adviser, Jack Wheeler,

> It was a small group of people. . . . Everyone thinks, "oh, the Reagan Doctrine, the Reagan Administration," like everybody was for. No. It was a small little cabal within the Soviet—within the Reagan White House, that really pulled this off. What united this small group of ours was the vision of bringing more freedom to the world, more security to the world, to actually get rid of the Soviet Union itself. As a result, supporting the freedom fighters became the premier cause for the entire conservative movement during the Reagan years. (Curtis 2004)

Fear, then, evokes a defense of righteousness, but it is also important to understand how the enemy is portrayed through fairly consistent mass-media reports that seldom provide alternative scenarios to treat the myths as "a perspective" rather than an objective description of "the way the world is now." My aim in this book is to clarify this process.

My argument in this book is that much of this misinformation is quite intentional. This does not mean that everyone in the mass media lies, although that is certainly true of a number of politicians (e.g., Richard Nixon about Watergate, George W. Bush about Iraq and weapons of mass destruction, and Bill Clinton about sex). Rather, as I point out in chapter 3, it is the emphasis on entertainment and making profits that leads to the major distortions. Consider the money, excitement, and intrigue associated with the massive expansion of surveillance in our lives.

Surveillance represents one of the most intrusive changes in our everyday life and can be traced to the politics of fear. For example, surveillance was initially promoted to protect us from crime, particularly during the drug war of the past three decades (Kappeler et al. 1999; Marx 1988; Staples 2000). A key aspect of surveillance is that it focuses on the "body" as an object rather than as a subject, with feelings, emotions, rights, and, in short, humanity. We can count bodies, photograph them, frisk bodies, peak inside them with drug tests as well as various scanners, and capture DNA information that contains the "truth." News media reports about crime and terrorism (chapter 4) stressed the need for surveillance and more cooperation between federal agencies. The "war on terrorism" promoted massive federal, state, and local surveillance policies, all of which were guided by the USA Patriot Act, which legitimated a wide range of technological intrusions on American citizens and the detaining of citizens and foreign nationals for extended periods of time without allowing them access to an attorney. These developments are examined in later chapters, but the important point for now is that surveillance becomes institutionalized and promotes, often subtly, the notion that all of us are under attack and need protection. For example, in 2004, students in a course I taught at Arizona State University wrote that one of their biggest fears was "identity theft"! Not coincidentally, of course, the previous six months had seen thousands of reports in the news media and popular culture, including several movies, that examined identity theft.

FORCE AND THE POLITICS OF FEAR

The politics of fear is not new to social life or to journalists, politicians, and social scientists who have studied politics and social order. I will not attempt a partial listing of the hundreds of political treatises on the political uses of fear. Arendt's (1966) conceptualization of tyrannical terror and more recently Robin's (2004) elucidation of fear in political theory suggest that many intellectuals separated fear from politics, seeing terror as a weapon rather than as a lens for understanding social inequality and political partisanship.

My focus is on the modern application of fear in politics in a media age. We must make a distinction between the actual use of force on the one hand and mobilizing support with fear on the other. Force can kill, but fear can defeat. Fear is the meaningful side of force. Living in fear is not synonymous with the politics of fear, but the latter does promote the former. Force without fear is futile and will achieve nothing but eradication of some enemies and ultimately the resolve of those who wield the force. If people do not fear certain consequences—and if they cannot anticipate and visualize these—then force will be more cruel than effective. Without sufficient fear, however, more enemies will follow those who have been killed. Anyone familiar with the decades of feuds and hatred in the Balkans (e.g., Serbs and Croatians), the Middle East (e.g., Israelis and Palestinians), Rwanda (e.g., Tutsis and Hutus), and elsewhere can recognize the cycle of killing, hatred, and revenge. The U.S. invasion of Iraq dramatizes this relationship between force and fear: many Iraqis volunteer for suicide missions because they believe that a martyred death is an opportunity for eternal life. One who does not fear death cannot be controlled by fear unless it is the source of their faith, their God. Zealous leaders of some nations, like the United States, have not considered this in their war plans. Thus, uninformed American war planners who planned the destructive bombing of Baghdad that began the Iraq invasion believed that Iraqi citizens and soldiers would be "shocked and awed" by the display, thus assuring a rather quick capitulation. This did not occur for the reasons noted previously; it was mere force and did not generate sufficient fear because the politics of fear were not meaningful to the Iraqis.

Leaders and politicians want to be fear effective. This requires manipulating symbolic meanings of actions and threats. This can be achieved through effective propaganda and the use of the mass media. Political leaders promote fear in order to ensure safety and, ironically, freedom. The very nature of political power and decision making entails an appreciation of the use of pressure, force, dominance, and a range of fear-like approaches. Observers for thousands of years have commented on the myriad ways to get power, maintain control, and exercise force to support one's goals. Indeed, political philosophers have offered numerous alternatives to the use of brute force to instill and sustain fear in the governed. In a sense, analysts and advocates of "civilization" have grappled with alternatives to fear as a political weapon. Indeed, reason and the Enlightenment aspired to promote understanding and consensus through common logics so that consensus could be achieved. What is often forgotten is that this was, by and large, offered in opposition to brute force and fear. From a political standpoint, fear is negative, while reason and the aspiration to higher values are positive. One looks in vain to find any philosopher who argued that the highest order of civilization was force and intimidation, although many acknowledged that it may be necessary from time to time, or that there may be stages in social and historical development that rely on such force and fear.

Many scholars have examined how terrorism, which may be defined as "the purposeful act or threat of violence to create fear and or compliant behavior in a victim and or audience of the act or threat" (Lopez and Stohl 1984, p. 4), is one dimension of force (Gale 2002; Offe 2002; Shirlow and Pain 2003a, 2003b; Sparks 2003; Thomaz 1997; Yavuz 2002). Studies of political oppression, torture, and random as well as targeted brutality reveal that fear is short lived as a political weapon, partly because it cannot be sustained indefinitely, even with some compliance from the governed. As noted by Sparks (2003),

> Overly fearful governments can lurch into panoptic governance, undermining the world they seek to preserve. In such situations, citizens come to be seen as actual or potential enemies within, vigilantes prosper, civility withers and, ironically, the uncertainties and dangers that lurk within the society become its defining and potentially terminating features. (p. 201)

Stated differently, fear needs to be understood against its opposite: predictability, certainty, and positive and sustaining action. In this sense, some segments of society live in perpetual fear yet may not be subject to the politics of fear. It is just that their everyday life routines operate so far below the comfort zone of their known contemporaries, that daily living is tenuous and problematic. As the prime minister of Belize, the Honorable Said Musa, stated in a commemorative speech inaugurating the National Assembly on April 4, 2003,

> At the Millennium Summit, UN Secretary General Kofi Annan stressed the need for securing for people the "freedom from want" and the "freedom from fear." As the lead paper at the ACS ministerial conference held in Belize last November states: "What is often not recognised: that a person that is not free from want can only live in fear, and that the greatest evil, the most effective and consuming terrorism of our age is the terrorism of abject poverty, a poverty in which millions of people live in terror because they know that sooner rather than later they or their loved ones will die from hunger or preventable diseases." (www.belize.gov.bz/pm/speeches/pm_speech.html)

This condition of fear is perceived to be a feature of indifferent others who wantonly seek to hurt or take advantage of them. While poverty and exploitation may provoke emotions and circumstances that cultivate the politics of fear, this is not an inevitable development.

People can live in circumstances that promote fear quite independently of the politics of fear. The politics of fear promotes fear through propaganda and symbolic manipulation. Indeed, in contemporary Western countries like the United States, it is not abject poverty and want that sustains the politics of fear but rather collective support for leaders, ideologies, and policies that claim to protect people from losing what they have as well as maintaining opportunities for them to improve their lives and obtain more economic and social security and well-being.

The key point is that fear is constituted through interaction and meaning with others. Several of the following chapters examine how terrorism has been defined for political reasons. Simply having a building bombed does not constitute the politics of fear; it is the reaction of leaders to the act and especially how those reactions are communicated to the audiences they govern that do matter. Like many aspects of social life, fear is blamed on outsiders or others. Thus, we see that terrorism, especially following the 9/11 attacks, was cast as something that was done to the United States as barbaric, as unfair. A number of officials stated or implied that the United States, by contrast, did not engage in terrorist activities—ever. Most official documents of the United States would support this claim; I include news reports as well. One searches massive news archives in vain to find many statements by elected officials—especially in high federal office—stating that the United States engages in terrorist activities. Yet other sources, including government documents, make it clear that the United States and many of our allies have engaged in assassinations, kidnapping, torture, civilian bombings, and so on. The United States, like most countries, provides rhetoric encased in certain narratives or complete stories of our history, character, and purpose:

> The omission element in the political construction of the propaganda message was equally powerful in shaping the war. It was an ideological battle to be sure, but it was fueled by secret international economic and trade interests, which meant that money and power were the secrets kept at the heart of Cold War fever. For this reason, nothing that risked exposing those secrets was anything less than "Top Secret"; and, it was the covert operations run by intelligence operatives and directed by members of the elite classes that were used to win the war against Communism that was also a war to protect their own, and their wealthy friends', interests. To conduct this covert war, Presidents and CIA directors relied heavily on paying bribes; international money laundering; illegal arms trade; drug smuggling; the seduction, intimidation, and blackmailing of officials; carrying out the occasional murder, assassination, or attempted assassination of leaders; and other violent, illegal acts labeled by our opponents as "state-sponsored terrorism" or "acts of aggression." (Goodall 2004, p. 19)

Cold War control efforts were extended to domestic issues, like the civil rights movement.

Authority and procedures to investigate U.S. citizens had been established as a feature of the politics of fear during the House Un-American

Activities Committee hearings of the 1950s as well as congressional committees concerned with racketeering and organized crime (e.g., the Kefauver Committee). Fear about enemies of the state, whether communists or "mobsters," provided ample media fuel to power careers and public entertainment. For example, Senator Kefauver's committee hearings received widespread press coverage, and the senator, who would later become Adlai Stevenson's vice-presidential running mate on the Democratic ticket, had his picture on the cover of *Time* magazine and became a household name. The villains to be controlled were organized criminals, later referred to as the "mob," "mafia," "Cosa Nostra," and other euphemisms. This committee's work on racketeering and political corruption was carried forth by other commissions over the next two decades (e.g., the McClelland Committee in 1957 and Attorney General Robert Kennedy's investigations of organized crime in the early 1960s). One of the most important developments of these commissions was legislation that would permit the forfeiture of the property of persons suspected of engaging in organized crime. Known by the acronym RICO (Racketeer Influenced and Corrupt Organizations), this act permitted the government to seize assets of suspects even if they were not found guilty of any crime. The application of this law was extended over the next forty years to various drug enforcement legislation. The abuses of this law have been well chronicled (Levy 1996).

This legislation, borne of the politics of fear about crime, has been extended to drugs through various "drug wars" and became another instance where individual guilt need not be proven to confiscate property. Like many policies and programs constructed in the politics of fear, police and state officials used the legislation to promote their own agendas, ultimately leading to gross injustice, particularly in the state of Arizona. Azscam was an eighteen-month sting operation run by the Phoenix chief of police and the county attorney and financed by nearly a million dollars from RICO forfeitures. Their intent was to prevent organized gambling in Arizona. They enlisted an ex-con to violate Arizona law and offer legislators money if they would agree to support organized gambling. Many of these conversations were surreptitiously recorded, and the tapes were released to the news media one day after seven members of the Arizona legislature, four lobbyists, and several others were indicted on a range of charges pertaining to the legalization of casino gambling in Arizona, on February 5, 1991 (Altheide 1993; Flatten 1993). Adjustments were made to the use of the RICO law in Arizona when the abuses were made public by a series of award-winning investigative reports (Flatten 1993). By 2005, there were twenty-two casinos operating in Arizona. The abuses of RICO in Arizona and elsewhere are examples of policy changes that can arise through the politics of fear.

American legislators learned from the experiences with centralized control in Nazi Germany and the Soviet Union that a police state not only operates on fear but is very coordinated as well. These lessons were renewed during the civil rights movement and anti–Vietnam War protests in the 1960s and 1970s when federal and state police agencies spied on U.S. citizens, conducted illegal wiretaps and surveillance, and committed burglaries and blackmail. Much of this came to a head during the Nixon administration with the infamous Watergate burglary at the national Democratic headquarters. The fallout from the Watergate investigation (e.g., Robert Woodward and Carl Bernstein's reporting for the *Washington Post*) and the cadre of Nixon operatives, also known as the "plumbers," revealed that they had ties to the FBI, the CIA, and several state-sponsored terrorist groups, including individuals involved with the unsuccessful Bay of Pigs invasion of Cuba in the 1960s. The Nixon administration claimed that these and other acts were warranted by "national security," a catchphrase that lost credibility and would not be used with the same fervor until the Iraq War in 2003.

The politics of fear, then, is made visible through various policy changes ranging from property forfeitures through RICO legislation to other abuses, like the federal government's violations of civil rights, the abuse of power in meddling in foreign affairs, and the breaking of the law. However, the legal and ethical violations become old news and are short lived, seldom remembered when the next "crisis" warrants a rebirth of the soiled policy. This happened with centralized state control during the Cold War, when domestic spying was applied to innocent citizens. Surveillance operations were scaled back, and legislation was enacted to prohibit agencies from working together to harm American citizens. All these criminal acts and violations of citizens' civil rights led Congress to pass strident legislation separating police powers and functions. This separation extended to lines of authority as well as limitations on interagency jurisdiction (e.g., the FBI and the CIA were not to work together to investigate U.S. citizens), and was intended to maintain some structural separation between agencies' information sharing. Some officials did not like these limitations and, as we have seen throughout history, simply chose to break the law in order to pursue their own interpretation of what was needed. (Chapter 8 describes how a number of U.S. officials began planning the war in Iraq in 1992, ten years before bombs fell on Baghdad.) A good example was the Iran-Contra scandal that was coordinated by the Reagan administration in the 1980s (www2 .gwu.edu/~nsarchiv/nsa/publications/irancontra/irancon.html). The plan was to violate congressional and United Nations laws and sell arms to Iran, then involved in a bloody war against Iraq. The profits were then used to fund rebel forces, the "Contras," opposing an elected government in Nicaragua. This plan was overseen by Marine Colonel Oliver North, who became a conservative radio talk-show host and motivational speaker, sometimes for fees of $35,000 (http://premierespeakers .com/1016/index.cfm).

After the 9/11 attacks, proponents of centralized police authority and information bases negated the lessons learned and the civil rights violations by overwhelmingly passing the USA Patriot Act, which gave the federal government tremendous power over civil rights, including surveillance of personal records. The appeal was to work together against the nation's common terrorist enemies. Numerous members of Congress would later claim that they neither read the act nor were given time to do so. Action was called for to protect Americans from the enemy in "these times," now that the "world is different." The passage of this act symbolizes perhaps more than any other recent legislation the renewal of the politics of fear. Several Americans and numerous foreigners were detained without charges and were denied legal counsel (Walker 2002). This did not happen solely because of the 9/11 attacks; the effort to focus central control against the "enemy" was relentlessly pursued by strong proponents of social control even after Watergate.

Most wars invoke the politics of fear to varying degrees. Unlike previous wars in the late twentieth century, such as Grenada, Panama, and the first Gulf War, the war against terror does not have an end in sight, partly because there is not a well-defined enemy or a clear objective, although in each case the enemy was appropriately demonized or else castigated as the personification of evil. Both Panamanian ruler Manuel Noriega and Iraqi President Saddam Hussein were apt targets for cartoons and tough street language (e.g., "kick your ass"). Noriega was also referred to as "pineapple face" because of acne problems and was said to like men, women, voodoo, and pornography.

Grenada and Panama were threats not to the United States but to U.S. interests. In 1983, Operation Urgent Fury in Grenada focused on toppling a new Marxist regime that was suspected of collaborating with Soviet and Cuban forces to build an airstrip that could be used for shipping arms to South American countries. A second reason given was to rescue some American medical students:

> In the early morning hours of October 25, 1983, the United States invaded the small Caribbean nation of Grenada. The fiery leftist President Maurice Bishop had been assassinated days earlier. The initial invasion consisted of some 1,200 US troops. At the time of the invasion, a delegation of 500 Cubans were in the country. They included doctors, engineers, teachers and construction workers, who were there to help build an international civilian airport for Grenada. When the US forces moved in they landed at the airport, they killed more than a dozen Cubans and more than 40 Grenadian soldiers.

The U.S. quickly consolidated its occupation of the island and expanded its force to more than 7,000. By December a pro-American government was established. (www.democracynow.org/article.pl?sid=04/06/10/1425246)

In 1989, Operation Just Cause in Panama was focused on capturing Noriega, who had fallen out of favor with the United States. Panama was important because of the Panama Canal and also because it was useful in reducing the transportation of illegal drugs. Noriega was supported in office by the United States and worked closely with President George Bush when he was director of the CIA. However, Noriega had become more politically independent of the United States, perhaps being influenced by Cuban President Fidel Castro, and had begun to profit from drug sales as well. The drug connection with Panama was very important for the politics of fear because of the long-standing war on drugs in the United States since the 1960s. Panama was the first explicit connection between a foreign invasion and the fight against drugs. Politicians would use this symbol of fear thirteen years later as part of the justification for fighting terrorism abroad and would claim that many terrorists were funded by drug sales. One scholar who investigated the invasion of Panama captures some of these issues:

> One of the policies that the United States was practicing during the period leading up to the intervention in Panama was rollback. Rollback is the theory that United States policy makers were determined to return to a pre-communist world. These policy makers sought to end communism in the Soviet Union and establish free-market capitalism worldwide. With the fall of Cuba to communism, the United States turned its attention to Latin America and became determined to establish and maintain democratic governments.
>
> The Ronald Reagan and George Bush administrations in the United States both used their War on Drugs to legitimize United States intervention in Latin American countries. The United States concluded that drug-trafficking and left wing social movements were closely related to each other. . . . The increasing cooperation in the world to curb drug trafficking made it feasible for the United States to use drug trafficking as an excuse to intervene in Panama, especially with Noriega's connection to drug cartels in Colombia. (Calderon 2003)

Grenada and Panama were tests of the U.S. military as well as confirmation of the Monroe Doctrine—that the United States had the right to defend its interests throughout the Western Hemisphere—the use of pre-emptive strikes. This new policy would be very important in selling the Iraq War to the American people a decade and a half later. Establishing new rules for controlling the press was another important aspect of the invasions of Grenada and Panama (Altheide 1995). The Pentagon, still smarting from the adversarial coverage of the Vietnam War, spent decades improving its image and skill in managing the press, although lessons were also learned about controlling the news from the British during the Falklands War (Morrison and Tumber 1988). The Pentagon controlled press access but still permitted journalists to observe bodies of U.S. soldiers in flag-draped caskets at Dover Air Force Base. There were a number of news reports that used emotional visuals of dead Americans; the Pentagon did not permit this in future wars.

The politics of fear was rejuvenated with the first Gulf War, as some five months of planning enabled the press to construct sets, develop film libraries, and even venture to Baghdad to interview Saddam Hussein. Control of journalism in previous wars was a very important precedent for spoon-feeding the press in the first Gulf War (1991 in Operation Enduring Freedom), which was predicated on driving Iraqi forces from Kuwait's oil fields. This action helped develop an international coalition of forces under the auspices of the United Nations. The elder President Bush compared Saddam Hussein to Adolf Hitler, and bellicose propaganda by Kuwait's royal family—produced by the U.S. public relations firm Clark and Knowlton—claimed that Iraqi soldiers pulled infants from hospital incubators and smashed their heads on the ground. This was a war of superior technology against a weaker foe; machines (e.g., tanks, jets, and helicopters) did most of the work as journalists and worldwide audiences saw many of the same bombsight visuals just prior to smashing into targets. There were few coalition casualties; indeed, it is estimated that more women military personnel became pregnant than the number of soldiers killed during the brief operation.

The war with Iraq, which the administration claimed to be the nation's flagship war against terrorism (Afghanistan was secondary, even though it was the original bombing target), will end, and the United States will declare victory regardless of the government that is in place. But the war on terrorism is much more open ended. Another battle or enemy will have to be discovered for the politics of fear to endure with terrorism.

THE POLITICS OF FEAR IN CONTEXT

The politics of fear can exist independently of the actual fear level of the population. This paradox requires some conceptual attention. Social control is the key element and criterion of the politics of fear. Increased control is justified by appealing to citizens or their interest groups. Crime provides a good example. Opinion polls, letters to decision makers, and mass-media emphasis on problems like gangs or drugs can amplify the problem and broadcast its consequences to a broader audience than the original groups that are most directly affected by the problem (Best 1995; De Young 2004; Hunt 1997; Jenkins 1998; Spector and Kitsuse 1987; Walker 2002). Thus, drugs became a societal issue that qualified as a moral panic, calling for strict action to save society from morally unraveling (Pfuhl and Henry 1993). Citizens are also likely to support officials taking action to protect them if rationales are provided that emphasize citizen safety and the salvation of social order. This support is likely to be ensured if any actual or potential opposition to the expanded control is couched in negative language (e.g., "soft on crime," "liberals," or, in the case of terrorism, "unpatriotic"). Associating dissenters or the opposition with outsiders, deviants, or the "other" is a common propaganda technique that neutralizes the opposition. This suggests that any analysis of the politics of fear must be sensitive to the language of membership, particularly insiders and outsiders (Becker 1973).

The politics of fear plays to the mass media–generated concerns of audiences, but it can continue long after the initial incidents have receded from public attention. As social control is increased, the state control agents that usually promote such efforts can simultaneously point to their efforts to ensure public safety as well as take credit for reducing the problem that prompted the expanded control. For example, the drug war is given credit for not only incarcerating thousands of offenders but also reducing the supply and use of illegal drugs, even though careful research shows that incarceration played little part in crime reduction or drug use. Nevertheless, the politics of fear sets the discourse for claims of its effectiveness. President George W. Bush's statement to the American Bar Association illustrates this claim. When asked his views about federal sentencing policy in view of growing evidence of the ineffectiveness of harsh sentencing, President Bush is reported to have replied,

> With respect to our overall sentencing policies, the United States is experiencing a 30-year low in crime. Nearly 27.5 million violent crimes were not committed in the last decade because of this reduction in crime. It is therefore hard to accept the claim that current sentencing policies are ineffective. Nor are they too costly when state prison budgets today account for less than 2 percent of state and local spending. Our crime rate is low because we are keeping violent, repeat offenders in prison and off our streets. (*ABA Journal* 2004)

The harsh sentencing guidelines remain after the initial media flurry about crime waves and drug wars was replaced by newer threats to public order, such as terrorism (the main topic of this book). The public and policy response to fear-induced social control are interlocked with the latest societal threats. Various audiences are affected by the social control efforts and gradually take them for granted. For example, gated communities, security guards, and home security systems—complete with camouflaged landscaping and aesthetic ram-proof fences—are now part of what has been referred to as the architecture of fear (Ellin 1997). The lesson, then, is that political enactments informed by fear can continue to communicate fear over a period of time. Indeed, enough time may lapse between fear-inspired events and dramatic media productions that some audiences may perceive that all the social control is no longer needed. However, most citizens will support the status quo and continue to cling to the prior definitions of fear-induced policies. The persistence of fear is illustrated by the actions of public schools.

Numerous changes were quickly adopted by many school districts during the 1990s as a result of widespread media reports about drugs, weapons, and gangs at schools. Consider the impetus to search/or abandon lockers, place metal detectors and armed police in schools, and require students to wear uniforms and undergo drug tests. Parents who opposed such policies were in the minority and were regarded as being unrealistic and "out of touch" with the changing harshness of social life. More parents, school officials, and researchers were skeptical about the efficacy of such policies by 2005, but by then these changes were institutionalized and were very difficult to change. Indeed, a number of Arizona school districts began equipping school officers with Tasers (electronic stun guns) to use against unruly students even though there had been virtually no call for armed response in the previous years. Arizona officials have been misled by numerous reports about the popularity and safety of these potentially lethal devices. After an initial flurry of well-managed positive public relations, Taser Inc. has come on harder times as more information has surfaced about this lethal weapon, including dozens of people who have been killed as well as a troubling report that the Securities and Exchange Commission is investigating Taser's sales reports "that some stock analysts have called dubious because it appears to inflate sales to meet annual projection" and ultimately stock prices (Anglen and Gilbertson 2004, p. A2).

Many of Arizona's schools are safe from almost everything except fear despite receiving less public support for buildings and teachers than every state except Mississippi. Parents aren't too fearful as a rule, but, as noted previously, there is a political process at work throughout the country to embed fear in our culture. There's the case of my neighborhood school, Broadmor Elementary, in Tempe, Arizona, where both my children attended. Even though there has never been a child abducted from this idyllic school or a shoot-out in the thirty years that I have lived in Tempe, the principal used $6,000 raised by the Parent-Teacher Organization to install two surveillance cameras:

> Nothing has ever happened at Broadmor Elementary School in Tempe to warrant installation of security cameras, and Principal Michael Fidler hopes nothing ever will. . . . But just to be on the safe side, Fidler, like a growing

number of elementary school administrators nationwide, has had two security cameras installed. He believes—and police agree—that cameras can deter crime on campus.

They are more affordable now, easier to use, and address every principal's biggest fear: a child disappears from campus, taken by a non-custodial parent or worse, a stranger.

"Every school administrator struggles with keeping a warm, welcoming environment for legitimate individuals who are supposed to be there, but also keeping out the individuals who are not supposed to be there," [Ken] Trump [president of National School Safety and Security Services in Ohio] said. (*Arizona Republic,* January 3, 2005, p. B3; www.azcentral.com/news/articles/0103edcameras03.html)

There are several points about these statements that are important. First, the principal states "to be on the safe side," as though we are not already, as though we can and should do more. And what is that? Buy some cameras that are claimed to make things safer? I discuss this point a bit more, but first the comment by Trump needs to be examined. Trump's statement illustrates the role that the mass media play in credentialing or legitimizing issues and spokespersons in promoting the politics of fear. Trump is with a consulting company in Ohio that is in the business of protecting schools and children. His organization is a key claims maker in promoting the lack of school safety, including such obvious—but fear-generating—assertions that most schools are "vulnerable to terrorism." Moreover, Trump and his associates regularly appear on the news media and use such appearances as part of their legitimacy. His organization's website states,

School leaders, law enforcement, and community safety officials in over 40 states have used our services because we understand K–12 school safety issues.

Our president, Ken Trump, has over 20 years school safety experience and is one of the nation's most widely quoted school safety experts in media and professional education publications. Ken has been featured as a school safety and crisis expert on ABC World News Tonight, ABC's Nightline, CBS This Morning, CNBC, CNN, Fox News Channel, Good Morning America, MSNBC, NBC Nightly News, Associated Press, Newsweek, Time Magazine, USA Today, NY Times, Education Week, and other national and international print, radio, and television media. On May 6th, 1999, he presented testimony at a school safety hearing of the United States Senate in Washington, DC. (www.schoolsecurity.org)

The previous example illustrates the circularity of the politics of fear: a problem or crisis occurs (e.g., the 9/11 attacks or the shooting at Columbine High School in Littleton, Colorado), school officials and parents are inundated with mass-media coverage of politicians and others defining the terrorist threat as imminent or that "Columbine could happen here," and businesses and social control organizations (e.g., the police and military) appear in the mass media informing school officials and others that they can protect them from the imminent threat.

Recall the cameras mentioned previously that were purchased by Broadmor Elementary School. What happened with schools in Tempe and throughout the United States illustrates an important principle about the use of technology. If a surveillance device is available at modest cost, then it will be used. This is one reason why there are so many cameras in buildings and schools today. Many people believe that cameras prevent violence and keep people safe, even though research shows that it is not this simple (Betin et al. 2003; Biressi and Nunn 2003; Coleman and Sim 2000; Ditton 2000; Lyon 2003; Musheno et al. 1978; Welsh and Farrington 2003). CCTV has been found to reduce some types of crime in England (Ditton 2000). Studies of the impact of CCTV in the United States show that the largest reductions in crime occurred in parking lots (Welsh and Farrington 2003). However, crime control strategies have been altered by CCTV; public acceptance of surveillance in urban settings has increased, and norms and expectations about public behavior have become more restricted as audiences adjust to their awareness of surveillance (Betin et al. 2003). In retrospect, any social scientist would have serious doubts about the utility of cameras by themselves. As we have learned with other technologies, like home burglar alarms, they are usually more trouble than they're worth; they send out numerous false alarms, they break easily, and many are no longer in use after a few years. Cameras, to be effective, must be widely dispersed, covering a range of areas and angles; they must be in working order, monitored by technicians, and have the tapes reviewed. To effectively engage in prevention, one would monitor tapes in order to find out if, for example, someone is "lurking" around the school grounds. This requires someone to view hours of tape every day; even fast-forwarding will take time and require someone to be responsible for this. It is also necessary to store tapes for later comparisons, such as to see if a suspect has been in the area previously. Will Broadmor Elementary set aside a closet for this, and, if so, who will catalog the tapes? If the tapes are not used in this way, then it will simply be a matter of luck if, say, a "bad person" is caught on tape doing something he or she shouldn't be doing.

Perhaps there's a bigger problem. What message are we sending to students? Widespread surveillance cameras also convey mistrust to students and others at whom they are directed. And why wouldn't students be creative enough to avoid the camera angles once they learned about them? If these points are known and are part of the research record, then why do school districts keep buying cameras? First, the research record isn't consulted, although this is easy to do with the availability of the Internet (or many researchers in universities, in this case, just blocks away from Broadmor Elementary School). Second, companies like Trump's actively market their wares and expertise to school districts, and, as noted previously, they are well known, being seen in the mass media. (I doubt that many of the scholars who have done the exhaustive studies about the problems with security cameras have been on national television.) The upshot is that what began as part of the politics of fear is now institutionalized in business, advertisements, and television programming. This is true of cameras and stun guns, but it is also the case with other cultural elements.

A number of things can influence the rise and maintenance of the politics of fear. A major focus in this book is on the role of the mass media and popular culture, and these will be examined in some detail in following chapters, but there are other factors that are indirectly related to the mass media. Recall that I have emphasized how the politics of fear becomes part of the culture. It is not only about what's on television or in the movies or the latest campaign speech. It is also about the language we use, the things we worry about, what we study, and even what we pray about. It is also about what we see in terms of fashion and "normal dress" in everyday life. Consider how business and universities play to the politics of fear.

THE HOMELAND SECURITY BUSINESS AND THE UNIVERSITY

The politics of fear is recognized during designated times of "crisis," such as occurred at the 9/11 attacks, but the foundation for these politics is far more basic, having begun much earlier. A key part of the politics of fear, as we discuss more in a later chapter, concerns crime, and the "crime entrepreneurs," mainly law enforcement agencies, play a large role in getting out the message about fear of crime through the local news media. Crime, after all, is the most common local news item. But city and municipal governments also play a large part in promoting fear by funding programs to deal with citizens' concerns about safety, establishing block watch programs, and dozens of other citizen involvement projects. Recall the previous discussion about how schools buy products and services. Many of the people working in these programs are businesspeople who, while community oriented, are also focused on the impact of crime and fear on business and products. These concerns inform a variety of routine and mundane decisions as well as policy directives.

The fear business is immense (Kappeler et al. 1999; Staples 2000). Aided by the politics of fear, many businesses provide services and products to help solve or reduce the alleged sources of fear. I will not dwell on the multi-billion-dollar defense industry, which continues to employ thousands of workers and generate a significant part of the gross national product, but its role in maintaining the baseline of fear (called "defense preparation") is critical.

There is a massive home protection and security industry; the gun industry has fired up many neighborhoods to get involved in personal security and home protection by buying weapons and taking weapons training and has spawned numerous hobbies involving firearms, such as "reloading" ammunition. Business also use security services that are very visible to customers in banks, offices, retail outlets, schools, and even places of worship. We see people in uniforms everywhere, and we tend to associate them with security and patrol work, which in turn implies that such protection is necessary in this place (even schools).

Universities also contribute to the politics of fear, although academics are more likely to be critical of fearmongering and its social consequences. The federal government supported the National Academy of Sciences in 1863 to help with the Civil War effort. By 1941, the National Institutes of Health had joined the National Science Foundation as one of the major research organizers. The contribution of universities to the Cold War and the proliferation of nuclear weapons and other deadly weapon systems throughout the world was accelerated after the Soviet Union launched Sputnik in 1957. Fearing that the communist country would dominate space, millions of dollars were spent to train more science teachers. One of these programs, the National Defense Education Act Loan (1958), was signed by President Dwight Eisenhower. This loan was quite attractive because anyone who taught for five years could cancel up to half the loan. This loan supported the undergraduate education of myself and my brothers.

Specific programs fared very well during the Cold War. Departments of physics, as well as major research institutions, essentially owe their start and sustenance to enormous government infusions. Consider the Massachusetts Institute of Technology (MIT):

> MIT is the number one non-profit Department of Defense contractor in the nation, according to the *Chronicle of Higher Education* (4/13/88). . . . In fiscal year 1988, MIT's total research funding was $539.238 million. Of this total, $433.680 million—80.4 percent—was Department of Defense funding. (www-tech.mit.edu/V109/N7/glenn.07o.html)

Many universities benefit from defense funding:

> Because there is broad consensus that university research is a long-term, national investment in the future, the federal government supports 60 percent of the research performed at universities. In 2002, federal research support to universities was about $22 billion: $17 billion in basic research, $4.4 billion in

applied research, and \$512 million in development. (www.aau.edu/resuniv/GvtFunding.pdf)

The bulk of this funding is in the sciences, medicine, and engineering.

Even the social sciences, which receive very little funding, have benefited from fear. Numerous universities offer degrees in criminal justice, a field of study that tends to focus on police, court, and correctional operations and procedures. Better programs will incorporate research and some critical assessment of the expanding use of incarceration, but much of the curriculum concerns straightforward descriptions, evaluations, models, and recommendations for the organization of criminal justice agencies and the roles that its workers (e.g., police officers, probation officers, and corrections officers) play in keeping crime under control and keeping us all safe. Critical criminology, seldom a key part of such programs, takes a much different look at the institutional operations of criminal justice in creating and sustaining structured inequality, racism, and discrimination.

Universities (and particularly social sciences) are very social control oriented. The dominant theoretical orientation of sociology—functionalism—posited a smoothly functioning social world that was occasionally upset by deviant acts that often reflected social disorganization. Gouldner (1970) strongly criticized this functional approach because it led social science (and particularly sociology) to study the nature and sources of these disruptions (dysfunctions/malfunctions) and offer solutions so that the social order—cast as a welfare state—could run more smoothly. While many social scientists reject this approach to serving the "welfare state," major research support reflects this emphasis. The lion's share of research support in sociology was oriented to this functional paradigm, typically coming from the National Institute of Justice, certain programs within the National Science Foundation, and a host of other government/social control–related agencies. This concern extended to drug use and addiction, which were widely perceived to reflect disorder and eventually lead to social mayhem. Indeed, the concern with drugs was framed within the politics of fear as a criminal problem rather than a public health issue, and, like all framing, there were massive consequences in relying on policing for addiction and treatment alternatives (Kappeler et al. 1999).

The university researchers who studied crime, deviance, and illegal drug use helped fund the university with their research grants. Ironically, the very social sciences that had historically been the most critical of government efforts at social control were also enabling the control efforts by accepting government research grants. The universities were, then, in the social control business as well. Their research reports, while occasionally critical of certain criminal justice practices (e.g., police behavior), were nevertheless a key component in the politics of fear.

The penchant of universities for chasing large research grants continued following the 9/11 attacks, but now the emphasis shifted from crime to terrorism. As with many institutions in the United States that pursued the multi-billion-dollar largesse to "fight terrorism," universities ramped up their typically slow bureaucratic processes to approve new academic majors by adding terrorism and security to their repertoire:

> Over the last three years, nearly 100 private and state colleges have introduced programs in terrorism and emergency management. In New York City, both Metropolitan College, which changed its name from Audrey Cohen College in 2002, and John Jay College of Criminal Justice have introduced master's programs that specialize in terrorism and disaster management. New York University is putting together a certificate program focusing on homeland security. (Hoffman 2004)

Some of the programs were tied to established areas of study involving disaster and emergency preparedness, but more was involved than just offering a timely curriculum to curious students:

> This year, the Department of Homeland Security has doled out about $70 million in grant money to colleges and universities. With the agency's annual budget of $32 billion, there is the powerful lure of new jobs at state and local agencies, as well as corporations that benefit from its grants. (Hoffman 2004)

The universities' most recent linkage to agencies perpetuates the framing of fear rather than offering alternative perspectives that may generate research questions to help uncover other takes on the problem. The politics of fear is self-sustaining, guiding even the "study of fear" along certain directions. Thus, these new programs were not oriented to such questions as, What do the 9/11 attacks (and other events) tell us about the place of the United States in the international order? Rather, the questions deal with reaction and adjustment within a fear framework:

> "All the students we have been involved with haven't seen this as a political issue, but as a way to come together for their country," said Melvin Bernstein, the director of university programs at the Department of Homeland Security. (Hoffman 2004)

The politics of fear is directly and indirectly related to everyday life perspectives and activities involving business and education, but it is also supported by religious rituals and institutions.

POLITICS OF FEAR AND RELIGION

The politics of fear is effective because it joins basic emotional motivations with social structural contexts. The most effective politics of fear promotes extensive social control efforts that reflect audience fears and resonate with collective identity about the legitimacy of protecting "us" against "them." Leaders who provide such directions are validated by their constituents because they reflect that they are presumed to share the same deep feelings of their audiences. The ultimate example of this consists of religiously motivated fears that connect personal safety with one's immortal soul; fearing for the well-being of one's soul goes well beyond the concerns of the flesh, the focus of most social control efforts.

PRAYER, RELIGION, AND THE POLITICS OF FEAR

Popular culture and mass-media marketing and promotion of fear can blend the politics of the soul with the politics of fear. So-called religious popular culture is a good example of this, particularly when the focus is on movies, music, and literature about righteousness, redemption, salvation, and, ultimately, survival as one of the elect. Virtually all religions teach the fundamental principle that life is pain but that, through self-sacrifice, proper cleansing, and/or good works, pain—and life—can be transcended for a higher form by the elect. Salvation rhetoric in popular culture has become very popular as a feature of media logic. While religious media have been a strong but small part of the total popular-culture market, they have grown rapidly since the middle of the 1990s, when major media organizations began producing and marketing religious salvation products for a much wider audience. Just as religion had been transformed earlier by the entertainment format of media logic, religious television programming, movies (e.g., *The Passion of the Christ*), and Christian novels greatly expanded. So-called rapture novels (e.g., *Left Behind*) chronicle the adventures of life as told by a reporter who describes earthly turmoil and suffering of all those who are not swept up on Judgment Day. These books have sold millions of copies and have earned the religious publishing industry earthly riches beyond their wildest dreams. These books appeal to many Christian and fundamentalist believers as well as others.

The beneficiaries of these books extend beyond the pulp fiction authors and their publishers. The role of popular culture and media logic in changing organized religion has been well known for decades (Altheide and Snow 1979). The organizations that help fund these projects are part of the media conglomerates that also own other publishing and popular-culture outlets (Tunstall 1994; Tunstall and Palmer 1991). Moreover, these organizations also support certain political candidates and political positions, such as Middle East policies (Goulden 1988; Halberstam 2000). The policies of the United States resonate with social control ideals and objectives that pervade the narrative accounts of these publications, including that evil is ever present and must be combated, that the devil is behind all evil and the threats from "false" religions (e.g., the worship of false gods), and that the battle with evil is scripted to end in the ultimate triumphal escape from a corrupt earth at Judgment Day (i.e., the "rapture," or the Second Coming of Christ). Tim LaHaye and Jerry Jenkins, whose twelve-volume apocalyptic series describes hell and mayhem visited on those who were "left behind," have sold more than 40 million copies (Frykholm 2004; Hendershot 2004). One reviewer's assessment of the genre seems apt:

> Loosely based on the biblical book of Revelation, these novels open with the rapture, when true believers are stolen away to heaven, leaving cars, contact lenses and unbelievers behind. Then come seven years of tribulation, brought on by a fiendish Antichrist who glories in famines, earthquakes and the proverbial wars and rumors thereof. In the end, Jesus makes his much-anticipated appearance and, with a fervor seemingly meant to avenge for each and every lashing doled out in Mel Gibson's "The Passion of the Christ," slices and dices his way through millions of evildoers. (Prothero 2004)

A political foundation of fear requires cultural and symbolic support that it is necessary, valid, and effective and that has practical payoffs. One of the helpful contributions of the religious mandate is that the ultimate payoff can always be assumed. Even when things are not going well in the battle or on the job or when browsing the newspaper and seeing evil pornographic ads, there is always the realization that eternal salvation is yours for the believing, if not also the buying of certain books and viewing of appropriate movies. Moreover, national slogans that claim directly or indirectly that God is on our side—including the national anthem, the pledge of allegiance, money, government seals, as well as our slang and profanity (e.g., "oh for Christ's sake")—help make invisible sentiments visible in symbols that have been, essentially, appropriated in their ultimate meaning and significance by the state. Thus, most presidents, after they declare war, position themselves with the audience and the heavenly elect with the words "God bless America." Increasingly, these words are also associated with the uniform dress of more of our citizens. I turn now to a brief discussion of how uniforms symbolize the politics of fear.

POLITICALLY FIT UNIFORMS

The politics of fear relies on nationalism and perceived consensus against an enemy. Engineering the appearance of consensus and applying pressure to get with the program and demonstrate consensus is part of the propaganda apparatus that underlies all efforts to achieve the politics of fear. What citizens see and hear day in and day out is a key aspect of this consensus. The mass media and popular culture play a large part in this process, but so do the uniforms that dominate social services and athletics in the United States. Proponents of the politics of fear would prefer that uniforms would look strikingly familiar across all services, as in fascist Germany and Italy, but this is very difficult to achieve in the United States because laws actually prevent certain agencies from working in concert against U.S. citizens. I turn briefly to an examination of the role of uniforms in communicating the politics of fear.

Several scholars have commented on the role of uniforms in promoting social control (Brunsma 2004; Brunsma and Rockquemore 1998; Joseph 1986, 1990; Joseph and Alex 1972; Malec 1993; Schneider 1997; Wojtusiak 1982). Nathan Joseph's analysis of clothing as communication suggests that uniforms, like other clothing, communicate information about values, beliefs, and emotions (Brunsma and Rockquemore 1998). Joseph (1986) suggests that for clothing to be considered a "uniform," it must fulfill the following criteria: (1) it must serve as a group emblem, (2) it must certify the institution's legitimacy by revealing an actor's status position, and (3) it must suppress individuality. It is no mere coincidence that uniforms have accompanied the expansion of the politics of fear. This can be seen with the application of the American flag to uniforms as well as the growth of student uniforms.

School uniforms also illustrate the push to control appearance. I noted previously that uniforms are important not only for the identity of the person wearing them but also for the audiences who recognize and affirm that identity. Students who deviated from school policy by wearing a visible sign of protest have also been censored. The politics of fear promotes uniformity through steps. Placing the flag on already established uniforms of athletes and police and fire departments escalated the standardization of uniforms to carry a common symbol. A similar process is under way for schoolchildren.

In his 1996 State of the Union Address, President Clinton stated, "If it means that teenagers will stop killing each other over designer jackets, then our public schools should be able to require their students to wear uniforms" (www.udel.edu/htr/Psc105/Tests/sotu.html). Clinton ordered the secretary of education to send the *Manual on School Uniforms* to school districts across the nation.

Until the early 1990s, school uniforms were associated mainly with parochial schools and other private "college prep" academies. They were markers of distinction to separate the wearers from the others. Most nonuniformed students regarded these distinctions as symbols of snobbery and superficial superiority. Indeed, many of the wearers respected this distinction and provide numerous accounts of how they would remove uniforms or try to conceal them when away from parents and teachers. But things changed in the 1990s when, partly because of the mass-media barrage of sensational crime reports, many public schools added uniforms, along with random drugs tests of students, metal detectors, searching student lockers, and employing police officers for security and "counseling." One survey of elementary school principals estimates that by 2004, nearly 11 percent of such schools were requiring uniforms and that many of these were being supplied by popular clothiers like Bugle Boy, Esprit, and DKNY (www.123helpme.com/assets/11318.html). Research has made the reasons very clear:

> The reasons for uniforms are almost always the same. Uniforms will decrease crime and violence in schools while improving the behavior of students, say experts. Students less concerned about who is wearing what brand name clothing are less likely to judge their fellow students or to form cliques. Also, they say, uniforms cause school pride to increase. Students feel more united, more connected, and therefore their school becomes a safer, healthier environment; students test higher on standardized tests and their grades improve, proponents of uniforms argue. (www.123helpme.com/assets/11318 .html)

These beliefs and a few anecdotes led school administrators to adopt uniforms prior to engaging in the most basic evaluation research. Several projects about the efficacy of uniforms that were completed a few years after they had been required in many schools found that uniforms did not have the uniformly positive effects of making kids smarter, stopping crime, or turning schools around. One of the best studies of the Long Beach School District, lauded by President Clinton for having a successful uniform policy, concluded,

> Our findings indicate that student uniforms have no direct effect on substance use, behavioral problems or attendance. A negative effect of uniforms on student academic achievement was found. These findings are contrary to current discourse on student uniforms. We conclude that uniform policies may indirectly affect school environment and student outcomes by providing a visible and public symbol of commitment to school improvement and reform. (Brunsma and Rockquemore 1998, p. 53)

In addition,

> Student uniform use was not significantly correlated with any of the school commitment variables such as absenteeism, behavior, or substance use (drugs). In addition, students wearing uniforms did not appear to have any significantly different academic preparedness, proschool attitudes, or peer group structures with proschool attitudes than other students. Moreover, the negative correlations between the attitudinal variables and the various outcomes of interest are

significant; hence, the predictive analysis provides more substantive results. (www.gate.net/~rwms/UniformBrunRock.html)

But if uniforms do not make kids smarter or more compliant, then what do they accomplish? One conclusion has been that uniforms are a symbolic crusade to promote the appearance of order that is desired by officials (Brunsma 2004). The authors of one major study of uniforms note a parallel effect:

> If the clothing that adolescents wear can be considered a sign, then that which they freely choose as individuals can be seen as conveying an expression of their personal identity. School uniforms, by contrast, are clothing which is selected by school officials and mandated to students. It is simple in style and color and it is intended to convey the institutional values of the school. . . . Within the context of an educational institution, school uniforms clearly function as a symbol of membership to the school community. The presence of a uniform in schools automatically implies a two-tiered hierarchical structure, those that wear uniforms (subordinates) and those that do not wear uniforms (superiors). School uniforms serve as a clear sign of this status distinction between students and faculty and therefore, certify the legitimacy of that distinction by all members. School uniforms act as suppressers of students' individuality by mandating standardization of appearance and removing student expression through clothing.

Given these characteristics of uniforms, it becomes clear that mandatory uniforms serve the function of maintaining social control within the school environment. The uniforms, as a sign of group membership, act as immediate cues that signal who does and does not belong to the school community. Among the community members themselves, uniforms seem to act as a dramaturgical device by establishing interactional boundaries between members of separate statuses (teachers and students) and promoting the internalization of organizational goals.

Social control takes many forms and generates resistance. Just as many students are rebelling against the imposition of uniforms today, students were protesting the politics of fear and its regulation of apparel more than forty years ago. During the 1960s, one of the organizational goals was to not have student protest. One of the first to gain public attention occurred in Des Moines, Iowa, in the 1960s, when three students, Mary Beth Tinker, John Tinker, and Chris Eckhardt, went to high school in Iowa wearing black armbands to protest the Vietnam War. The students were suspended. Some four years later in 1965, the U.S. Supreme Court, in *Tinker v. Des Moines,* ruled that students do not "shed their constitutional rights to freedom of speech or expression at the schoolhouse gate" and declared that "state-sponsored schools may not be enclaves of totalitarianism" (http://archive.aclu.org/features/f110499a.html).

Working together was promoted by appearing to be on the same team. The commonality of uniforms was enhanced when the American flag began appearing on numerous outfits in 1991 in support of the Gulf War. For the first time in U.S. history, athletic teams, along with police and fire departments, corrections officers, and private security operations, wore American flags on their uniforms. This was an important change that was sparked by supporters of the Gulf War, who reigned over numerous paramilitary organizations that were commensurate with military regimens. Other organizations that symbolized patriotic fervor and sought to demonstrate common values with their fans, such as professional athletics and the National Collegiate Athletic Association, would follow suit in the coming months. Soon, virtually all teams—athletic, police, and fire—wore American flags on their uniforms to symbolize that they belonged to the same team.

There were some ironic twists to the pressure to promote the flag on uniforms. In 1991, an employee union for the Pennsylvania Department of Corrections petitioned the Department of Corrections for permission to wear flag patches on their uniforms. They wanted to be associated with the military operation in Iraq and to visibly show their support. Wearing the flag decal became mandatory in 1993. A patriotic Vietnam veteran, Dieter Troster, refused to place a flag on his Pennsylvania Department of Corrections uniform. Troster sued the Pennsylvania Department of Corrections, stating that he was very supportive of the flag and displayed it proudly but that being ordered to wear it actually cheapened the meaning of the flag. He claimed that his First Amendment rights were being abridged. A lower court's ruling against him was upheld by the U.S. Court of Appeals for the Third Circuit (*Dieter H. M. Troster v. Pennsylvania State Department of Corrections, et al.*, No. 94-3162.). In the words of the appeals court,

> Troster is a deeply patriotic American citizen with obvious devotion to his adopted country and to the principles of freedom and democracy embodied in out system of government. Troster has a sincere reverence for the American flag and the principles it symbolizes. For Troster, the American flag, properly displayed, symbolizes the principles of freedom and democracy embodied in our system of government. He voluntarily displays his father-in-law's burial flag, properly folded and in a lighted display case, in his home. He also voluntarily flies another American flag outside of his home on national holidays and other occasions. . . . Troster objects to being compelled to display the American flag. He believes that state-compelled display desecrates the flag and debases it. Troster considers the required displays deeply objectionable . . . because of his conviction that the American flag symbolizes freedom from state-coerced political or patriotic speech. (ACLU 1995)

At issue in the case was whether wearing a flag or any other symbol should be a matter of choice or part of one's duty as an employee. Other rulings indicated that police officers could not wear insignia representing certain political organizations on their uniforms. The significant point is that a uniform is a space that represents an organization, not an individual point of view. This makes wearing the national flag on a uniform very significant; the uniform becomes a space that is policed by the nation as well as the particular organization, even a university basketball team. Thus, the court of appeals' ruling against Troster stated,

> The court concluded that, "sympathetic as we may be to Troster's genuine patriotism as well as with his predicament, we cannot accept his suggestion that we hold, as a matter of 'common sense' and law, that the mere act of wearing a uniform with a flag patch on it constitutes an expressive or communicative 'use' of the flag." (ACLU 1995)

The ACLU petitioned the Supreme Court to hear his case. They pointed out that the court of appeals just a year prior had ruled that a Missouri firefighter could wear the flag to show his support for the Gulf War (not then required for his uniform) and that this act was protected by the First Amendment, adding,

> The ACLU's petition asks the Supreme Court to consider whether the compelled flag display "constitutes compelled expressive conduct subject to First Amendment scrutiny." The ACLU suggests to the Court that the case presents an opportunity to define when expressive conduct falls within the First Amendment. (ACLU 1995)

The court supported the state-endorsed uniform regulation just as legislators and others have sought to exercise more control over individuals.

The symbolic value of a uniform could also be measured monetarily. Firefighters who were killed when buildings collapsed as a result of 9/11 attacks were also described as "heroes" even though they were just doing their job. The monetary value of "heroism" on 9/11 was about $1 million. As part of a reported $38 billion paid to families and relatives of persons killed in the attacks, the largest payouts went to businesses, followed by disparate compensation for individuals who died. The funds available to those killed included the federal government's Victim Compensation Fund, various charities, and insurance payments:

> The families or loved ones of civilians killed on Sept. 11 received, on average, $3.1 million in government and charitable awards. The families of those who died in uniform that day—including police officers and firefighters— received more, their average compensation exceeding $4.2 million. . . . The Rand study determined that the families of the more than 400 uniformed

men and women who died, out of a total of 2,976 victims, received a total of $1.9 billion. On average, the families received, in addition to a $250,000 death award for public safety officers, an average of $880,000 more in charitable awards than civilians with similar economic losses. (Chen 2004)

The disproportionate attention to the 9/11 victims was influenced by the number of uniformed people who died that day. Police officers, especially firefighters, who entered burning buildings symbolized not only valor but also people doing their jobs. Most Americans, while saddened at the loss of any lives at the hands of the hijackers, were particularly upset with the deaths of uniformed personnel, partly because all Americans see representatives of police and fire departments in their own communities and most Americans actually know a police officer or firefighter. This made it very personal, much more than, say, wealthy stockbrokers. The class or group of firefighters and police officers was joined to the very meaning of the attacks and America's resolve to get revenge. These people, after all, were entrusted to protect us, but this implied a kind of contract with the universe: that these protectors would not themselves be harmed. If our protectors were harmed, then we were all more vulnerable to danger, and that was frightening. From a social-psychological standpoint, then, it made a lot of sense to continue the tradition of honoring men and women in certain uniforms, partly to symbolically resurrect our symbolic protection.

I stated that the politics of fear rests on a foundation of meanings and cultural symbols, practices, routines, and social institutions. It is helpful to look at the contributions of these factors for several conflicts over a period of years. While most of the remaining chapters examine the emphasis on terrorism and the politics of fear since 2001, none of this would have occurred without the foundation in narratives about crime that will be examined in chapter 4 or the previous wars that developed and packaged narratives about America's enemies. The mass media, especially news reports, play a major role in the propaganda process and shaping audience perceptions of "us" and "them." The next chapter provides an overview of the operation and significance of the mass media as a social institution.

3

The Mass Media
as a Social Institution

The politics of fear relies on a compliant mass media that will carry news reports and other popular-culture messages that promote fear. My argument is that the politics of fear works best when the messages and meanings are part of the broader culture and are recognized and taken for granted by a mass audience. Communication scholars have known for years that Hitler and his top propagandist, Josef Goebbels, were correct in proposing that the "big lie" would be believed if it was reduced to very simple black-and-white terms and repeated often. The politics of fear reflects important changes that have occurred in the mass media over the past fifty years. Popular culture provides the experiences and meanings for audiences about fear, social control, and scenarios for relying on the state to protect us. As chapter 2 stressed, formal agents of social control are often the source of many images and concerns as well as "news" updates about how well the policies are working. A large part of the politics of fear involves mass-media formats to promote familiarity and repetitive images and slogans about crime, fear, and terrorism. This chapter examines the media logic that joins entertainment with reality.

Imagine this. A posh English wedding, costing $35,000, was videotaped, but the wedding was reenacted because the mother of the bride was dissatisfied with the footage. "The video was dreadful. . . . There were no shots of the reception, and the video man missed the bride going up the aisle" (*Arizona Republic*, October 19, 1988). This reflects media logic and the growing impact of mass-media formats on our everyday lives and social institutions. The mass media are significant for our lives because they are both form and content of cultural categories and experience. As form, the mass media provide the criteria, shape, rhythm, and style of an expanding array of activities, many of which are outside the "communication" process. As content, the new ideas, fashions, vocabularies, and a myriad of types of information (e.g., politics) are acquired through the mass media. This chapter offers an analysis of social institutions transformed through media to illustrate how the logic and forms of media perspectives have transformed much of the social stock of knowledge we share.

A medium is any social or technological procedure or device that is used for the selection, transmission, and reception of information. Every civilization has developed various types of media, transmitted through such social elements as territory, dwelling units, dress and fashion, language, clocks and calendars (Zerubavel 1985), dance, and other rituals (Couch 1984). But in the modern world, these types of media have been overshadowed by newspapers, radio, and television. Groups aspiring to power seek to gain leverage and legitimacy through media. In addition, select media promote a public portrayal of everyday life and political power according to the logic of the dominant institutions.

The mass media refer to information technologies that permit "broadcasting" and communication to a large audience. The mass media are critical carriers and definers of popular culture. Traditionally, these media have included print (e.g., books, newspapers, magazines, and billboards) and electronic media (e.g., cinema, radio, and television) and, more recently, various computer communication formats, particularly the Internet. They also include personal communication devices (e.g., audio CD players and video games), iPods, as well as pagers and cell phones, especially when the latter are used for "broadcasting" messages to subscribers of paging and telephone services.

The mass media are enigmatic for social scientists. Traditional sociological analysis of the mass media tends to treat them as a "separate institution" and regards them as just one "functioning" part of the other social institutions (DeFleur and Ball-Rokeach 1982). The nature and impact of the mass media in social life are difficult to discern because they are so much a part of culture (Comstock 1991; Comstock and Scharrer 1999). I consider the mass media to be our most important social institution. I regard the "definition of the situation" as the key theoretical construct for the study of social life. Indeed, this is why I study the mass media: they contribute to the definitions of situations in social life. Moreover, I regard social power as the capacity to define a situation for oneself and others. If the mass media contribute to social definitions, then they are also relevant for any attempt to understand "power in society."

A symbolic interactionist approach to the mass media stresses social interaction and social context in understanding the social impact of new information technology (Maines and Couch 1988; Surratt 2001). Symbolic interactionism focuses on the origins of definitions and their enactment in interaction, and the consequences of such actions are rich theoretically and, most important for our analyses, grounded in the time, place, and manner of action. From this perspective, meanings are derived through a process of symbolic interaction between an actor and another (e.g., an audience), even between a television viewer and a program; mass-media interaction is not "monologic" as poststructuralists assert but involves two-way (dialogic) and even three-way (trialogic) communication. Theory suggests that we exist as social beings in the midst of process. We don't own an "identity" but are featured and acknowledged as such in situations defined as such; we live in the identity process. The mass media are part of the identity process and thereby influence social interaction, everyday life, and social institutions.

Social power rests on information technology and communication. This includes symbol systems as well as assumptions about how, what, and when we communicate. Changes in information technology are rapidly altering social routines, assumptions, and social institutions.

This approach represents another generation of media studies. McQuail's (1983) insightful demarcation of "phases of media effects" lists the following approximate dates and focus:

Phase 1. (1900 to late 1930s): The emphasis was on the nature and impact of the mass media to shape public opinion.
Phase 2. (1930s to 1960s): Attention turned to the role of film and other media for "active persuasion or information, including some of the unintended consequences of media messages."
Phase 3. (1960s to 1980s): Interest in studies of media effects but with a shift toward long-term social change, beliefs, ideologies, cultural patterns, and "even institutional forms."
Phase 4. (1990 to the present): The contemporary focus is on cultural logics, social institutions, and public discourse (Ferrarotti 1988; Gronbeck et al. 1991). This phase focuses on media and modes of representations as significant features of social life (Best 1995; Cerulo 1997; Furedi 1997).

During this latest phase of media analysis, attention shifts from the content of communication to the forms, formats, and logic of the communication order. Phase 4 benefited from insights by Harold Innis and Marshall McLuhan (McLuhan 1962; McLuhan 1964; McLuhan and Fiore 1967; McLuhan and Powers 1989) about the importance of technology for social change. These authors not only directed attention to the contribution of the technology of media for any message but further argued that it is the technology that is most important in altering information and social relationships. However, it has remained for others to examine their thesis and incorporate the surviving corpus within an awareness of culture and, especially, popular culture commonly associated with mass production, including mass-media programming and other information (Couch 1984; Couch et al. 1996). A key concept to emerge during this period is media logic.

Media logic consists of a form of communication: the process through which media present and transmit information. Elements of this form include the various media and the formats used by these media. Format consists, in part, of how material is organized, the style in which it is presented, the focus or emphasis on particular characteristics of behavior, and the grammar of media communication. My focus is on the process and impact of this logic on other domains of social life. Formats of communication and control are central elements of this phase; communication modes are no longer regarded merely as "resources" used by powerful elements; rather, communication formats become "topics" in their own right, significant for shaping the rhetoric, frames, and formats of all content, including power, ideology, and influence.

In this period, significant social analysis is inseparable from media analysis. Here the key concept is "reflexivity": how the technology and logic of communication forms shape the content and how social institutions that are not thought of as "media arenas," such as religion, sports, politics, and the family, adopt the logic of media and are thereby transformed into second-order media institutions.

According to the media logic perspective, ideas, interests, and ideologies are clothed in communication logics and formats; it is the negotiability of the latter that enlivens the former. The research agenda for innovative work in mass communication will involve its "cultural reflexivity," including how "news codes," "entertainment codes," and mediated logics, styles, and rhythms have transformed our postmodern experiences through an "ecology of communication" that clarifies the complex relationships between information technology, new communication formats, and social activities. For example, research shows that significant "news sources," such as the police and politicians, now use the reflexive media logic and formats through which they have learned to "successfully communicate" via news media agencies to their various publics. Indeed, the media increasingly control the negotiation process for setting the themes and discourse through which those agenda items are to be addressed (Ericson et al. 1989). These developments prompted the introduction of a more expansive view of communication in the social environment: the ecology of communication.

In its broadest terms, the ecology of communication refers to the structure, organization, and accessibility of information technology, various forums, media, and channels of information (Altheide 1995). Contemporary social life increasingly is conducted and evaluated on the basis of organizational and technological criteria that have contributed to the development of new communication formats that modify existing activities and help shape new activities. Social life is a communicated experience, but the rules and logics of communication have changed drastically in recent decades with the maturation of magnetic recording devices, television broadcasting, and information-processing machines (e.g., computers). Many of these points are particularly applicable to "postindustrial" societies where an increasing array of work and play involves symbols and symbolic manipulations. It is in this sense that our lives increasingly are mediated.

There are several points to consider when assessing the process and extent to which popular culture and communication formats contribute to the changing face of identity. First, the United States and many Western countries are deeply involved with media and the entire gamut of popular culture. Whether measured in terms of hours viewing television, movie attendance, music and CD purchases, popular brands of clothing, and so on, the experience, while far from uniform in our pluralistic society, is enormous (Comstock and Scharrer 1999). Second, popular culture affords individuals a plethora of styles, personas, and potential role models. Third, popular-culture audiences are also participants, albeit in varying degrees. Fourth, the physical and symbolic environment reflects media culture as theme parks, theme cities, shopping malls, and even wars adopt media forms. Fifth, the criteria and frameworks for authenticity, credibility, competence, and acceptability can be widely shared and, indeed, taken for granted as audiences interact in this media context.

More of our daily activities are symbolic, often requiring access to some electronic media or working to comply with "document requirements" that will be processed electronically. As Carey (1989, p. 123) and others note, the expansion of electronics into everyday life, or what they term the "electrical sublime," did not produce the utopia sought and predicted by many, but it has had consequences for adding machinery, formats, and "logic" for getting things done, for communicating; in our age, one's competence is often judged by communicative performance, but this performance increasingly involves the direct or indirect manipulation of information technology and communication formats.

ACCESS TO MEDIA AND POPULAR CULTURE

Changes in information technology within a capitalistic context have altered mass communications processes, products, and social impacts. (Later chapters note how important Aljazeera [aljazeera.com] was for a

Middle Eastern perspective on the Iraq War. Most of the world relied on CNN for coverage of the first Gulf War.) Images of the audience and the purpose of the "media communicators" have also been affected. Let's begin with a few points about information technology.

Information technology has increased media access tremendously, particularly in the industrial countries. The availability of inexpensive paper and high-speed printers and other "presses" provide ample supplies of newspapers and magazines, although the economics of the newspaper industry can detract from "massive" circulation to more narrow, targeted consumers. Likewise, technological changes involving transistors and microprocessors have not only lowered costs per volume tremendously but also helped "miniaturize" electronic media (e.g., personal media players, telephones, pagers, and personal computers) so that they can be carried or easily accessed in a vehicle. This makes people more "reachable" and has resulted in a geometric increase in communications activity.

Changes in information technology had profound effects on how the "audience" was conceived, including what motives and capabilities were attributed to audience members by those who owned, operated, and regulated mass communication. "Broadcasting" has changed, essentially, to "narrowcasting," or more specific marketing. It was the commitment to reach a mass audience, which in turn would produce the highest possible advertising revenue, that led programmers to define their "target audience" to include a heterogeneous audience and especially women between the ages of eighteen and forty-nine. Much of this has changed.

Technological changes influenced the content and form of the mass media, especially television news and entertainment programming. Traditional viewer choices and demographic "loyalties" shifted with the expanding choice of media and "channels." For example, network television news audiences have been declining for several years, with less than half of potential viewers now watching one of the "big 3" nightly newscasts (or CNN).

"Taste" cultures and "media communities" accompany broadcasting (i.e., narrowcasting) alternatives. Communication is part of everyday life, personal style, and identity. Products and services are geared for age and consumption identities that crosscut age, gender, social class, and ethnicity. Researchers estimate that the typical family in the United States will spend approximately $600 on communications services (e.g., Internet connections and wireless telephone) in 2001, which is nearly a 200% increase from the previous five years. While there are variations in media use, it is an understatement to emphasize how pervasive and widespread mass-media involvement has become in everyday life. Consider just a few trends in media access and use noted by a family research organization:

- By 2003, major companies hope to cover the earth with wireless phone and data networks, launching nearly 1,000 telecom satellites.
- The average time spent in front of electronic screens (televisions, computers, and video games) is nearly four and a half hours per day among two- to seventeen-year-olds.
- Eighty-two percent of children surveyed (ages ten to seventeen) say they play video or computer games at home. Forty-two percent play every day.
- The average American child grows up in a home with two televisions, three tape players, three radios, two VCRs, two CD players, one video game player, and one computer.
- Sixty-nine percent of American households have computers.
- Forty-three percent of American households have access to the Internet from their home.
- Seventy-eight percent of children surveyed (ages ten to seventeen) say they have a computer at home. Of these, 73 percent say they use the Internet or e-mail at home.
- More American families own a television set than own a telephone.
- Seventy-eight percent of adults surveyed report that they have home cable or satellite television.
- By the year 2003, there will be more than 500 million Internet users worldwide.
- Approximately 96 percent of teens listen to the radio each week.
- Most children and teens use the Internet for e-mailing, search engines, games, music, and schoolwork.
- When using a search engine, preteens are likely to log on to Pokemon, television, and game sites. Teens are likely to log on to music and game sites.
- Fifty-four percent of children surveyed (ages ten to seventeen) use their computer at home to access chat rooms.
- Thirty-one percent of children surveyed (ages ten to seventeen) report having seen a pornographic site on the Internet.
- There are now an estimated 100 million Internet domain hosts in the world, most of them in the United States, with a disproportionate number of these in California.
- Some 80 million U.S. citizens use cell phones on a daily basis (www .mediafamily.org/research/fact/mediause.shtml).

Clearly, our communication environment has changed, particularly for young people.

Increasingly, "media consumptions and use" influences how we spend time and regulate daily routines, including reading the newspaper at breakfast, listening to drive-time radio for traffic and news, surfing the

Internet for sports scores (sometimes at work), checking e-mail messages, and watching television news while fixing dinner and before bed (Snow 1983).

Normal use of media is also related to identity and how we are known to others. Three things happen in a media age where identities and products are marketed interchangeably and synergistically: (1) we experience them in the same time, place, and manner; (2) the product and process are reflexive (the product is the identity); identity appears explicitly and implicitly in numerous advertisements; and (3) media images "loop" (Manning 1998) through various media and messages, moving, for example, from initial claim to established fact to background information to standard. Product labels as key membership categories are a triumph for popular culture and mass mediation. And the freedom to purchase and become a member—and participant—reflects the actor's individual freedom and decision making. Social interaction with peers begins to reflect and turn on such familiarity.

An important aspect of the definition of the situation is social identity. The mass media are key to the identity process in the postmodern world (Altheide 2000; Cerulo 1997). Media logic that contributes to the definition of situations and identity has been examined in various studies of political reporting and action. Numerous examples of comparative studies of the political relevance of the news process illustrate how context, elite news sources, and communication formats guide news content (Doyle 2001; Hunt 1999; Wasburn 2002).

The presentation of self has changed drastically. When both actor and audience have at least one foot in popular culture, they hold shared meanings for validating the actor's performance. The mass media promote identity as a resource to satisfy individually oriented needs and interests to "be whomever you want to be." Popular culture's emphasis on entertainment and commodification of the self informs this emphasis. Grossberg, Wartella, and Whitney (1998) agree with numerous researchers who have documented the impact of media logic on everyday life: "Ultimately the media's ability to produce people's social identities, in terms of both a sense of unity and difference, may be their most powerful and important effect" (p. 206).

The impact of mass media on social identity is also evident in the current development of massive electronic communication, or what I term the "E-audience." The E-audience refers to those individuals who dwell partially in cyberspace and engage in substantial amounts of electronic interaction and communication (e.g., e-mail, Internet surfing and specific Internet use, pagers, cell phones, and so on). A distinctive feature of this audience is a sense of control and entitlement to communicate whereby the communicative act is demonstrated and displayed to self and others through electronic technology. This audience is constantly interactive but does not exist in relation to a fixed medium (e.g., television). Rather, this audience is very active and reflexive, meaning that it takes into account other communication experiences and renderings of them in other mass media and popular culture. Moreover, the communication process transcends work and play.

This characteristic of a communication identity raises the specter of an information technology persona (Gattiker 2001; Langford 2000; Porter 1997; Sieber and Schmiedeler 1996; Slevin 2000). The E-audience is an elusive membership that is controlled by a meaningful interaction process involving audience expectations, anticipated audience responses, and identity formation in everyday life contexts that extend increasingly to familiarity, ownership, and use of information technology (Markham 1998).

Public space is communicative space, but rather than dealing with people in one's immediate surroundings, the existential actor reaches for meaning and involvement as display and communication with those more familiar, even if they are not immediately in one's physical presence. One's personal definition of the situation and of self is what matters, not that shared by others in one's surroundings. So we carry on private conversations out loud on cell phones in public places. Civility gets compromised, manners are called into question, and individual rights are set forth in defense. It is happening all over the world.

Any format that sustains identity will be valued, pursued, and mastered. I suggest that the E-audience, largely because of its visible communicative nature and the implications for identity, increasingly "wear" communicative skill as fashion and as an extension of their technological persona. Of course, all this has implications for marketing and "commodification" of format:

> Users of leading-edge cell phones know that custom ring tones are out and ring melodies, which signal an incoming phone call by playing short clips of well-known tunes, are in. . . .
>
> Like cell phone faceplates, ring melodies are becoming "a fashion item," says Your Mobile CEO Anthony Stonefield. . . .
>
> Seamus McAteer, senior analyst at Jupiter Communications, says ring tunes are a way "to customize this very personal device. Everyone wants to be different but still fit in." (www.usatoday.com/life/cyber/tech/net023 .htm)

In contemporary society, the logic of media provides the form for shared "normalized" social life. Indeed, Meyrowitz (1985) has argued provocatively that social hierarchies are communication hierarchies and that access to the codes of various media varies inversely with support for social hierarchies. Historically, powerful people used media to define the time, place, and manner of certain activities, including the knowledge to participate in them (Couch 1984). Thus, Meyrowitz suggests, because television is so widely available and exposes audience members to the same information, it tends to reduce social hierarchies. As the dominant medium in our age, television becomes even more important than print because of the visual nature of the information being transmitted as well as its capacity to transcend temporal locations of experience. Thus, young people can learn at an early age how to be older.

The present-day dominance of media has been achieved through a process in which the general form and specific formats of media have become adopted throughout society so that cultural content is basically organized and defined in terms of media logic. It is not a case of media dictating terms to the rest of society but rather an interaction between organized institutional behavior and media. In this interaction, the form of media logic has come to be accepted as the perspective through which various institutional problems are interpreted and solved.

MEDIA LOGIC AND SOCIAL INSTITUTIONS

Today, all social institutions are media institutions. A major effect has been on entertainment as content and also as a perspective, orientation, and expectation of audience members. Entertainment and news programming provide "content" that may influence political agendas. There are numerous analyses of mass-media content and programming, and only a few points will be made here (Barnouw 1990). While the major media impact, in my view, goes beyond the mere content of such programs, they are relevant for how many people, especially politicians, make decisions. A key part of the communication order is to give the audience what the message "producers" believe they will accept and find entertaining. According to Snow (1983), one formula that has been used for this is following "ideal norms."

Ideal norms generally refer to those rules and strategies that are regarded as the best possible way to live. Honesty, modesty, fidelity, and hard work are examples of ideals that people will agree to at the public level, even though deviation from those ideals is quite common in everyday life. (Later chapters illustrate how ideal norms are appealed to in propaganda campaigns to promote more social control.) The ideal-norm format resonates through most prime-time offerings, including the news and some daytime programs. Viewers may object to specific acts of violence or scenes and dialogue that emphasize sex, but the ideal of justice and family that forms the heart of the program is rarely challenged. One of the most common "scenarios" to convey these ideal norms is the family or group context.

A quick scan of programming lists over several decades (e.g., in *TV Guide*) indicates how the ideal-norm format operates (Altheide and Snow 1991). For example, situation comedies (sitcoms) stressing ideal norms, law and order, and family life (but often quite broadly) dominated television entertainment from the 1960s to the 1980s. Family- or group-oriented shows continued to dominate the airwaves throughout the 1990s (e.g., *Seinfeld* and *Friends*) and, or course, criminal justice shows that feature camaraderie and loyalty (e.g., *NYPD Blue* and *LA Law*).

A great deal of public life takes on the "frames" or interpretive perspectives offered by the mass media and especially television news. News is the most powerful resource for public definitions in our age. The legitimacy of media logic now underlies claims about the nature of public disorder that in turn point to the constructive process for social worlds (Altheide and Snow 1991; Couch 1984; Snow 1983). The renewed interest in "culture" and the symbolic systems and processes through which social order is constructed, constituted, defined, interpreted, and enacted calls for an expansive perspective incorporating the processes of communication, interpretation, and meaning. This awareness has taken us beyond the point where the mass media merely set the public agenda (Altheide 1976; Carey 1989; Ericson, Baranek, and Chan 1991; Ericson et al. 1987, 1989; Maines and Couch 1988; Meyrowitz 1985).

Media logic becomes a way of seeing and of interpreting social affairs. This involves an implicit trust that we can communicate the events of our daily lives through the various formats of media. People take for granted that information can be transmitted, ideas presented, moods of joy and sadness expressed, major decisions made, and business conducted through media. But at the same time, there is a concern that media can and will distort what they present. This fear of media has been defined by some as a conspiracy in which powerful media moguls willfully set out to determine the character of behavior: how people vote, what they buy, what is learned, and what is believed (Chomsky et al. 1992). No doubt there is an intent to shape attitudes and "sell soap," but this is not the most critical factor in understanding the mass media.

I suggest that it is more important theoretically to understand mass communication as an interactive process between media communication as interpreted and acted on by audiences. It has long been recognized that television news was entertainment oriented, but now there are indications that entertainment programs are becoming more like news programs as standard formats mold programming for a culture geared to a media logic that subtly folds television criteria, discourse, and perspectives into everyday life. One indication was when surveys revealed that a majority of viewers (and especially younger ones) thought that the program *America's Most Wanted* was a news show. From the standpoint of media logic, this is hardly surprising since this show (and many like it) incorporates a number of standard television news formats within its production formula. Another indication is the way in which extended news coverage of events foreshadows future television movies and, in a sense, becomes a kind of preview or advertisement for "coming attractions."

The Waco, Texas, debacle that ended in multiple deaths in April 1993 is a good illustration of "news as advertising." Waco was the scene of a confrontation between the FBI and a religious leader, David Koresh, and his followers, who would not vacate their compound to answer a range of charges, including child mistreatment and possessing illegal weapons. The fifty-one-day standoff ended when a government assault resulted in a horrendous fire that consumed all the inhabitants of the compound. This much-debated action has achieved epic proportions in American popular culture, particularly among "survivor" and "antigovernment groups," and was said to be the major motivation for Timothy McVeigh's bombing of the federal building in Oklahoma City half a decade later. What matters for our purposes is that NBC was working on a docudrama of this event before it concluded. As the docudrama formula has been learned and refined from the production end, the time period between a real event and its prime-time airing as a television movie has been reduced to a matter of weeks and in some cases days. Commenting on NBC's quick production of a television movie while the Waco standoff was continuing, ABC's senior vice president, Judd Parkin, stated, "Dramatizing such events before they're fully resolved can be irresponsible. In a way, it almost preempts the news" (*Newsweek*, May 24, 1993). As television networks continue to pursue lucrative ratings, they appear to have stumbled on a surefire way to attract audiences to their fare: simply take news events, which are increasingly being cast in television formats rich in entertainment value, and then follow up with a made-for-television movie. After noting that ABC had its own Koresh docudrama in the works, a *Newsweek* reporter article discussed what could be termed "advertising news":

> It isn't just their odor of exploitation or their penchant for selling fiction as fact: we've become all too accustomed to that. What's less obvious is the genre's habit, exacerbated by haste, of reducing a complex story to the simplest, most viewer-friendly terms. . . . Still, get ready for a lot more. In high-visibility disasters like Waco, the networks see a way to survival: instantly recognizable "concepts" with a presold market. . . . "We've reached the point," says ABC's Parkin, "where TV movies and news shows are competing for the very same stories."

Audience familiarity is nurtured as repeated news coverage of an event provides the familiarity of an event and its connection (often quite distorted) to dominant values and beliefs in order to "make the report relevant." More than 30 million viewers—one-third of the viewing audience—watched NBC's spectacle about Waco. News as a form of knowledge was transformed through news as entertainment into news as advertising, a preview of coming attractions on television, in turn adding to the context of experience, understanding, and perspective for future "news events." The collapsing of several formats with the aid of innovative information technology in the context of Waco would seem to reflect Carey's (1989) statement several years earlier:

> Modern media of communication have . . . a common effect: they widen the range of reception while narrowing the range of distribution. . . . Consequently, modern media create the potential for the simultaneous administration and control of extraordinary spaces and populations. No amount of rhetoric will exorcise this effect. The bias of technology can be controlled only by politics, by curtailing the expansionist tendencies of technological societies and by creating avenues of democratic discussion and participation beyond the control of modern technology. (p. 136)

As news organizations and the parties they cover share similar views and approaches to what is newsworthy, the line between the journalist and the event has essentially disappeared, producing a "postjournalism" condition:

> First, journalistic practices, techniques and approaches are now geared to media formats rather than merely directing their craft at topics; second, the topics, organizations and issues which journalists report about are themselves products of media-journalistic formats and criteria. In a sense, it is as though journalists, and especially TV journalists, are reporting on another entity down the hall from the newsroom. (Altheide and Snow 1991, p. x)

This collapsing of symbolic boundaries has produced a hybrid array of messages and views of social reality that has been delineated as a postjournalism news media (Altheide and Snow 1991). As McDonald (1994) provocatively notes,

> Formats are complex and multidimensional. They include a constellation of people, activities, and the implements important to them, as well as the kinds of discourses and relations that result. . . . The formats of technology and power are intimately connected because formats structure social fields of behavior—the possibilities for human perception and relationships. These techno-formats blur and redefine the boundaries between public and private self in the learning process. (p. 538)

Journalists and "news sources" or "event managers" shared the same logic in producing reports, but audience members also were socialized into expecting abbreviated "stories" with clear, familiar, and emotionally enticing narratives. This marked the emergence of the problem frame.

THE PROBLEM FRAME AS ENTERTAINMENT

The "problem frame" is an important innovation to satisfy the entertainment dimension of news. The major impact has been on the way organizations produce news about "fear." A key strategy to develop audience identification and interaction with the message is to provide "new information," such as "here's what's happening now," within a familiar context of meaning, such as "another killing in the Valley today."

The problem frame is a secular alternative to the morality play. Its characteristics include the following:

- Narrative structure
- Universal moral meanings
- Specific time and place
- Being unambiguous
- A focus on disorder
- Being culturally resonant

The problem frame combines the universal and nonsituational logic and moral meanings of a morality play (Unsworth 1995) with the temporal and spatial parameters of a news report—something happened involving an actual person in an actual location, such as a street address. Unlike a morality play in which the characters are abstractions facing death and damnation, news reports focus on "actual" people and events to package the entire narrative as "realistic." Complex and often ambiguous events and concerns are symbolically mined for moral truths and understandings presumed to be held by the audience, while the repeated presentation of similar scenarios "teaches" the audience about the nature and causes of "disorder" (Ericson et al. 1989). It is immaterial whether the audience has other experiences with crime or related problems; the resulting messages both reinforce certain experiences and perceptions and provide a meaning about the pervasiveness of fear and the emotional attractiveness of terms like "victim" and "victimization." Unlike morality plays in which the audience is reminded of eternal threats and truths, the problem frame features everyday life filled with problem-generating fear. In sum, the problem frame is reflexive of media formats, especially television, but is easily adjusted to oral and linear media as well (Ericson et al. 1991). The problem frame incorporates a particular temporal/spatial relationship (here or "close by" and "now") to make it relevant to the audience (Altheide and Michalowski 1999).

PUBLIC PERCEPTION AND SOCIAL ISSUES

Mass-media materials are organized through an entertainment format that promotes conflict and drama, vicarious and emotional identification, and spontaneity. The mass media and popular culture are relevant in the production of meaning by providing significant symbolic meanings and perspectives that may be drawn on by individuals in specific social situations (Altheide 2000). One example is the increased use of fear. Research on the use and extent of the word "fear" in news reports indicates a sharp increase during the middle 1990s, suggesting the emergence of a discourse of fear (Altheide 1997, 2002c; Altheide and Michalowski 1999). The combination of entertaining news formats with these news sources has forged a fear-generating machine that trades on fostering a common public definition of fear, danger, and dread (Furedi 1997; Glassner 1999). Crime and violence have been a staple of entertainment and news programming for decades but have become even more graphic and focused (Surette 1998), particularly with numerous daytime talk shows and reality television programs featuring "real cops" and so on (Fishman and Cavender 1998).

An impressive literature on popular culture in the United States, particularly concerning crime, suggests multiple effects of media messages (Warr 1980, 1983, 1985, 1987, 1990, 1992), including the rise of "cultural criminology" (Ferrell and Sanders 1995) and "perceptual criminology" or the notion that "many of the problems associated with crime, including fear, are independent of actual victimization . . . because it may lead to decreased social integration, out-migration, restriction of activities, added security costs, and avoidance behaviors" (Ferraro 1995, p. 3).

Researchers have argued for decades that such concerns are connected to the mass-media coverage of news as well as entertainment (MacKuen and Coombs 1981; Surette 1998). An abundant body of research and theory suggests that the news media contribute to public agendas, official and political rhetoric, and public perceptions of social problems as well as preferences for certain solutions (Graber 1984; Shaw and McCombs 1977). For many people, the mass media in general and the news media in particular are a "window" on the world. How the public views issues and problems is related to the mass media, although researchers disagree about the nature of this relationship (Gerbner and Gross 1976; Gunter 1987; Hirsch 1980; Katz 1987; Schlesinger et al. 1991; Skogan and Maxfield

1981; Sparks 1992; Zillman 1987). This is particularly apparent when fear is associated with popular topics like crime, violence, drugs, and gangs, which have become staples of news reports as well as of entertainment media. What audiences perceive as a "crime problem" is a feature of popular culture and an ecology of communication (Bailey and Hale 1998; Ferrell and Sanders 1995).

Mass-mediated experiences, events, and issues are particularly salient for audiences lacking direct, personal experience with the problem. Indeed, many observers have wondered how it is possible for a comparatively healthy and safe population to perceive themselves to be so at risk. Research on media violence suggests that violent content can lead viewers to perceive life as "scary," dangerous, and fearful (Gerbner and Gross 1976; Signorelli and Gerbner 1988; Signorelli et al. 1995). Linda Heath and Kevin Gilbert note in a review of more recent research on mass media's relevance to crime that "because the media often distort crime by over-representing more severe, intentional, and gruesome incidents, the public overestimates its frequency and often misperceives reality" (Heath and Gilbert 1996, p. 371). Broader effects of mass-media presentations include the ways in which public perceptions of problems and issues (the texts they construct from experience) incorporate definitions, scenarios, and language from news reports (Bennett 1988; Ericson 1995; Ferraro 1995). Indeed, how the mass media report risk suggests that journalists need to be more conscientious and informed in their accounts (Willis 1997).

While crime and violence are part of the "fear story," there is more to it. For example, the constant coupling of crime and other aspects of urban living with fear has produced a unique perspective about our effective environment. While crime is certainly something to be concerned about, as is any potentially dangerous situation, the danger per se does not make one fearful, just cautious. Fear is not a thing but a characteristic attributed by someone (e.g., a journalist). Often associated as an attitude pertaining to danger, fear is multifaceted in its actual use in popular culture and especially the news media.

CHANGING SOCIAL INSTITUTIONS

Virtually all social institutions have been affected by the mass media, popular culture, and changes in information technology. The most general impact has been a move toward an entertainment orientation that is widely shared by "audiences" that participate in institutional activities. The consequences may be described as "media culture" (Altheide 1995; Altheide and Snow 1991). In a broad sense, media culture refers to the character of such institutions as religion, politics, or sports that develops through the use of media. Specifically, when a media logic is employed to present and interpret institutional phenomena, the form and content of those institutions are altered. The changes may be minor, as in the case of how political candidates dress and groom themselves, or they may be major, such as the entire process of present-day political campaigning in which political rhetoric says very little but shows much concern. Or the changes may be more significant, as in the way that foreign policy, diplomacy, and "war in prime time" is very much informed by satellite and Internet capability. Religion has adopted a television entertainment perspective to reach the people. In sports, rule changes, styles of play, sports stadiums, and the amount of money earned by players are directly related to the application of a television format.

MEDIA LOGIC AND THE POLITICS OF FEAR

Media politics have entered the framework of all institutions. Several examples will be offered about domestic issues and media politics, then I'll turn to the international terrorism scene. Any discussion about crime and justice or war and terrorism in the United States today must begin by correcting the audience members' assumptions about crime, law and order, and evil. Serious personal criminal attacks happen rarely, but they are regarded as typical and quite common by American citizens because virtually all mass-media reports about crime focus on the most spectacular, dramatic, and violent. With the images of blood, guns, psychopaths, and suffering in front of them and inside their heads, it is quite difficult to offer programmatic criticisms of our current approach to crime and accompanying issues such as prisons and other modes of dispute resolution, including restitution and negotiation. As long as crime and mayhem are presented in such familiar and fun formats, new information will not be forthcoming, only a recycling of affirmations tied to previous popular culture. And in general, as long as experience is enacted by human beings who participate in mass-mediated imagery and orient consumption toward markets and products that look like those of the status groups, personal identities and forms of conduct displayed through a host of mass media, media, and culture will not only be electronically and technologically joined but meaningfully united as well.

Highly dramatized school shootings illustrate how formal agents of social control work through the entertainment-oriented problem frame to promote social images of impending doom that in turn fuel public fears and promote more surveillance and social control of social institutions like schools. Notwithstanding the rare nature of school violence, including a "downward trend" since 1992 (and the fact that each American child has one chance in two million of getting killed on school grounds), the exceptional cases that occur have been "linked" as part of an epidemic and trend calling for stringent surveillance and "zero tolerance" of "weapons" (e.g., pen knives) in school, possibly resulting in expulsion (Hancock 2001). The discourse of fear can be illustrated with the impact of publicity about the shootings on April 20, 1999, at Columbine High School in Littleton, Colorado. Extrapolating Cerulo's (1998) conceptual framework, school and fear have been joined through the repetitive news reports that emphasized narrative sequences as "victims" (twelve dead classmates) and "performers" (senior students Harris and Klebold) along with icon-like electronic and magazine visual images of students shot by students. The joining is so complete that the term "Columbine" implies school but also fear, social control, and, above all, loss. One report argues that students' admission essays to colleges and universities are heavily influenced by Columbine's images and meanings:

> The word "Columbine" is shorthand for a complex set of emotions ranging from anxiety to sadness to empathy. . . . "Violence has seeped into their daily lives. . . . The once-tranquil school has become a place of lockdown drills. Young people are being robbed of what traditionally has been the carefree time of adolescence. . . ." The essays show how violence in distant schools changed students' habits, and how they came to terms with a newfound recognition that safety is not guaranteed. . . . "I think students today heard the word Columbine and they are horrified by the image that they have, the negative feelings." ("'Columbine' Essays Inundating Colleges," *Arizona Republic*, April 20, 2001, p. A13)

Research suggests, then, that there is a clear media presence and impact on cultural symbol systems from which societal members draw to make sense of routine and extraordinary events (Altheide and Snow 1991; Carey 1989; Denzin 1991; Holstein and Gubrium 2000; Manning 1998; Manning and Cullum-Swan 1994). Symbols occupy public spaces that, with the aid of expanding research capacities and innovative designs, can be identified and queried in order to comparatively examine cogent relationships over time. Such perspectives or discourses are shaped over time, and these guide but do not determine perceptions and interpretations to provide meaningful assessments of both specific and general conditions.

The interaction and shared meanings of news workers who follow the entertainment format and audience members who "experience" the world through these mass-media lenses promote sufficient communication to achieve the news organization's goals of grabbing the audience while also enabling the audience member to be "informed" enough to exchange views with peers. Shared knowledge about the social world in a mass-mediated society tends to be about "bad news."

Public order increasingly is presented as a conversation within media formats, which may be envisioned as a give-and-take, point-counterpoint, problem-solution (Ferrarotti 1988; Furedi 1997). For example, when mass-media depictions stress the breakdown of social order, and suggest a failing by agents of social control, we can expect those agents to present dramaturgical accounts of their resolve and success in order to increase citizens' confidence in them.

The combination of various media constitutes an interactive communication context. For example, in a study of the "missing children problem" we found that messages about "thousands" if not "millions" of missing children who were abducted, molested, and mutilated by strangers were carried on television news, docudramas, newspapers, billboards, posters, T-shirts, mailings, and milk cartons (Fritz and Altheide 1987). Such claims were exaggerated and traded on widespread beliefs about crime and dangerousness (Best 1985). This can also be illustrated with crime news that seemingly celebrates the inability of the state agencies to protect its citizens. In some cases, this will involve vigilante scenarios by individuals, while in others it will involve vigilante actions by entire audiences. An example is the television program *America's Most Wanted*, hosted by John Walsh, the man behind much of the "missing children" furor. This show draws some 5,000 calls per week from viewers who report that their neighbors, work associates, and fellow consumers "fit the description" of a "wanted suspect" flashed on television.

Another example is "gonzo justice," which has emerged as a new cultural form to address the mass-mediated public perception of unsuccessful social control (Altheide 1992). A combination of "public spectacle" (Edelman 1985), moral authority, and news legitimacy, gonzo justice is specifically oriented to mass communication formats and is often celebrated and applauded by mass-media writers and commentators. Popular culture provides a way to participate or play with horror, banditry, crime, and justice, as we are presented a range of scenarios and enactments through which we can interactively arrive at meaningful interpretations. The scenario of "out of control" evil calls forth a heroic retort as a kind of narrative response in the mediated drama. Consider a few examples. This one is from Pennsylvania:

> A 311-pound man who hasn't made child-support payments for more than a year because he's too overweight to work is under court order to lose 50 pounds or go to jail. . . . "I call it my 'Oprah Winfrey sentence,'" [Judge] Lavelle said. . . . It's designed to make him lose weight for the benefit of his children, while Oprah (a talk-show host) lost weight for the benefit of her job and future security. (United Press International and *Arizona Republic*, June 18, 1989)

And from Tennessee:

> A judge ordered Henry Lee McDonald to put a sign in his front-yard for 30
> days declaring in 4-inch letters that he "is a thief." U.S. District Court Judge
> L. Clure Morton instructed McDonald to erect the sign Tuesday as part of his
> three-year probation for receiving and concealing a stolen car. . . . The sign
> must be painted black and have 4-inch white capital letters that read: "Henry
> Lee McDonald bought a stolen car. He is a thief." (United Press International
> and *Tempe Daily News*, January 5, 1984)

Analysis of news materials suggest some identifiable features of gonzo
justice that join the news media to legal authority: (1) there must be an act
that can be defined and presented as extraordinary, if not excessive and
arbitrary; (2) it must be protective or "reclaiming" of a moral (often mythical) dimension; (3) individual initiative (rather than "organizational" initiative) is responsible for the reaction; (4) the act is expressive and evocative; (5) the act is intended to be interpreted and presented as an exemplar
for others to follow; (6) audience familiarity with other reports about the
problem provides a context of experience and meaning; and (7) reports seldom include contrary or challenging statements. In short, what makes
gonzo justice peculiar and unique is that we can expect it to be associated
with those agencies that are less likely to be seen as affirming and supportive of the cultural myths.

The previous examples suggest that formal agents of social control increasingly use the mass media to reach into more areas of the public order. Just as judges use gonzo justice to demonstrate (and promote) their
moral character and resolve to audiences who know little about their
work routines, other bureaucratic workers, such as politically ambitious
county prosecutors, rely on the news media not only to publicize their
"achievements" but also to actually work with and through the news formats to "do good work." With an escalating number of interest group
concerns, the domain of state control has expanded considerably, and the
orientation and tactics of state power have also increased beyond the traditional domains of "public life" to more proactive investigation and surveillance. As Marx (1988) notes,

> Social control has become more specialized and technical, and, in many
> ways, more penetrating and intrusive. In some ways, we are moving toward
> a Napoleonic view of the relationship between the individual and the state,
> where the individual is assumed to be guilty and must prove his or her in-
> nocence. That state's power to seek out violations, even without specific
> grounds for suspicion, has been enhanced. With this comes a cult and a cul-
> ture of surveillance that goes beyond government to the private sector and
> the interaction of individuals. (p. 2 ff.)

The exponential growth of the surveillance and undercover options across international, national, state, county, and city jurisdictions has been widely documented (Marx 1988; Staples 1997). While much of this work has focused on the increased use of "agents provocateurs," our interest is in the way certain state tactics and orientations can be blended with prevailing mass communication routines and patterns.

Media logic was a key part in Azscam (referred to in chapter 2). To reiterate, Azscam was a political sting operation in Arizona that joined the work of journalists and formal agents of social control through television news formats (Altheide 1993). The million-dollar operation, which ultimately contributed to the resignation and replacement of 8 percent of the state legislature and also influenced an ongoing election, was orchestrated by the Phoenix Police Department and the Maricopa County attorney. Azscam agents offered bags of money to numerous legislators in order to find out who could be tempted to support organized gambling legislation. The liberal use of racketeering statutes or RICO (Racketeer Influenced and Corrupt Organizations Act) legislation that permitted property forfeitures and seizures gave the local authorities in excess of a million dollars to use at the discretion of the county attorney. The videotaped materials and transcripts were featured in television and newspaper reports prior to any legal hearing. The mass media, and especially television, were integral features of the entire operation; the outcome was certainly consistent with any intention to entrap people, publicly expose them on videotape, and then get them to plea-bargain and resign. The presumption seems to have been that the publicity effect would exact a toll, and it did. The transcripts of conversations and edited video materials showing legislators making such statements as "I want to die rich" were released to the news media one day after arrests were made. Most of those indicted pleaded guilty in order to avoid greater charges. Others would later be named in conjunction with a civil racketeering suit filed to recover the $1 million cost of operation Azscam.

The mass-media formats that promote visuals packed with dramatic action were certainly consistent with the entire operation. It was regarded as "made for television evidence," even if it may not have been perfect for "courtroom" evidence. As with the "wedding video" that began this chapter, visual reality increasingly is what counts. Several chapters that follow illustrate how visuals of the enemy, such as "the falling towers" from the 9/11 attacks and the videotape of combat in Iraq in both Gulf wars, contributed to the public perception of danger and victory against a strange enemy.

Popular culture entertainment and media logic contribute to the international landscape as well. The politics of fear is apparent in mass-media coverage of negative war news. Ironically, much of the news reporting will be propaganda about positive developments rather than fear itself. Major news media do not present bad news, such as casualties, in a prominent place. Deaths of soldiers seldom appear on page 1. When not at war, any American killed abroad—especially if they are affiliated with the government—is quite newsworthy and is featured in major news sections. Not in wartime, however, especially the most recent Iraq war. News organizations have been told to not dwell on negative news, so many newspapers bury reports about American casualties in small-print headlines deep inside the newspaper. The exception to this is when a "local" soldier is killed, in which case the story will be framed as a patriotic one. The young man's or woman's death will be celebrated as an example for all of us to follow. Often we will be told that the person always wanted to join, for example, the Marines and be a soldier, and the article may include a statement that he or she was motivated by the 9/11 attacks and felt that it was his or her duty to join. Seldom will a statement appear like the one in *Newsweek* about Marine Staff Sergeant Russell Stay, who, a short time before he was killed, gave this advice in a letter to his five-year-old son: "Be studious, stay in school and stay away from the military. I mean it" (*Newsweek*, December 6, 2004, p. 21).

If the politics of fear lasts long enough, the lack of negative coverage about the costs of war or other military adventures will become commonplace. Indeed, the news discourse largely constitutes the politics of fear for mass audiences because this is their main source of information about the state of the political world. Soon, curtailing negative reports about the government, especially foreign policy, becomes the baseline for journalists and editors and, over time, their audiences as well. News media do not like to be cast as unpatriotic or "left" or "liberal." Those terms, especially "liberal," were popularized during the Reagan administration and have continued to dominate news discourse and commentary about news content. One study found that the phrase "media bias" occurred within a few words of "liberal" far more often than it did with "conservative."

The politics of fear is apparent not only in news content but also in the basic framework of news. This means that the dominant framing and organization of news material is intended to support the government and the status quo. While there are a few news organizations that are less compliant, their exceptionalism makes them appear to be even more deviant from the way that news reporting is expected to be done. Journalists understand that any critical reports will be interpreted as editorializing against the administration. Yet a few still report negative and controversial materials, but they are heavily documented.

One example is the news reporting about the prisoner abuse in U.S.-controlled prisons in Iraq (Abu Ghraib) and Guantanamo Bay, Cuba. According to reports in the *New Yorker*, *Newsweek*, the MoveOn.org website, and others, the problem began when the Bush administration approved a plan to treat terrorist suspects differently than prisoners of war. The latter are protected (in civilized nations) by the Geneva Convention's guidelines for the treatment of prisoners (Hersh 2004).

President Bush approved a policy that the Geneva Convention wouldn't apply to suspected al Qaeda and Taliban fighters held in Guantanamo Bay. When the war in Iraq started to go badly, Secretary of Defense Donald Rumsfeld extended these aggressive interrogation policies to Iraqi prisons. According to *Newsweek*,

> It was an approach that they adopted to sidestep the historical safeguards of the Geneva Conventions, which protect the rights of detainees and prisoners of war. In doing so, they overrode the objections of Secretary of State Colin Powell and America's top military lawyers—and they left underlings to sweat the details of what actually happened to prisoners in these lawless places. While no one deliberately authorized outright torture, these techniques entailed a systematic softening up of prisoners through isolation, privations, insults, threats and humiliation—methods that the Red Cross concluded were "tantamount to torture." (Barry et al. 2004)

Photographs of prisoners being beaten and sexually humiliated were obtained by some journalists, and others were sent to relatives of guards at the prison in Iraq. The visuals were compelling and raised critical comments by congressional leaders as well as human rights organizations. The reports were heavily documented with many facts and quotations from various government and military officials. Official inquiries were held, and several enlisted men and women were court-martialed, while senior-ranking officers were allowed to resign or were exonerated with typical bureaucratic accounts (e.g., other intelligence officials were in charge):

> High-level officials in the Pentagon were sent from Guantanamo Bay to Iraq to implement the more aggressive policies, and it appears that command of the prison was placed in the hands of military intelligence officers. Techniques that had been approved only for suspected al-Qaeda terrorists were suddenly applied to Iraqi prisoners (up to 90% of whom were mistakenly detained, according to the Red Cross). (Higgins 2004)

CONCLUSION

The politics of fear relies on public perceptions of threats and enemies. These are promoted by repeated news and popular-culture (e.g., movies) images of the "bad guys." The mass media and popular culture contribute to the definition of situations and audience expectations and criteria for self-presentations for themselves and others. A good example is the popular series *24*, starring Kiefer Sutherland, who plays an agent for the Counter Terrorist Unit, a fictional convergence of the FBI, the CIA, and the less public Homeland Security operations. The key backdrop is the 9/11 attacks, setting the stage for seemingly endless threats from ruthless Middle Eastern terrorists. The series of twenty-four episodes takes the viewer through an entire day of hard-hitting, fast-paced action of a renegade agent against a very well-organized group of terrorists. What is very important for our purposes is that this is the first television show that shows and legitimizes U.S. agents torturing suspects in a "race against time" to get information before the terrorist weapon kills millions of U.S. citizens. This introduction to torture by Americans on American television screens was a preview of photos and accounts of U.S. soldiers and other "contract workers" torturing Iraqi prisoners in Abu Ghraib prison in Iraq.

The reality of torture is muted by popular-culture depictions that are important for familiarizing and desensitizing audiences to grotesque cruelty. The news media provide sparse coverage of torture and conduct that is reprehensible to most Americans. Like many of the semisecret "black operations" engaged in by the U.S. terrorist forces during the past thirty years, murderous activities are not regarded as part of U.S. foreign policy, but when they do come to light, the brutal tactics are likely to be presented as tough but necessary. We have already seen how the United States handles charges of torture, but what is more astounding is when suspects are turned over to other countries that will apply torture on behalf of the United States. The practice is referred to as "extraordinary rendition" and was practiced against a Canadian citizen who was suspected of being involved in terrorist activities. On September 26, 2002, Maher Arar, a thirty-four-year-old man who had emigrated to Canada from Syria as a teenager, was picked up at Kennedy International Airport. American officials handed Arar over to Syria, a nation condemned by the Bush administration and others as an "outlaw nation" that supports terrorism. Arar was tortured for a year, all the while insisting on his innocence. Of course, he had never been charged with anything, just shipped out of the United States. According to *New York Times* columnist Bob Herbert (2005),

According to the State Department, torture was most likely to occur at one of the many detention centers run by the Syrian security forces, "particularly while the authorities are trying to extract a confession or information about an alleged crime or alleged accomplices."

Extraordinary rendition is antithetical to everything Americans are supposed to believe in. It violates American law. It violates international law. And it is a profound violation of our own most fundamental moral imperative—that there are limits to the way we treat other human beings, even in a time of war and great fear.

As audiences spend more time with these formats, the logic of advertising, entertainment, and popular culture becomes taken for granted as a "normal form" of communication. As Couch (1995) noted, evocative rather than referential forms of communication now dominate the meaning landscape. The referential forms fall before the electrified rolling formats that change everyday life with the look and swagger of persona, entertainment, and action.

One way power is manifested is by influencing the definition of a situation. Cultural logics inform this process and are therefore powerful, but we are not controlled (and certainly not determined) by them, particularly when one's effective environment contains meanings to challenge the legitimacy, veracity, and relevance of certain procedures. Resistance can follow, but it is likely to be formatted by ecologies of communication. Indeed, the contribution of expanded discourses of control to the narrowing or expansion of resistance modes remains an intriguing area of inquiry:

> We must locate the modes in which believing, knowing, and their contents reciprocally define each other today, and in that way try to grasp a few of the ways believing and making people believe function in the political formations in which, within this system, the tactics made possible, by the exigencies of a position and the constraints of a history are displayed. (Couch 1995, p. 185)

Some of the most significant cultural logics can be conceptualized within the ecology of communication that is part of the effective environment that competent social actors must take into account as they forge definitions of the situations. Just as "markets" contain a leveling dimension (e.g., anyone with the price of admission can play), so too does the increasingly technical information technology, with its "common key" to a host of activities. And while the price of admission excludes many, so too does the activity built on formats not easily accessible to everyone. It is within these symbolic boundaries that freedom and constraint are routinized and dramaturgically played out through an expanding array of social definitions in the social construction of reality.

4

Crime and Terrorism

The crime scene, marked off in yellow police tape, doesn't move; no matter when the reporter arrives there's always a picture to shoot, preferably live. No need to spend off-camera time digging, researching, or even thinking. Just get to the crime scene, get the wind blowing through your hair, and the rest will take care of itself.

—Grossman (1997, p. 21)

Objective indicators of risk and danger in American life suggest that most U.S. citizens are healthier and safer and live more predictable lives than at any time in history, yet numerous surveys indicate these same citizens perceive that their lives are very dangerous. The politics of fear requires specific topics or events to promote fear. In the United States, crime policies lead the way in promoting crime as a major public issue that citizens should fear and that authorities should control. Crime and fear dominate most U.S. newspapers and television news reports. This chapter examines how crime coverage is linked to entertainment formats that provide the basic underlying logic of commercial television (and newspapers). I draw from more than a decade of research on the social construction of fear (Altheide 1997, 2002b; Altheide and Michalowski 1999). I will also argue that one reason crime is so popular is that it is almost always linked to "fear," the most basic feature of entertainment in popular culture. This emphasis has produced a discourse of fear, defined in chapter 1 as the pervasive communication, symbolic awareness, and expectation that danger and risk are a central feature of everyday life. The discourse of fear has important consequences for social policy, public perceptions of social issues, the demise of public space, citizens who are becoming more "armed" and "armored," and the promotion of a new social identity—the victim—that has been exploited by numerous claims makers, including politicians, who promote their own propaganda about national and international politics. These points will be followed by a brief discussion of alternative news formats.

Crime news has been a staple of journalism for decades (Surette 1992). For many years, newspapers emphasized sensational and even erotic aspects of homicides and brutal assaults, sex crimes, and kidnappings (Soothill and Walby 1991). This emphasis became more "rational" with the emergence of movie "newsreels" as well as television news and the ability to "see" crime scenes, victims, and the accused. Another major change is the rise of a pervasive mass-mediated popular culture that virtually engulfs everyday life. In another age, there was the mass media, and there was reality; in our age, there is popular culture—everywhere—and even "reality" is presented to us as entertainment programming. In the United States, for example, dozens of "reality" television programs are about crime and "crime fighting," as caricatures of criminals and police officers (Fishman and Cavender 1998) are presented back-to-back with sexually evocative images of people roaming "remote islands" in search of love, treasure, and security.

Running through all this programming is the commercially inspired entertainment format. As suggested by Snow's (1983) analysis of "media culture," the entertainment format emphasizes, first, an absence of the ordinary; second, the openness of an adventure, outside the boundaries of routine behavior; and, third, a suspension of disbelief by the audience member. In addition, while the exact outcome may be in doubt, there is a clear and unambiguous point at which it will be resolved. Packaging such emphases within dramatic formats (visual, brief, and action oriented) produces an exciting and familiar tempo for audiences. Moreover, as audiences spend more time with these formats, the logic of advertising, entertainment, and popular culture becomes taken for granted as a "normal form" of communication.

There are two reasons why crime is so prevalent in American television and, increasingly, throughout the world. First, as noted, crime is connected to fear, a staple of the entertainment format. Second, crime is very easy to cover and therefore fits well with scheduling and personnel constraints of local television. As one vice president of several local stations pointed out, "Covering crime is the easiest, fastest, cheapest, most efficient kind of news coverage for TV stations. News directors love crime" (Grossman 1997, p. 21). A clear bias of this coverage is that those crimes that occur very rarely, such as homicides and brutal physical assaults, receive the majority of coverage, while those crimes that are more likely to occur, such as theft and burglary, are seldom mentioned. One consequence of this coverage is to give viewers (and readers) the sense that "crime" means "violent crime." There is strong evidence that this perception of the "crime problem" contributes to voter support for "tough crime legislation," including mandatory sentencing, "three strikes and you're out," and capital punishment (Cavender 2004).

Numerous studies of crime reporting stress how pervasive crime and danger are in American news media, especially television (Budzilowicz 2002). Crime reports make up 25 to 35 percent of news in some local markets. A recent study by the *Columbia Journalism Review* (Grossman 1997) noted that nearly 20 percent of all "people" featured in local news are involved with crime reporting:

> Consider this statistic: one has to add up all the educators, school board members, city council members, mayors, state agency officials, state legislators governors, members of Congress and all other local elected and appointed officials combined just to match the number of criminals and suspects on screen. . . .
>
> Who are the people shown in local TV news stories? After criminals and suspects (who make up 10 percent of all people n screen) the most common group featured is crime victims or their families (9 percent). . . .
>
> Crime is the perennial No. 1 topic, in large markets and small, but on the largest markets stations are most likely to pad their crime coverage with tales of mayhem from distant places.
>
> One consequence is that "local" news about the "community" looks like "crime," but numerous other aspects of life are not covered.
>
> 1. Forty percent of the stories last 30 seconds or less.
> 2. One in four stories is about crime, law or courts.
> 3. Less than 1 percent of stories could be called "investigative."
> 4. Health stories outnumber all other social issues by 32 percent.
> 5. There are as many stories about the bizarre (8 percent) as there are about civic institutions.
>
> . . . Poverty, welfare, and homelessness are all but absent in local news. Out of the nearly 6000 stories studied, only nine dealt with these topics, not enough to even register a single percentage point. . . . [According to a National Endowment for the Arts study, citizens spend more money each year attending performing-arts events than either the movies or professional sports]. Yet on local TV news, the arts and culture are almost invisible, accounting for just 24 stories—again, less than one percent of the total studied. (Project for Excellence in Journalism 2001)

According to a report by the Project for Excellence in Journalism (2005), crime news is important for the economics of television news; crime news is apparently institutionalized as a good way to "hook" an audience and "hold" them throughout the newscast.

> This approach ["hook and hold"] shows up quite clearly in an examination of the data collected by the Project for Excellence in Journalism during its local TV news study from 1998 to 2002. While "public safety" news accounted for 36% of stories over all, it constituted nearly two-thirds of the stories that led newscasts (61%), the stories given the most time and resources. And public safety news continued to make up the majority of stories until the fifth story in the newscast. (Indeed, 13% of all newscasts began with three crime stories in a row, back to back to back.)

The major television networks in the United States tend to not present a lot of crime news since crime tends to be "local." Yet there has been a remarkable increase in the amount of violent crime news presented on network television. Indeed, in recent years, journalism has begun to take a look at the impact of such distorted coverage about crime and fear on American life. Two journalists (Westfeldt and Wicker 1998) who are very critical of the news coverage of crime observed,

> In 1997, even as the prison population was going up and the crime rate was falling the public rated "crime/gangs/justice system" as "the most important problem facing the country today"—and by a large margin. (p. 2)

As they chronicled the preoccupation with crime by local newspapers and television broadcasters in promoting a fear of crime agenda, the authors observed the culpability of national and prestigious news outlets in pushing the same views, including television network news:

> The Center for Media and Public Affairs reported in April 1998 that the national murder rate has fallen by 20% since 1990—but the number of murder stories on network newscasts rose in the same years by about 600% . . . not including the many broadcasts of or about the O. J. Simpson trial. (Westfeldt and Wicker 1998, p. 2)

FEAR AND CRIME

In my book *Creating Fear: News and the Construction of Crisis*, I tracked the nature and extent of the use of the word "fear" in major newspapers from 1987 to 1996 and examined ABC news coverage for several years. This project was informed by numerous studies and insights by criminologists and media scholars, particularly the conceptual development of a model—the "problem frame"—of how entertainment inspires news reports about fear (Altheide 1997). The basic findings were that use of the word "fear" increased substantially—often 100 percent in stories as well as headlines, peaking around 1994. This usage also "traveled" across various topics over time, meaning, for example, that at one point fear would be closely associated with AIDS, while a few years later it was gangs or violence. Two terms closely associated with fear in the 1990s were "children" and "schools." Numerous news reports about fear pertain to children (Altheide 2002a). The news media's emphasis of fear with children is consistent with work by Warr (1992) and others on the significance of "third-person" or "altruistic fear"—the concern for those whom you love or are responsible. Specifically, Warr found that children are the most common object of fear in households. Much of this concern is generated around crime and drugs. Such coverage of crime promotes more communication of fear and control by authorities. One example is the "Amber Alert" program that has been adopted by most states in the United States as well as federal legislation. Named after Amber Hagerman, who was kidnapped and killed in 1997, Amber Alerts are public messages broadcast on radio, television, and freeway signs that a child has been abducted.

Frequent association of terms like "fear" (rather than other descriptors, e.g., "danger" or "risk") promote a discourse of fear. Moreover, while the association of certain words (topics) with fear varies, this does not mean that they are no longer connoted as fear. Rather, analysis suggests that words used frequently together in public discourse may become "meaningfully joined," as sign and signifier, as connotation and denotation, so that, over time, it becomes redundant and unnecessary to use "fear" with "violence," "crime," "gangs," and "drugs": the specific word itself implies fear. The rationale for this approach is that the meaning of two words is suggested by their proximity, their association. Indeed, over time, terms merge in public discourse and the actual use and meaning of terms. Consider the example of "violence" and "crime" in the following three sentences:

1. An act of violence that might be regarded as a crime occurred Saturday night.
2. A violent crime occurred Saturday night.
3. A [crime (violence)] occurred Saturday night.

The first sentence treats both "violence" and "crime" as nouns, as separate but perhaps related. In the second sentence, "violence" is an adjective for "crime," part of its description and meaning. But the third sentence shows what happens when terms are continually used together, often merging. This sentence suggests that "crime" has incorporated "violence" into its meaning and that the word "violent" need not be used. As the audience becomes more familiar with the meaning of the term and the context of its use, it becomes redundant to state "violent crime" since the mass-mediated experience suggests that "crime is violent" (despite research to the contrary, such as that most crimes are property crimes). Other work in cultural studies, deconstruction, and semiotics has demonstrated how this happens with numerous social problems and issues (cf. Manning and Cullum-Swan 1994). Not only is the event distorted by this coupling, but our capacity to deal with it in different ways may be compromised as well. A similar coupling occurs when television reports about crime and violence show individuals of certain racial and ethnic groups. The news reports tend to stress individual causation and responsibility and very seldom place these acts in a societal context that includes poverty (Budzilowicz 2002). Thus, television visual formats can contribute to social definitions. Conversely, coupling may not occur between words and topics if they have traditionally been viewed as quite separate. There is reason to suspect that this is part of the difficulty in convincing people that domestic violence is "really violence" and also a "crime." The notions of "family" and "crime" and "violence" have seldom appeared within close proximity in routine news reports until fairly recently.

SOCIAL CONSEQUENCES OF THE DISCOURSE OF FEAR

The evidence is quite strong that mass-media reports about topics inform public opinion on such matters and contribute in no small way to setting social and political agendas (Chermak 1995; Chiricos 2000; Chiricos et al. 1997). As Warr (1985) notes, "And like criminal victimization itself, the consequences of fear are real, measurable, and potentially severe, both at an individual and social level" (p. 238). From the standpoint of media content as "cause," researchers ask whether news reports can "cause" or "lead" people to focus on and fear crime, including the extent to which relevant values and perspectives may be "cultivated" (Gerbner et al. 1978). From this perspective, the mass media play a large role in shaping public agendas by influencing *what* people think about (Shaw and Mc-Combs 1977). While there is scant data on "fear" per se among public opinion polls, most measures of fear in recent years are associated with crime. Chiricos and colleagues (2000) note, "With regard to fear, the most consequential of those messages are received from local news, and the volume of crime stories in that medium has achieved proportions that concern many critics" (p. 780). As noted previously, numerous public opinion polls show that fear of crime and personal safety reign above most other concerns. Indeed, many Americans feel that their lives are unsafe and more subject to harm than at previous times (Surette 1998).

Crime coverage contributes to perceptions of danger and the emergence of the discourse of fear. Ferraro (1995) suggested the concept "perceptual criminology," or the notion that "many of the problems associated with crime, including fear, are independent of actual victimization . . . because it may lead to decreased social integration, out-migration, restriction of activities, added security costs, and avoidance behaviors" (p. 3).

Researchers have argued for decades that such concerns are connected to the mass-media coverage of news as well as entertainment (Comstock 1980; MacKuen and Coombs 1981; Surette 1998). For many people, the mass media in general and the news media in particular are a "window" on the world. How the public views issues and problems is related to the mass media, although researchers disagree about the nature of this relationship (Gerbner and Gross 1976; Gunter 1987; Hirsch 1980; Katz 1987; Schlesinger, Tumber, and Murdock 1991; Skogan and Maxfield 1981; Sparks 1992; Zillman and Wakshlag 1987). This is particularly apparent when fear is associated with popular topics like crime, violence, drugs, and gangs, which have become staples of news reports as well as in entertainment media. What audiences perceive as a "crime problem" is a feature of popular culture and an ecology of communication (Bailey and Hale 1998; Ferrell and Sanders 1995). Mapping how fear has become associated with different topics over time can clarify how the mass media and popular culture influence public perceptions of danger and risk. Indeed, Surette's (1992) "social ecology of crime" model suggests that the "world of TV entertainment" resembles "citizen-sheep" being protected from "predator wolves—criminals" by "sheep dogs—police" (p. 43).

Several projects have suggested that the media do contribute to political agendas as well as people's perceptions and interests in everyday life (MacKuen and Coombs 1981). Iyengar and Kinder (1987) employed an experimental design to demonstrate " that television news shapes the relative importance Americans attach to various national problems" (p. 113). Focusing on energy, inflation, and unemployment, they argued that television is most powerful at "priming" or providing accessible bits of information that viewers may draw on to help interpret other events. Making it clear that ultimately it is the viewers' perceptions and everyday life experiences that help interpret social life, nevertheless, television contributes "by priming certain aspects of national life while ignoring others, television news sets the terms by which political judgments are rendered and political choices made" (Iyengar and Kinder 1987, p. 4).

In other work, Iyengar (1991) suggests that priming and framing of reports as either "episodic," focusing on individual circumstances and responsibility, or thematic, focusing on contextual and societal responsibility, has a bearing on what viewers take from television news reports

(Ericson 1993). For example, Budzilowicz (2002) notes that most of these reports emphasized individual responsibility rather than the social conditions and context that led to the acts.

Other work has shown that fear and victim are informed by perceived membership (Altheide et al. 2001). Crime and threats to the public order—and therefore to all good citizens—is part of the focus of fear, but, as noted throughout this book, the topics change over time. What they all have in common is pointing to the "other," the outsider, the nonmember, the alien. However, Schwalbe et al. (2000) have shown that "othering" is part of a social process whereby a dominant group defines into existence an inferior group. This requires the establishment and "group sense" of symbolic boundaries of membership. These boundaries occur through institutional processes that are grounded in everyday situations and encounters, including language, discourse, accounts, and conversation. Knowledge and skill at using "what everyone like us knows" involves formal and informal socialization so that members acquire the coinage of cultural capital with which they can purchase acceptance, allegiance, and belonging. Part of this language involves the discourse of fear:

> Discourse is more than talk and writing; it is a way of talking and writing. To regulate discourse is to impose a set of formal or informal rules about what can be said, how it can be said, and who can say what to whom. . . . Inasmuch as language is the principal means by which we express, manage, and conjure emotions, to regulate discourse is to regulate emotion. The ultimate consequence is a regulation of action. . . .
>
> When a form of discourse is established as standard practice, it becomes a tool for reproducing inequality, because it can serve not only to regulate thought and emotion, but also to identify others and thus to maintain boundaries as well. (Schwalbe et al. 2000, pp. 433–34)

It is not fear of crime, then, that is most critical. It is what this fear can expand to, what it can become. Sociologists have noted that we are becoming "armored." Social life changes when more people live behind walls, hire guards, drive "armored" vehicles (e.g., sport-utility vehicles), wear "armored" clothing (e.g., big-soled shoes or clothing with the phrase "No Fear!"), carry Mace or handguns, and take martial arts classes. The problem is that these activities reaffirm and help produce a sense of disorder that our actions perpetuate. We then rely more on formal agents of social control to "save us" by "policing them," the "others," who have challenged our faith.

The major impact of the discourse of fear is to promote a sense of disorder and a belief that "things are out of control." Ferraro (1995) suggests that fear reproduces itself, or becomes a self-fulfilling prophecy. Social life can become more hostile when social actors define their situations as "fearful" and engage in speech communities through the discourse of fear. And people come to share an identity as competent "fear realists" as family members, friends, neighbors, and colleagues socially construct their effective environments with fear. Behavior becomes constrained, community activism may focus more on "block watch" programs and quasi-vigilantism, and we continue to avoid "downtowns" and many parts of our social world because of "what everyone knows."

Another consequence of the nature and extent of crime reporting is that the discourse of fear becomes taken for granted as a description of reality. What are very rare events are assumed to be common occurrences. For example, audience members not only talk about brutal assaults and even child kidnappings—which are very rare—but they also begin to enact them as hoaxes and to "play with fear" in order to get attention:

> A mother in Mesa, Arizona, claimed that she was sexually assaulted in her child's school restroom when a "man with cigarette breath, dirty fingernails and long, messy hair had placed a sharp object to her neck, knocked her unconscious and assaulted her." Actually, she wounded herself and cut up her clothing in order to get some attention, particularly from her husband. ("Mom: 'Rape' Was a Hoax," *Arizona Republic*, August 18, 1999, p. A1)

Stories of assaults and kidnappings blasted across headlines—even when false or greatly distorted—make it difficult for frightened citizens to believe that schools are one the safest places in American society. It is becoming more common to "play out" scenarios of danger and fear that audiences assume to be quite common. Researchers find that many of these hoaxes rely on stereotypes of marginalized groups, such as poor people and racial minorities. The oppositions that become part of the discourse of fear can be illustrated in another way as well. Repetitious news reports that make connections between fear, children, schools, and suspected assailants who fit stereotypes are easy to accept even when they are false. Russell's (1998) study of sixty-seven publicized racially tinged hoaxes between 1987 and 1996 illustrates how storytellers frame their accounts in social identities that are legitimated by numerous reports and stereotypes of marginalized groups, such as racial minorities. For example, in 1990 a George Washington University student reported that another student had been raped by two black men with "particularly bad body odor," in order to "highlight the problems of safety for women."

A schoolteacher in Tucson, Arizona, wrote herself threatening letters before shooting herself. She had claimed that discipline and security were too lax. She implied that a twelve-year-old Hispanic youth sent the letters and then shot her. In the spring of 1999, two Mesa, Arizona, fifth-grade girls, playing a game of Truth or Dare, told a detailed story about a knife-toting transient who grabbed them as they were leaving an elementary school. They fought off the man, whom they said "chewed his nails," and escaped to a neighbor's house. Police and neighbors patrolled the neighborhood questioning various people, only to have the girls admit that it was false. When people "pretend" that they have been assaulted, abducted, or in some way harmed by strangers, they are acting out a morality play that has become part of a discourse of fear, or the notion that fear and danger are pervasive.

Fear is part of our everyday discourse, even though we enjoy unprecedented levels of health, safety, and life expectancy. And now we "play with it." More of our "play worlds" come from the mass media. News reports are merging with television "reality programs" and "crime dramas" ripped from the front pages, in turn providing us with templates for looking at everyday life. The increase in "false reports" is an example. We have long known that some officials use fear to promote their own childish agendas. The expanding interest in fear and victimhood also contributes to (1) audiences who play with the repetitive reports as dramatic enactments of "fear and dread in our lives" and (2) individual actors who seek roles that are accepted as legitimate "attention-getters" in order to accomplish favorable identity vis-à-vis particular audience members.

Research also shows that the news coverage of the 9/11 attacks brought out a lingering and pervasive preoccupation with fear that has been exploited by government officials seeking to expand social control and limit civil liberties. After all, fear—more than danger or risk—is a pervasive emotional orientation that calls for strong action against those responsible. The remedy usually involves state authorities taking more control. The 9/11 terror attacks were presented, essentially, as a "crime story," albeit a "big crime," and language that was developed over two decades of crime reporting was applied to terrorism. President Bush said that "it's important for Americans to know that trafficking of drugs finances the world of terror, sustaining terrorists." The focus on fear provides more revenue for news organizations and related popular-culture outlets (e.g., *America's Most Wanted*) while giving police and law enforcement agencies more credibility and control. The audience participates through hoaxes of fear.

The massive number of news reports about terrorism and alleged links to anthrax mailings sparked numerous "hoaxes" in the United States and around the world. The Postal Service received nearly 16,000 anthrax reports, and an additional sixty reports have been investigated in which people claimed to have mailed or received anthrax in a letter. Clayton Lee Waagner, a petty criminal and self-proclaimed "antiabortion warrior," is suspected of sending some 550 letters containing harmless white powder to abortion clinics with the words "Army of God." While this zealot clearly intended to frighten and intimidate recipients, several dozen people around the world sent similar "harmless" letters, intended as a "practical joke," to friends, coworkers, neighborhood foes, and news organizations. At least one postal worker has been indicted for scrawling a note on a package about anthrax in order to take advantage of the public's fear "to settle a score to pull off a prank." Several others claimed that they received anthrax-filled letters. One Missouri woman who initially claimed to have been sent a poisoned letter admitted that she put flour and roach killer in the envelope and then delivered it to police some eighty miles from her home.

Fear also makes us more compliant in seeking help or being "rescued" from formal agents of social control. This is very apparent with the rise of "victimization" as a status to be shared and enjoyed. Fear is a perspective or orientation to the world rather than "fear of something." Fear is one of the few things that Americans share. The discourse of fear is constructed through evocative entertainment formats that promote visual, emotional, and dramatic experience that can be vicariously lived, shared, and identified with by audience members. However, it is not just "fear of crime" or a particular thing but rather a sense or an identity that is held in common by many Americans that we are all actual or potential victims. Research indicates that the "object" of fear (e.g., crime, drugs, AIDS, or children) shifts or "travels" across topics over time. The sense that something has happened to us, could happen to us, or probably will happen to us connects the present moment with resentments and blame about the past as well as anxieties about the future.

The most pervasive aspect of this "victim" perspective is crime. Politicians and state control agencies, working with news media as "news sources," have done much to capitalize on this concern and to promote a sense of insecurity and reliance on formal agents of social control (and related businesses) to provide surveillance, protection, revenge, and punishment to protect us, to save us. Even foreign policy and threats of external enemies support fear:

> The constant articulation of danger through foreign policy is thus not a threat to a state's identity or existence: it is its condition of possibility. While the objects of concern change over time, the techniques and exclusions by which those objects are constituted as dangers persist. (Campbell 1998, p. 13)

In addition,

> The postwar tests of United States foreign policy certainly located the dangers they identified via references to the Soviet Union. But they always acknowledged that the absence of order, the potential for anarchy, and the fear of totalitarian forces or other negative elements that would exploit or foster conditions—whether internal or external—was their initial concern. (Campbell 1998, p. 30)

There can be no fear without actual victims or potential victims. In the postmodern age, victim is a status and a representation and not merely a person or someone who has suffered as a result of some personal, social, or physical calamity. Massive, concerted efforts by moral entrepreneurs to have their causes adopted and legitimated as "core social issues" worthy of attention have led to the wholesale adaptation and refinement of the use of the problem frame to promote victimization. Often couching their "causes" as battles for "justice," moral entrepreneurs seek to promote new social definitions of right and wrong (Johnson 1995; Spector and Kitsuse 1977). Victims are entertaining, and that is why they abound. They are evocative, bringing forth tears, joy, and vicarious emotional experience. But a victim is more. "Victim" is now a status, a position that is open to all people who live in a symbolic environment marked by the discourse of fear. We are all potential victims, often vying for official recognition and legitimacy.

BEYOND THE LENS OF FEAR

Continual news coverage about crime and mayhem gradually transforms public discourse into victimization and threat. Without minimizing the dangers of everyday life, we can speak of danger and risk rather than fear, except when it is warranted. It is possible to take more control of our social environment. But much of this action begins not with "cleaning up the streets" but with focusing on our symbolic environment, understanding how our meaning machines are operating, and trying to provide some options. A responsible news media will take action to move away from fear-oriented infotainment. Recent changes (since 1997) in select journalistic organizations are encouraging, as stations like KVUE in Austin, Texas, began following a different protocol for presenting crime stories. This station's news management examined how crime news was being covered and agreed essentially with several decades of social science research that much of the coverage was sensational and dramatic and had no social value whatsoever. Accordingly, they set forth five rules of thumb for covering crime news:

1. Does action need to be taken?
2. Is there an immediate threat to safety?
3. Is there a threat to children?
4. Does the crime have significant community impact?
5. Does the story lend itself to a crime prevention effort?

Many in the industry as well as newspaper writers criticized them for not presenting "all the news." The strongest claim was that their ratings would fall and that people would switch channels to the traditional blood and guts that leads local television newscasts across the country. To KVUE's credit—and perhaps their relief—the ratings have held, and their new brand of television journalism has become more popular, at least to the extent that other stations across the country are talking about change.

CONCLUSION

The politics of fear is fed by popular culture. Crime news and fear influence national and international affairs. Fear is a key component of the entertainment format that has shaped news reports for several decades. This usage has intensified in the United States around certain topics such as crime and terrorism. I suggest that the U.S. militant policy against Iraq was fueled by decades of crime reports and harsh efforts in pursuing the drug war. Citizens became accustomed to giving up civil liberties to surveillance and enforcement efforts by formal agents of social control. Numerous "crises" and fears involving crime, violence, and uncertainty were important for public definitions of the situation after 9/11. Government officials used the foundation of fear to build even more fear in the United States and to enact draconian legislation that has negated civil liberties. The drug war and ongoing concerns with crime led to the expansion of fear with terrorism. News reports and advertisements joined drug use with terrorism and helped shift "drugs" from criminal activity to unpatriotic action. A $10 million ad campaign that included a 2002 Super Bowl commercial stated that buying and using drugs supports terrorism, or, as President Bush put it, "If you quit drugs, you join the fight against terror in America." Criminals and terrorists are now joined in popular-culture narratives of evil, control, and conquest. The war on drugs increased our prison population 600 percent since 1970 and destroyed numerous minority communities in the United States. The war on terrorism brought death and destruction to untold thousands of Iraqis. And still we receive messages promoting fear, asking for more security, and promising more surveillance. Crime news has gone global. The American public and their legislators apparently accepted the Bush administration's trumpeting of the necessity of the various Patriot acts despite unprecedented violation of civil liberties at the expense of more surveillance and less law enforcement accountability. As I concluded in *Creating Fear*,

> Fear accumulates and is deposited over a wide social terrain. Like agates that were formed some 40 million years in the interstices of cooling magma and have been transported by rivers to oceans and then beaches ever since, fear retains its essential elements. The chemistry of agates can be uncovered

through analysis, although most people who find them don't really care about that; they are merely pretty rocks, which, when polished, assume a gemlike character that separates them from other earthen surfaces. The origin of a specific fear can also be uncovered in specific instances, but most people do not care about where it began; one fear merely gets compiled with others on the beaches of our experiences and social encounters. (Altheide 2002b, p. 195)

5

Consuming Terrorism

When a whole nation is roaring Patriotism at the top of its voice, I am
fain to explore the cleanliness of its hands and purity of its heart.

—Ralph Waldo Emerson

Keep America Rolling.

—General Motors

The war on terrorism reflects the power of the politics of fear while also
reinforcing policies and social changes that invigorate public fears.
This chapter examines some of the subtle and not-so-subtle ways that this
"new threat" was blended with previous threats. The longer-term effects
on public discourse and perspectives about the future will be examined in
the next chapter.

The terrorist attacks on September 11, 2001, awakened the American
spirit of giving and spending. The tragic loss of lives and property fueled
patriotic slogans, thousands of commercial advertisements, public contributions of more than $2 billion, major domestic and foreign policy
changes, and the largest increase in the military budget in thirty-five
years. Stores sold out of flags, businesses linked advertising to patriotic
slogans (e.g., General Motors' "Keep America Rolling"), baseball fans
sang "God Bless America" instead of "Take Me Out to the Ball Game,"
and children helped raise money for the Afghani kids who were "starv-
ing" (and being bombed). Analysis of news reports and advertisements
suggests that popular-culture and mass-media depictions of fear, patriotism, consumption, and victimization contributed to the emergence of a

"national identity" and collective action that was fostered by elite decision makers' propaganda. Initial declarations about recovery and retaliation to promote patriotism became a "war on terrorism" with no end in sight.

This chapter discusses how "patriotic" giving and spending to help victims and combat terrorism were linked to an expanded military posture. I wish to propose that popular-culture and mass-media depictions of fear, patriotism, consumption, and victimization contributed to the emergence of a "national identity" and collective action that was fostered by elite decision makers' propaganda. As suggested by Vidich (1991), any adequate social theory must consider the central trends and tendencies in our bureaucratic order, including the following:

1. The penetration of bureaucracy as a form of organization in all institutional orders
2. The development of mass communications and mass media and their pervasive global penetration
3. The consequences of industrial capitalism and the machine process of traditional sodalities, communal relations, universities, economics, political totalism, religion, and war

I argue that the communication order is a critical foundation for constituting social and political changes and that the logic of this order underlies how power is communicated. My analysis is informed by recent work on commensuration, communalism, the politics of fear, and institutional logics.

Examining the propaganda, advertisements, and public reactions reveals emergent cultural scripts about individual and national character and identity. Espeland's (2002) analysis of commensuration as "the expression or measurement of characteristics normally represented by different units according to a common metric" conceptually joins individually oriented consumption and communally oriented giving to patriotism and national unity. I suggest that elites and advertisers promoted cash donations and expenditures as commensurate with personal caring and national identity within the context of popular culture.

Unlike reactions to previous "external attacks" (e.g., Pearl Harbor) that stressed conservation, personal sacrifice, and commitment, a prevailing theme of consumption as character and financial contributions as commitment and support pervaded mass-media messages surrounding the 9/11 attacks. These messages made giving and buying commensurate (Espeland 2002) with patriotism and national unity. The key metaphor was investment for victims and against "evil" victimizers. More specifically, the argument is that the widely seen (and repeatedly replayed) visuals of the Twin Towers' destruction became an icon of membership in a common victimization and, ultimately, that "all" who viewed/cared/ opposed destruction could fight back by giving and spending. Citizens were asked to not only give blood and money but also grant elites and formal agents of social control all authority to take whatever measures were deemed necessary to protect citizens, take revenge, and prevent such a deed from reoccurring. This would take a lot of investment and "giving up" certain conveniences for the sake of protection. The metaphor of "investment" covered a context of meaning that joined contributing to "victims" of 9/11, buying products to "Keep America Rolling," and supporting military action and budget increases. These messages promoted a national identity (Shapiro 1992; Thiele 1993) based on the politics of fear that was later used by President Bush to pursue a "first-strike" policy against U.S. enemies.

It is the context and promotion of "spending" that most concerns me in this chapter. I propose that (1) fear supported consumption as a meaningful way for audiences to sustain an identity of substance and character, (2) consumption and giving were joined symbolically as government and business propaganda emphasized common themes of spending/buying to "help the country get back on track" (and related euphemisms), (3) the absence of a clear target for reprisals contributed to the construction of broad symbolic enemies and goals, and (4) consumption as investing promoted a massive increase in military spending.

PROPAGANDA AND THE MILITARY–MEDIA COMPLEX

It is helpful to distinguish the loss of life and property associated with 9/11 from its meaning. How would this situation be interpreted, defined, and accepted? While the terrorists were implicated in the technology of explosives and strategic deceptions to hijack four aircraft that were used as missiles of death, the meaning was provided essentially by the United States. This involved propaganda.

Chapter 1 stressed that propaganda of any event is tied to the historical and social context as well as basic structural arrangements. It is worth reviewing some of those key points. Propaganda thus reveals certain symbolic foundations for meaning and identity in social life. Crisis provides opportunities for heads of state to present themselves as leaders and to dramatically define the situation as tragic but hopeful and to bring out the "resolve" of national character. Symbolic interaction theory suggests that identity and meaning are socially constructed by applying familiar experiences and routines to specific situations (Altheide 2000; Cerulo 1997; Cerulo et al. 1992; Holstein and Gubrium 2000; Perinbanayagam 1974).

Thus, continuity and novelty are linked in meaningful ways. The theorist Hans Gerth (1992), who was familiar with the brilliant Nazi propaganda efforts in World War II, discussed the context of national conflicts and propaganda during the Cold War in the 1950s:[1]

> Loyalty to a national state is implemented by means of public educational systems. . . . Since the territory dominated by the nation is typically larger than that dominated by, say, the blood or religion, modern nationalism has had to rely more on mass education and propaganda. (p. 338)

In noting that leadership is challenged and demonstrated by joining the power of large organizations with occupational, professional, religious, and club associations, Gerth stressed that "in order to avoid unexpected and unwanted results, social and political administrations require a deep and extensive understanding of the total equilibrium of the given social structure" (p. 342). In the final analysis, Gerth emphasized that "propaganda, however, can be fully understood only if we recognize its most significant purpose, namely, to define the level of reality on which people think, discuss, and act" (p. 347).

Like many analyses of propaganda, Gerth's experience with World War II was tied to propaganda as representation, as media content that was distinctive from nonpropaganda and other realms of everyday life. But communication formats that link experience with meaning are part of everyday life. As McDonald (1994) provocatively notes,

> Formats are complex and multidimensional. They include a constellation of people, activities, and the implements important to them, as well as the kinds of discourses and relations that result. . . . The formats of technology and power are intimately connected because formats structure social fields of behavior—the possibilities for human perception and relationships. These techno-formats blur and redefine the boundaries between public and private self in the learning process. (p. 538)

The reality of a social order grounded in media logic (Altheide 1995; Altheide and Snow 1979) is constituted by shared understanding of communication formats and symbolic meanings conveyed increasingly by visual media that blur the lines between fantasy, news, and reality:

> A mimetic war is a battle of imitation and representation, in which the relationship of who we are and who they are is played out along a wide spectrum of familiarity and friendliness, indifference and tolerance, estrangement and hostility. It can result in appreciation or denigration, accommodation or separation, assimilation or extermination. It draws physical boundaries between peoples, as well as metaphysical boundaries be-

tween life and the most radical other of life, death. It separates human from god. It builds the fence that makes good neighbors; it builds the wall that confines a whole people. And it sanctions just about every kind of violence. (Der Derian 2002)

The importance of media formats in the communication process is apparent in the rise of the military–media complex that followed the decline of the Soviet Union and played a major role in the emergence of nationalism (Altheide 1999). It was not until the 1960s that television surpassed print media as a cultural force. The military–media complex is a feature of programming in an entertainment era dominated by popular culture and communication forms that share sophisticated information technology promoting visual media and evocative content. Der Derian (2002) noted that "the first and most likely the last battles of the counter/terror war are going to be waged on global networks that reach much more widely and deeply into our everyday lives," but this development turned on shared media logic between nightly newscasts and military planners. With an expanding revenue base, the emergence of the concept as well as actual "target audiences," and sophisticated marketing techniques, the mass media, and especially television, flexed its technology and discovered that visuals not only sold products but also conveyed powerful messages about social issues, such as civil rights, that could sell products. A flood of information technology—from CDs to cable to VCRs to the Internet to video games—produced a popular culture inspired by entertainment forms and the visual image. These technological and organizational changes influenced the renewed convergence of the military and the mass media.

The symbolic boundaries drawn by decades of war coverage with "Middle Eastern" (Adams 1981, 1982) foes were reconfigured as the crashing towers of the World Trade Center. The background work had been done by the military–media complex that produced the Gulf War (Altheide 1994; Gattone 1996; Kellner 1992). Coalition formation, "surgical strikes," and bomb-site videos were seen in briefings, news reports, movies, and commercials.

The "level of reality" for action against an uncertain enemy with no clear state identity involved the use of mass media and information technology to connect patriotism and membership with consumption and giving. This approach was related to emergent redefinitions by President Bush and others of the terrorists (from "those folks" to "evil ones") and the hijackings (from "terrorist attack" to "act of war"). Anger at loss of life and property would prompt revenge and vengeance, which it surely did. However, Americans and our "leaders" did not just drop words and bombs in anger; citizens also bought, gave, and participated in an identity ritual of membership even before the bombs fell. Such communalism, Cerulo (2002) notes, emerges when

> social actors become connected via a specific task, event, or characteristic. . . . Similarities are stressed over differences; common knowledge is stressed over specialized knowledge. The good of the citizenry takes precedence over any subgroup or individual. (p. 163)

The communal reaction involved drawing on national experiences of fear, consumption, and the role of national leadership in molding a response that would also constitute and justify future actions and relationships between nations, state control, and citizens. As Shapiro (2002) noted,

> The Euro-American approach to war and peace sees sovereignty as an expansive, cooperative venture. Cooperation is no longer constituted as merely an alliance against a common threat; it is enacted as a continuing preparation for engagement with what are regarded as disruptive modes of violence (threats to "peace") within sovereign territories. The new venture requires, in the words of one analyst, whose observation fits the current attack on Afghanistan, "a coalition of war and humanitarianism," where politics is deployed in the form of humanitarian war.

While the military–media complex familiarized audiences with coalitions against evil, the collective response to the terror attacks was framed as a communal patriotic experience that provided opportunities to "come together" and be "united." Numerous messages also appealed to a nostalgic past about U.S. moral and military dominance, authentic lifestyles, traditional values (e.g., family and respect), and institutions of social control (e.g., police, fire departments, and the military). Buying and selling was commensurate with communal goodwill in a context of fear and uncertainty.

MATERIALS AND PERSPECTIVE

A plethora of mass-media materials were provided by news accounts and extensive advertising that followed the events of 9/11 and subsequent political, military, and social action. Preliminary collection and review of print and television reports began during a seminar project for JUS 588, "Justice and the Mass Media," during the fall of 2001 immediately following the attacks. This exploratory project focused on news media reports pertaining to "charitable giving," "victims/victimization," and "fear." Nine students examined a range of print and electronic news media, including Lexis/Nexis, as a way of becoming familiar with qualitative media analysis, which is based on ethnographic content analysis. Such analysis refers to an integrated method, procedure, and technique for locating, identifying, retrieving, and analyzing documents for their relevance, significance, and meaning (Altheide 1987a, 1996). The emphasis is on discovery and description, including search for contexts, underlying meanings, themes, patterns, and processes, rather than mere quantity or numerical relationships between two or more variables. The process entails asking "questions" of an initial six to twelve reports on a particular topic, then refocusing inquiry on the basis of those "answers," and then selecting a "theoretical sample" of additional materials to pursue "constant comparative" analysis. Nearly 200 news reports, editorials and op-ed pieces, and numerous television news reports and commercials were collected, documented, and analyzed this way as students wrote analytical essays. These materials informed subsequent analysis over the next six months of videotaped news reports, advertisements, and numerous Internet newsgroups. The four key themes that emerged from this analysis are examined in the following.

1. *Fear supports consumption as a meaningful way for audiences to sustain an identity of substance and character.* The meaning of the attacks was constructed from the context of previous domestic and international events and, especially, well-established cultural narratives surrounding fear, justifying both it and the place of fear in the lives of many citizens. Gerth's (1992) mastery of character and social structure was applied to making sense of the Cold War, but the logic holds in contemporary times as well:

> The advent of war, no matter how long it has been anticipated, inevitably comes as a shocking surprise. Its outbreak is experienced as a great crisis full of stress and uncertainty. This sense of insecurity is not nourished solely by the particular event which sets it off, such as a surprise attack by an enemy, but also upon whatever factors may give rise to personal insecurity in industrial society: competitive pressures in markets, achievement competition, gaps between personal aspirations for success and frustration endeavors, etc. The intensity and volume of insecurity at the outbreak of war focuses and polarizes all otherwise dispersed and segmented feelings of insecurity. . . . The lasting virtue of representative government is that it integrates the whole people and all vital currents in society. (p. 341)

Terrorism from the sky inspired political terrorism in the mass media. One definition of terrorism certainly describes the thrust of news media reports after 9/11: "The purposeful act or threat of violence to create fear and or compliant behavior in a victim and or audience of the act or threat" (Lopez and Stohl 1984, p. 4). By this definition, the U.S. citizenry was being terrorized by strategic news sources providing entertaining news to a compliant audience willing to support all efforts to save them.

A history of numerous "crises" and fears involving crime, violence, and uncertainty was important for public definitions of the situation after 9/11. A major source of insecurity was a pervasive fear that was promoted in news reports, popular culture, and politicians' mantras about the "cure" for what ails America (Shapiro 1992). This mantra may be referred to as the discourse of fear, or the pervasive communication, symbolic awareness, and expectation that danger and risk are a central feature of everyday life (Altheide 2002c).

Americans' answer to the 9/11 attacks by giving and spending was informed by a long tradition of dealing with fear, especially fear of crime. Fear is related to cultural values and social structure (Glassner 1999). Ironically, Americans rely on fear to save them; it is fear in general as well as a specific "fear of X" (often crime) that is responsible for shortcomings in a market-dominated culture. This uncertainty and concern is expressed in numerous narratives of fear. While life in the United States for most citizens is quite safe, public perceptions are that everyday life is filled with risks, and thereby people are quite fearful.

Other analysis of the contributions of narratives of fear suggests that fear plays a part in identity statements about what is lacking in an otherwise (nearly) perfect world (Altheide 2002c). The dominant popular culture promotes identities, vision, and futures that reflect social affluence in a market economy. Technical, chemical, and psychological information is combined to produce a commodified social order that is valued for its symbolic meanings as well as the utility of the products. If we can solve the problems and sources of fear, the argument goes, then we could find salvation in a secular age that is very affluent, mobile, yet disconnected from community, or a shared sense of identity, purpose, and concern. Specific objects and targets of fear (e.g., crime, drugs, and immigrants) reflect an underlying cultural value for fear. Fear has been transformed from natural events, catastrophes, and "uncontrollable phenomena" that characterized life in the Middle Ages to social life. It is neither the plague, typhoid, tuberculosis, nor polio that troubles most Americans; it is fear of crime, drugs, gangs, and youth—and now terrorism.

Fear is used to deal with what social life lacks. It can be a substitute or catchall explanation for numerous troubles and disjuncture between what is and what ought to be. Fear provides a rationale for the management and control of social order. Fear provides explanations and solutions that often involve formal agents of social control, involving police, control, and surveillance:

> It is nothing as sharp as panic. . . . It is low-level fear. A kind of background radiation saturating existence. . . . It may be expressed as "panic" or "hysteria" or "phobia" or "anxiety." (Massumi 1993, p. 24)

The terror attacks were unsettling, but the subsequent campaign to integrate fear into everyday life routines was consequential.

2. *Consumption and giving were joined symbolically as government and business propaganda emphasized common themes of spending/buying to "help the country get back on track" (and related euphemisms).* Consumption messages that dominated popular culture after the attacks reflect elite management of a nation-state held together by mass-mediated markets, desires, and expectations (Ewen 1976). A nation's grief was directed to giving and spending dollars. Cultural scripts of generosity and sympathy were processed through organizational entertainment formats emphasizing market participation and consumption (Ewen 1976). "The imagery employed to inspire the consuming impulse can be transparently revealing of both social values and neuroses' (Kingston 2002).

Business became a key symbol of fighting terrorism. The World Trade Center towers were powerful symbols to the terrorists and Americans. Advertising and the market economy joined with giving and "selfless" assistance to others. Americans gave millions to charities to help the victims of 9/11. Indeed, businesses and corporate America offered rebates and contributions to charities from individual purchases. The slumping U.S. economy was in a recession prior to 9/11 and plummeted thereafter. Fear of air travel topped public perceptions that more attacks may follow and that it may be best to stay close to home. Purchases of "big-ticket" items like automobiles and appliances dropped rapidly.

The U.S. advertising industry sprang into action. For example, the Ad Council (Advertising Research Foundation) adopted a strong coalition stand against terrorism, noting in one communication that "it was originally founded as the War Advertising Council during World War II in the aftermath of the bombings of Pearl Harbor." Following an "all advertising industry meeting," a strategy was adopted on September 18, 2001, to "inform, involve and inspire Americans to participate in activities that will help win the war on terrorism." Advertising "creatives" (Jackall and Hirota 2000) developed the theme of "Freedom," and several public service announcements were created to stress "I am an American," "Laura Bush: Comfort Your Children," and "Mental Health Awareness" (Advertising Research Foundation 2001).

Showing support meant travel. Bush implored Americans to "fly, and enjoy America's great destination spots. Take your families and enjoy life, the way we want it to be enjoyed. Greatness is found when American character and American courage can overcome American challenges, and we will." United Airlines and other carriers presented messages of caring employees who were part of "United's family" (but also the entire country) as "we're United." Arizona Congressman John Kyl authored a bill to give $600 tax deductions for family vacations. As one of my irreverent colleagues, who is also a decorated Vietnam War veteran, stated in a postcard from Disney World, "We came here so the terrorists wouldn't win!"

The travel industry was not alone in commercial empathy. Numerous ads appeared for products and services that would benefit individuals yet serve the country (e.g., American flags, tooth whiteners, the Ithaca Gun Company's "Homeland Security" pump-action shotguns, anthrax antibiotics, cars, and vacation "deals").

American news media promoted the reopening of the American Stock Exchange as a major symbolic victory, quoting President Bush, "We'll show the world" that we can get American economic life back to normal. One writer commented,

> We were being asked to bounce back in the name of commerce. Somehow running out and buying stuff or suffering through TV's increasingly excessive commercials would serve as a rebuke to Osama bin Laden and all those who had helped perpetrate the atrocities. It didn't quite scan, but as part of the new patriotism, we complied. The new patriotism itself became an industry, as entrepreneurs cranked out American flags in various sizes and shapes, CDs of patriotic songs, tokens and totems meant to commemorate the catastrophe and supposedly honor the dead and injured. . . .
>
> What's sacred to broadcasters and cablecasters is not the programming but the commercials. Rarely if ever, then, do networks continue their crawls across space that has been bought and paid for—although if there's a way to do that for added profit, it might some day become common. Perhaps General Motors could buy only a part of the screen and Ford Motor Co. another part. The TV picture is turning into a collection of animated billboards, with viewers challenged to ferret out actual information as it vies for space with ads and promos and visual junk. We're not just back to business-as-usual. We've gone on to business-with-a-vengeance. (Shales 2001)

The gun industry and the National Rifle Association (NRA) urged fearful Americans to buy their slogans and products. Many Americans responded to the 9/11 attacks by arming themselves. As one reporter noted, "People may say: 'Let Tom Ridge watch out for our shores. I'll watch out for my doors'" (Baker 2001, p. 1). Gun sales were up nationwide 9 to 22 percent despite the concern of police officials: "We are always concerned with the overall numbers of guns that are available and out on the street making things unmanageable for law enforcement," said William B. Berger, the police chief of North Miami Beach, Florida, who is president of the International Association of Chiefs of Police, the nation's oldest and largest group of law enforcement executives, with 19,000 members worldwide (Baker 2001, p. 1). The gun industry accommodated the public concerns with creative advertising such as "Ithaca Gun Company is selling its Homeland Security model for 'our current time of national need.'" Its advertising pitch states, "In our current time of national need Ithaca Gun is ready to meet the challenge. . . . In every respect, these new Homeland Security Model shotguns are up to the demanding tasks which lay before us as a nation." The Beretta gun company has its "United We Stand," a 9-millimeter pistol bearing a laser-etched American flag. The company sold 2,000 of them to wholesalers in one day in October (Baker 2001, p. 1). The company lists the New York Police Department and the Survivors Fund of the National Capital Region as the charities to which they will donate. Another gun manufacturer, Tromix, publicized a soon-to-be-released 50-caliber rifle nicknamed the "Turban Chaser." The announcement on the company's website was accompanied by an American flag design.

Similar to the fear generated by a decade of "drug war" and "rampant crime" reports, the 9/11 attacks implied that all Americans were vulnerable. Investing in a gun made sense to a lot of people. The California Rifle Association (an NRA affiliate) placed a billboard that read, "Society is safer when criminals don't know who's armed." Such marketing led Congresspeople Henry Waxman and Carolyn McCarthy to join the Washington-based Alliance for Justice at a news conference to draw attention to gunmakers' marketing efforts (Associated Press 2001). Gun sales continued to climb. According to one report,

> Guns are being bought with the feeling that they will make the buyer safer. Scott Abraham, a Long Island investment broker in his 30's, said he never dreamed of buying a gun until Sept. 11. Last month he bought a Mossberg shotgun because "I don't want to be caught shorthanded," and made a spot to hide it in his house. Thomas M. Iasso, 53, a former police officer who stopped carrying a gun two years ago, bought a .40-caliber Glock after the terrorist attacks—and he carries it.
>
> "You can't sit there and tell me you can protect me anymore, because you can't," Mr. Iasso said, explaining his purchase. (Baker 2001, p. 1)

Notwithstanding Gun Industry Watch's caution that "there's nothing patriotic about flooding our streets with lethal weapons," their research found that gun manufacturers are also using the events of September 11 to sell weapons:

> At the Firing Line, a South Philadelphia gun shop and pistol range where gun sales have increased 20 percent since Sept. 11, the owner, Gregory J. Isabella, said economic fears have not stopped sales. He said he sold 58 guns in the first 20 days after the attacks, an increase of 20 percent or more over the same period last year, and sold 18,000 rounds of ammunition in the same period, an increase of more than 30 percent. Sales at his shop have steadied, but are still ahead of last year's pace. He said women were buying their own guns, or ammunition for their husbands as a Christmas stocking stuffer. Other customers, he said, come by just to shoot at the Osama bin Laden targets.

"I got him!" Mr. Isabella said he could hear shooters saying, or, "I got even with him!" He said: "It's a way to blow off steam and, perhaps, practice for some nebulous future event." (Baker 2001, p. 1)

Efforts by others to add context and perspective made little difference.

The Red Cross efforts reflect the widespread communalism spirit, although some money was donated in anger, as a type of "vengeful philanthropy"—giving not out of sympathy but out of anger—against the terrorists (Strom 2002). The country had become "unified" through various giving campaigns, but there remained doubt, skepticism, and opportunism about the process, amount, and appropriateness of the settlements. Numerous appeals were made for citizens to donate blood and money. Heeding the voices of politicians and pop-culture celebrities, Americans contributed more than $2 billion to a host of charities. They also gave thousands of pints of blood that were destroyed when not used. The donations were part of a symbolic healing (and vengeful) act that fused individuals with a national identity that was sustained by seeing and hearing television commentators, coworkers, and family members discuss how generous Americans were, how they always pulled together in times of crisis, and how a new resolve was being constructed. The most important point of the communal narrative was what Americans held in common rather than what separated them. Such outpouring was unprecedented in the history of U.S. generosity:

> Much of the frustration has arisen because many charities, from the Sept. 11 Fund to the city firefighter union's Widows' and Children's Fund, have yet to distribute a total of roughly a billion dollars in aid. The Robin Hood Relief Fund, administered by the Robin Hood Foundation in Manhattan, has $23 million left; the World Trade Center Relief Fund, administered by New York State, still has $29 million of the $65 million it has raised; the Uniformed Firefighters Association is locked in a fight with families about its plan to allocate only a portion of its $60 million. (Strom 2002, p. 29)

But all was not well with the giving and especially with the distributing of the funds:

> The massive giving foretold an impending crisis in trust and social justice as the rules for dispersing the fortunes smacked of social inequality and privilege. This was the first time that those unfortunate to be "in the line of fire" were officially entitled to compensation. While later congressional action and lobbying would include individuals killed in previous attacks on U.S. embassies, the entitlement status was new.
>
> Sept. 11, they say, challenged the basic principles of many charities and the assumptions underlying them as never before. In many respects it obliterated the question of need, which has traditionally defined aid distribution.

For instance, many people, including financially well-off victims, were given hundreds of thousands of dollars and stand to receive perhaps millions more from the federal government. (Strom 2002, p. 29)

Indeed, the larger organizations like the American Red Cross had more money than was necessary for the current need, so another fund (Liberty Fund) was established to help prepare for future terrorist attacks and emergencies. Bernadine Healy, head of the American Red Cross, was fired for allegedly withholding more than $250 million donated to families of people who were killed in the attacks. The Red Cross came under increasing pressure to spend all the funds for the deserving, and this led to an expanded category of what victimization was and who would deserve it.

The Red Cross expanded its program to include a wide range of "victims" in order to satisfy those monitoring the dispersal of funds. Applicants for Red Cross help included drivers of luxury sedans whose big-spending clientele was reduced by the attacks. Even though the 2,000 to 3,000 drivers were still working and earning around $1,000 a week, they could pick up disaster relief funds of $5,000 to $10,000 if they could prove that their company had accounts near the World Trade Center (*Newsweek*, February 11, 2002, p. 40).

The Red Cross funds were in addition to the billions of dollars of the federal Victim Compensation Fund set up to reduce lawsuits against airlines and other businesses. Special master of the fund, Kenneth Feinberg, estimated that his "economic scale" of compensation that took into account occupation, age, and other assets would provide an average payment of nearly $3 million in government and charitable contributions for each person who died in the attacks, with firefighters and police officers receiving an additional $1 million (Chen 2004). However, there were grave problems associated with dispersing these millions. Family members of those killed in the attacks were reluctant to accept the government's victim compensation fund:

Nearly six months after the federal government opened its checkbook to the relatives of the 3,200 people killed or seriously injured on Sept. 11, fewer than 10 families have filed completed applications, illustrating the complex nature of the process, the anguish or wariness some families still have about settling a victim's financial affairs and lingering concerns about the government fund's fairness.

In all, about 500 families have filed partial claims with the government's Victim Compensation Fund, many of which need to be verified or lack crucial information from employers and other sources. But even that figure has been smaller than expected, disappointing some supporters of the fund and surprising detractors, too. (Chen 2002b, p. B1)

The problems grew as, on the one hand, family members battled over "inheritance rights" and several dozen "dueling claims" (Chen 2002a, p. A1) and, on the other, compensation to foreigners got bogged down in cultural differences regarding taxation and inheritance rights (e.g., polygamous marriages) (Chen 2002c). One example is a young man who had been sending money he earned to his parents in Peru:

> Mr. Carpio, a black belt in martial arts who aspired to be a lawyer, was his family's primary breadwinner, sending about $400 home to Lince, Peru, each month. But according to the Internal Revenue Service, non-Americans like Ms. Bautista and her husband do not count as dependents. As a result, Ms. Bautista would receive about 30 percent less than what an American family would.
>
> "It seems to me that they are being treated like second-class victims based on just the aberration of geography," Ms. Steinberg said. "And I think that would be unfair." (Chen 2002c, p. A1)

Collective participation in consuming and giving would also help "battle terrorism" as scripted by the military–media complex.

3. *The absence of a clear target for reprisals contributed to the construction of broad symbolic enemies and goals referred to as "terrorism."* Patriotism was connected with an expansive fear of terrorism and enemies of the United States. The term "terrorism" was used to encompass an idea as well as a tactic or method. The waging of the "war on terrorism" focused on the "idea" and "the method," depending on the context of discussion and justification. The very broad definition of terrorism served the central authorities' purposes while also justifying action of others (e.g., Israel) in their own conflicts. Fear reflected the military–media complex:

> But how men and women interpret and respond to their fear—these are more than unconscious, personal reactions to imagined or even real dangers. They are also choices made under the influence of belief and ideology, in the shadow of elites and powerful institutions. There is, then, a politics to fear. Since September 11, that politics has followed two distinct tracks: First, state officials and media pundits have defined and interpreted the objects of Americans' fears—Islamic fundamentalism and terrorism—in anti-political or non-political terms, which has raised the level of popular nervousness; and, second, these same elites have generated a fear of speaking out not only against the war and US foreign policy but also against a whole range of established institutions. (Robin 2002)

Virtually all the major news media bolstered this view of terrorism, as network anchors cried on camera, evoked an angry tone, wore flags in lapels, and draped their sets and visual signatures (e.g., backgrounds) in patriotic slogans. Dan Rather, the CBS anchorman, acknowledged the pressure to comply with propaganda and that many of the tough questions were not being asked. Rather told a British journalist,

"It is an obscene comparison . . . but you know there was a time in South Africa that people would put flaming tyres around people's necks if they dissented. And in some ways the fear is that you will be necklaced here, you will have a flaming tyre of lack of patriotism put around your neck," he said. "Now it is that fear that keeps journalists from asking the toughest of the tough questions. . . .

"It starts with a feeling of patriotism within oneself. It carries through with a certain knowledge that the country as a whole—and for all the right reasons—felt and continues to feel this surge of patriotism within themselves. And one finds oneself saying: 'I know the right question, but you know what? This is not exactly the right time to ask it.' . . .

"Limiting access, limiting information to cover the backsides of those who are in charge of the war, is extremely dangerous and cannot and should not be accepted. And I am sorry to say that, up to and including the moment of this interview, that overwhelmingly it has been accepted by the American people. And the current administration revels in that, they relish that, and they take refuge in that." (Engel 2002)

These were extraordinary times requiring extraordinary measures. Patriotism and American resolve were central parts of the U.S. response, and numerous government and business messages of support ruled the day. There were few specific targets as "nation-states," so the focus was on a key individual, Osama bin Laden, and his "terrorist network" of camps that were located in Afghanistan, although the official message was emphasized that the United States was not at war with Afghanistan or Muslims but rather with terrorism and those who harbor them. Thus, even though Afghanistan was attacked, the official target was global terrorism whether it was connected to bin Laden or not (e.g., South America). One consequence of this was to promote more fear from potential terrorists and enemies of the United States.

The atmosphere of alarm and fear was heightened as federal law enforcement officials warned that more attacks were likely. On October 12, 2001, the House of Representatives advanced "antiterrorist" legislation to grant broad surveillance and detention powers to the federal government. The USA Patriot Act passed by a vote of 337 to 79 with little debate despite pleas from civil liberties advocates that the legislation could be a dangerous infringement on rights. Some members of Congress acknowledged that they had not read the legislation. This act removed restraints that had been placed on the FBI and CIA because of their numerous civil rights violations (e.g., those associated with COINTELPRO) (Churchill and Vander Wall 1990). One of the major changes was to permit warrantless e-mail and Internet searches. One of the dissenters, John Conyers Jr.

(D-Mich.), stated, "But we must remember that just as this horrendous act could destroy us from without, it could also destroy us from within" (*New York Times*, October 13, 2001, p. B6). Representative Conyers was concerned with, among other points, the provisions to relax civil rights and expand state power. The ease with which these extraordinary measures were passed foreshadowed an expanding circle of "terrorism control" to other areas of American life.

Leaders in the United States added to communalism and promoting a like mind among U.S. citizens by insisting that terrorists could be anywhere and ratcheted up various Homeland Security measures. Americans were implored to seek not only retribution but also salvation from fear by supporting a series of draconian measures. The common identity flowing from popular culture post-9/11 echoed support of leadership as identity. As Campbell (1998) argued, U.S. foreign policy actions and definitions are oriented to establishing its identity to citizens and others. Dangerousness, or the "evangelism of fear," with death as its impetus and salvation as its goal, required concern not only with external issues but with the self as well.

Elite propaganda efforts promoted joining the self with the state. This was operationalized as security. Security was expanded at airports, borders, and public events, particularly major popular-culture performances (e.g., the World Series, the Super Bowl, and the winter Olympics). The general message to the public was that security was being provided by the state. This included federal regulation of airport security. Security rituals reminded thousands of Americans at airports and millions of television audience members that it was essential to take off one's shoes, endure invasive "pat downs," and even frisk "little old ladies in wheelchairs" in front of guards armed with automatic weapons. It was barely mentioned that nine of the eleven hijackers who took over the deadly jets had been stopped and checked by the security system in place on that tragic day (Eggen 2002). Clearly, the problem was not primarily with airport security.

The situation was not unlike the paranoia about spies during World War II and especially the Red Scare during the Cold War (Barson and Heller 2001; Jenkins 1999). How would terrorists be distinguished from law-abiding followers of the Muslim faith? After all, the terrorists had been in the country for months before striking; they had been "sleepers," infiltrating American life and institutions, even receiving flight training from private flying schools. What could be done to prevent those "sleeping" from engaging in further attacks? Such questions were answered with more surveillance. More state control and regulation was accepted as a collective view of the struggle against terrorism. Rallying around the flag in fear of our survival was the key theme.

Chapter 2 discussed how popular-culture programs help defuse concerns about civil liberty violations, including torture. There was little criticism and dissent about administration incursions into civil liberties and violations of due process. Authorities called for relaxing civil rights and detention protections as several thousand immigrants and some citizens were questioned and more than 1,200 detained without due process. The social definition of impending attacks by terrorists among us was unchallenged in public discourse, with the exception of some Internet traffic. The major news media presented virtually no detractors from this view. Major political leaders were all but silent in opposing such action. Indeed, major news magazines like *Newsweek* offered a columnist who promoted more secret police at home with a "domestic" CIA:

> There's only one way to get security and liberty at the same time. Authorize the FBI to engage in domestic intelligence with clearly demarcated powers; put the agency under much stronger "civilian" oversight, including from Congress, and let it know specifically what it can and cannot do. "Without a national reorganization, every agency in government will get into domestic intelligence furtively, and that will be much worse for civil liberties," says Zelikow. "As last week's frenzy makes clear, no one will want to be blamed for missing a lead after the next terrorist attack." (Zakaria 2002, p. 39)

Civil libertarian Alan Dershowitz argued that judges should issue "torture warrants" when terrorist suspects were jailed (Walker 2002), and ABC's *Nightline* discussed using torture. As a producer for Ted Koppel's show stated in an e-mail to prospective audience members,

> One of the questions that Ted is going to ask tonight, and probably the first one, is about torture. Now I think it's fair to say that six months ago, before the attacks, no one would have thought that there was any question about a total ban on torture. We, as a country, don't believe in that. *We take people's rights very seriously.* We criticize those countries that don't.
>
> But as we all know, *things have changed.* Now no one is really advocating that anyone in the U.S. resort to torture, but let me lay out the question as Ted has laid it out to us. Say that you knew that a bomb was going off somewhere in your city in the next 12 hours. Say that you had captured one of the terrorists, and you knew he knew where the bomb was. In order to save innocent lives, would you still be willing to say no to the idea of torture, if nothing else was working? How far are we willing to go in this war against terrorism? Especially when we're talking about trying to save lives? Hopefully, no one will ever be in this situation, but it does raise some interesting questions." (*Nightline*, March 8, 2002; emphasis added)

The discussion of how we should treat the enemy also included prisoners. The writ of habeas corpus was greatly compromised. According to a report by Amnesty International,

It states that a "disturbing level of secrecy" continues to surround the deten-
tions and suggests "that a significant number of detainees continue to be de-
prived of certain basic rights guaranteed under international law. . . .

   "These are really issues that cut to the heart of our American understand-
ing of justice, to say nothing of international standards," said William F.
Schulz, executive director of Amnesty International USA. (*Washington Post*,
March 13, 2002, p. A13)

With a few exceptions, most of the criticism was against the detractors.
Criticism was limited as Bush gained 90 percent approval in opinion
polls. The "younger generation" was implored to meet the new challenge;
this was, after all, their war, and the mass media carried youthful testi-
monies of newfound loyalty and awakening that would have made a tent-
meeting evangelist proud. For example, *Newsweek* published two statements by young people, one "confessing" her naïveté about the "real
world" and another by a former university student who criticized "antimilitary culture" with a call to arms:

   "Before the attack, all I could think of was how to write a good rap. Now I'm
putting together a packet on our foreign policy toward the Middle East. . . .

   "In an ideal world, pacifism is the only answer. I am not eager to say this,
but we do not live in an ideal world. . . .

   "Americans may want peace, but terrorists want bloodshed. I've come to
accept the idea of a focused war on terrorists as the best way to ensure our
country's safety. In the words of Mother Jones, what we need to do now is
'pray for the dead and fight like hell for the living.'" (Newman 2001, p. 9)

Nearly three weeks later, university campuses were chastised in a "My
Turn" column from a Marine Corps officer:

   "As anyone who has attended a top college in the past three decades knows,
patriotism in the eyes of many professors is synonymous with a lack of sophistication at best, racism at worst. . . .

   "Yet, it is clear to me that the antimilitary culture that exists on many campuses is remarkably out of step with the views of the vast majority of Americans. . . .

   "Now is the time for America's brightest young adults to enlist in this
good fight against global terrorism—to join organizations like the military's Special Forces, the FBI and the CIA, whose members risk their lives
on the front lines of this battle. It is also time for America's universities to
support and encourage—not undermine—this call to service." (Sullivan
2001, p. 12)

Such pronouncements would be used by elites in the weeks after the attacks not only to claim a national consensus for a massive infusion of so-

cial control and military intervention but also to push for the reinstate-
ment of the ROTC at Harvard and other campuses.

Academics and traditional critics were all but silent, and *Sacramento Bee*
president and publisher Janis Besler Heaphy was booed off the stage during a commencement address at California State University, Sacramento,
after she suggested that the national response to terrorism could erode
press freedoms and individual liberties. One professor in attendance
stated, "For the first time in my life, I can see how something like the
Japanese internment camps could happen in our country" (*New York
Times*, December 21, 2001, p. B1). Attorney General John Ashcroft made it
clear that anyone concerned with the civil rights of the suspicious was
also suspect. Ashcroft told members of a Senate committee that critics
"aid terrorists" and undermine national unity:

> "To those who pit Americans against immigrants and citizens against nonci-
> tizens, to those who scare peace-loving people with phantoms of lost liberty,
> my message is this: Your tactics aid terrorists, for they erode our national
> unity and diminish our resolve," he said. "They give ammunition to Amer-
> ica's enemies, and pause to America's friends." (*Minneapolis Star Tribune*, De-
> cember 9, 2001, p. 30A)

Academics and other critics were targeted for their critical comments,
even though they were not well publicized. One nonprofit group, the
American Council of Trustees and Alumni (one founding member is Lynne
Cheney, wife of Vice President Cheney), posted a Web page accusing
dozens of scholars, students, and a university president of unpatriotic behavior, accusing them of being "the weak link in America's response to
the attack" and for invoking "tolerance and diversity as antidotes to evil"
(*Arizona Republic*, November 24, 2001, p. A11). (This association also issued a report, "Defending Civilization: How Our Universities Are Failing
America and What Can Be Done about It.")

Students of propaganda know that the mass media are central propaganda instruments, not only in content but also in the format and overall
presentation and "look" (Altheide and Johnson 1980; Doob 1966; Ellenius
and European Science Foundation 1998; Jackall 1994; Powell 1999; Speier
1969). With network and local nightly newscasts draped in flag colors,
lapel flags, and patriotic slogans reporting events "primarily through the
viewpoint of the United States (e.g., "us" and "we"), news organizations
presented content and form that was interpreted by the publisher of
Harper's magazine as sending

> signals to the viewers to some extent that the media are acting as an arm of the
> government, as opposed to an independent, objective purveyor of informa-
> tion, which is what we're supposed to be. (Rutenberg and Carter 2001, p. C8)

Such unanimity added pressure to say and do the right thing and above all to avoid saying the wrong thing. The formal and informal pressure on dissent were enormous:

> "We've never seen a rollback of free speech like this," says Will Doherty of the Electronic Frontier Foundation, a San Francisco-based organization that advocates for freedom of expression in new technology.
>
> "Dissent exists," insists Anthony Romero, executive director of the American Civil Liberties Union, sounding like a man trying to convince himself. "But it's not heard as loudly as it should be."
>
> A number of factors have virtually silenced America's culture of dissent. One central element is a tidal wave of public opinion, forged by both anger and fear, supporting the broad goals of defeating terrorists and protecting against terrorism. The Bush administration has used that mandate to convey a message that dissent is, if not downright un-American, at least dangerous. But there is more to it than that.
>
> Institutions that would typically offer opposition—the Democratic Party, college campuses, and the political left—are all reeling from September 11, too traumatized, polarized, and disorganized to produce much more than a peep of protest. And the powerful forces that control society's megaphones— the news media and entertainment industry—are too wary, too corporate, and too concerned about audience share to give voice to anything other than mainstream views. (*Boston Globe*, January 27, 2002, p. 10)

Indeed, even the former head of Students for a Democratic Society, New York University Professor Todd Gitlin, approved blasting Afghanistan. September 11, 2001, he stated,

> is a watershed for the left. To fail to see the virtue of the necessity of self-defense is to rule yourself out of any political discussion to the end of time. (*Boston Globe*, January 27, 2002, p. 10)

The drug war and ongoing concerns with crime contributed to the expansion of fear with terrorism. News reports and advertisements joined drug use with terrorism and helped shift "drugs" from criminal activity to unpatriotic action. As the destructive acts were defined as "war" rather than "attacks," it became apparent that the propaganda about one war would replicate the other war. By this I refer to the demonization of drugs/terrorists, the call for harsh measures against both, and the unanimity—especially among news media—that force was the best weapon. Messages demonizing Osama bin Laden, his Taliban supporters, and "Islamic extremists" linked these suspects with the destructive clout of illegal drugs and especially drug lords.

One of the strongest public statements linking the "drug war" and drug use with terrorism was a $10 million ad campaign that included a Super Bowl commercial produced by Ogilvy and Mather, stating that buying and using drugs supports terrorism, whether by al Qaeda in Afghanistan or guerrillas in Colombia, where Ogilvy and Mather also has offices.[2] The ad Web page, www.theantidrug.com, repeats a slogan from President Bush: "If you quit drugs, you join the fight against terror in America." The importance of the ad campaign was to not only reduce drug use—several critics noted that most addicts probably were not watching the Super Bowl—but also to blur boundaries between crime and terror and to suggest that both have international relevance and can warrant military intervention. One implication, then, was to extend the war against terrorism to those countries producing drugs:

"Twelve of the 25 groups designated as terrorist organizations by the State Department have ties to drug traffickers," administration officials say.

"Drug traffickers benefit from the terrorists' military skills, weapons supply and access to clandestine organizations," the State Department's ambassador at large for counterterrorism, Francis X. Taylor, told the Senate subcommittee. "Terrorists gain a source of revenue and expertise in illicit transfer and laundering of proceeds from illicit transactions."

The head of the Drug Enforcement Administration, Asa Hutchinson, urged Congress to free up $18 million to permit the agency to resume drug interdiction efforts in Afghanistan.

"We have to understand that by reducing demand for drugs, we will also reduce the financial structure that supports terrorist groups," Hutchinson told the senators. "There is multisource information that Osama bin Laden himself has been involved in the financing and facilitation of heroin trafficking activities. . . .

"It seems to me that we have an opportunity today to really change the farm processes in Afghanistan," he said. "If we can't do it today, when our people are there, we are never going to be able to do it."

Hutchinson and the State Department's assistant secretary for international narcotics suggested there might be significant impediments that keep the United States from destroying the upcoming crop. (*Dallas Morning News*, March 14, 2002, KO487, reprinted in *Arizona Republic*, March 14, 2002, p. A8)

The politics of fear extended beyond the U.S. borders as policymakers at home and abroad defined their "problem" as a terrorist threat that also needed strong government action. The broad use of terrorism as an idea and as a method that required (and justified) extensive retaliation was seized by other countries to define and legitimize control and military policies. Numerous "internal" conflicts and revolutionary movements were classified as "terrorism," and any government that opposed them would, presumably, be joining the United States in its fight against global terrorism. Within a matter of days, several countries vowed to join the United States in its fight against terrorism, including Colombia, Peru, and Israel. President Bush's call for an end to global terrorism and his vow to do whatever it takes to win the struggle was quickly seized on by Israeli Prime Minister Ariel Sharon to justify and intensify the conflict with the Palestinians and Palestine Liberation Organization leader Yasser Arafat:

> "Arafat chose a strategy of terrorism and established a coalition of terrorism," Mr. Sharon told the Parliament today. "Terrorist actions against Israeli citizens are no different from bin Laden's terrorism against American citizens." (Bennett 2001, p. 1)

Placing virtually all "opposition" forces in the terrorist camp was consistent with the military–media script of pervasive fear and opposition. The serious opposition that disappeared with the end of the Cold War was reconstituted worldwide as "global terrorism." More marketing and investing would be required.

4. *Consumption as investing promoted a massive increase in military spending.* The military support was part of a larger effort to market security for homes, families, and businesses. These efforts were sustained by weekly reports about terror alerts, asking Americans to be more vigilant and report suspicious activities. Truck drivers were enlisted as another line of defense against terrorism. Of course, the public's confidence in the American military to protect it was related partly to a heightened respect for key institutions and their leaders. For example, the *Washington Post* reported that a National Opinion Research Center survey found that more than three-fourths of respondents had a "great deal" of confidence in the military, nearly double from a year ago (*Arizona Republic*, no date). Certainly all public employees—and especially the military, police, and fire department workers—benefited from this outpouring of support that underscored a major message that varies with social issues over time: that "they" are "us" and are working on our behalf. Reports and images resonated communal themes of support for our "heroes." The participatory rhetoric was aimed even at children who were asked to send a dollar to Afghani youngsters.

One of the largest increases in military spending since World War II quickly followed September 11. By mid-2005, the war in Iraq was costing the United States $1 billion per week. The Department of Defense and the reborn military–industrial complex heeded President Bush's pledge to combat terrorism with "whatever it takes, whatever it costs." Fueled by the burning message that the United States was ill prepared to wage war against terrorism abroad and still protect its mainland, a proposed 20 percent increase in the military budget was hardly debated, although the exact benefits to homeland security were far from clear. The general message was less about shoring up military coffers than it was about investing in the nation's future to protect the country against terrorism in "far-flung" Afghanistan—at a cost of $1 billion per month—but also at home (Westphal 2001). Vice President Cheney noted in an interview that such investment was essential for the security of the United States:

> "I don't see . . . how anybody can argue that we cannot afford to defend America," he said. "And we're going to have to defend it against conventional threats. We're going to have to defend it against ballistic missile threats. We're going to have to defend it against the threat of terrorism." (Westphal 2001, p. 5A)

A military and defense budget was proposed that was commensurate with the communal "fear of terrorism." A military budget that dwarfed other nations' got even bigger over the next few weeks (Knickerbocker 2002). The call to arms strengthened the "iron triangle"—Congress, the Pentagon, and the defense industries—that had been subdued during the "peaceful 90s," as a projected defense budget of nearly $400 billion was emerging from reconstructed domestic and global responsibilities. Business and industry were called on to help: "Within weeks of the terrorist attacks, the Defense Department issued a "Broad Agency Announcement" in which military contractors were asked for "help in combating terrorism." Thousands of proposals have been submitted since then (Knickerbocker 2002). British journalists noted,

> The attacks and the subsequent war in Afghanistan—not to mention two sharp annual rises in US military budgets by President George W. Bush—have persuaded investors to pay attention to defence stocks after years of neglect. (Burt and Nicoll 2002, p. 18)

Another analyst noted that investment was good for business and the military and also for former administration officials (e.g., Frank Carlucci, former secretary of defense, and James Baker, former secretary of state):

> The "military-industrial complex" that General Eisenhower warned of presents potential political landmines for any administration. For example, many former Republican officials and political associates of those now in the Bush administration are associated with the Carlyle Group, an equity investment firm with billions of dollars in military and aerospace assets. (Knickerbocker 2002, p. 2)

The House of Representatives passed a $383 billion defense budget on May 9, 2002. The Senate passed (71 to 22) a $31.5 billion counterterrorism bill on June 6, 2002. This was $2 billion more than the measure approved in May by the House. This legislation reflected the mood of leaders who sought to be decisive and appear strong to their constituents, who were receiving virtually no contextual or historical information about underlying issues that may have contributed to the attacks.

The widespread support for military expenditures and the public's tacit approval of civil liberty restrictions—including profiling of Arab Americans—reflected fear-induced communalism surrounding terrorism. The politics of fear was becoming more visible in numerous social policies. The military expenditures were commensurate with a socially constructed morality play of the enemy and its horrendous acts. News reports reflected the mass media's use of routine "elite" news sources to "get the story" of attacks and promote entertaining reports such as "America Strikes Back." The public support quickly became a resource to use in "striking back" when the Bush administration proposed a "first strike"— not against Afghanistan or al Qaeda networks but against sovereign nations that either support terrorist activities or engage in threatening acts. Iraq and several other nations were part of the "axis of evil" that was targeted by President Bush for possible first strikes by the United States. President Bush implored Pakistan and India to resolve their ongoing dispute peacefully. But just a few days after posing at World War II cemeteries for a "photo op," the blustering Bush threatened international law and order when he told West Point cadets that the only strategy for defeating America's new enemies was to strike first.

> "If we wait for threats to fully materialize, we will have waited too long," the president said, speaking at the commencement of the 204th graduating class of West Point, the nation's oldest military academy. "We must take the battle to the enemy, disrupt his plans and confront the worst threats before they emerge."
>
> In a toughly worded speech that seemed aimed at preparing Americans for a potential war with Iraq, Mr. Bush added, "The only path to safety is action. And this nation will act." He did not mention Iraq by name, but warned that "even weak states and closed groups could attain a catastrophic power to strike great nations." . . .
>
> Looking directly at the graduates, he added: "I am proud of the men and women who have fought on my orders. The nation respects and trusts our military, and we are confident of your victories to come." (Busmiller 2002, p. 1)

CONCLUSION

The politics of fear benefited from terrorism. The 9/11 attacks were defined in the news media and popular culture as an assault on American culture. News media and popular-culture depictions of the U.S. reaction to terror attacks reflects a culture and collective identities steeped in marketing, popular culture, consumerism, and fear. Elite news management and propaganda by the military–media complex produced terrorism scenarios that were reflected in national agendas and everyday life.

Communalism and commensurability were joined reflexively through consumption as social participation. On the one hand, mass-media symbolic constructions of victims and terrorism contributed to a "national experience" oriented to communal values and reaffirmation of cultural narratives. Citizens were asked to give, buy, and support. On the other hand, these powerful symbolic definitions supported open-ended commensurate increases in military and police authority while expanding governmental surveillance and diminishing civil liberties. Opinion polls indicated that American citizens accepted reduced civil liberties because the "world has changed." It is as though "pre-9/11" civil liberties were there to protect citizens but "post-9/11" civil liberties could endanger citizens. Indeed, political bluster about engaging in "first strikes" against sovereign countries suggests that "risk policing" will be proactive (Ericson and Haggerty 1997).

The collective identity of victims of terrorist attacks was promoted by news reports stressing communal suffering as well as opportunities to participate in helping survivors and defeating terrorism. More traditional and culturally resonant narratives about crime, drugs, and evil were, essentially, transformed into the "terror story." Sorrow, suffering, empathy, and pain were merged with fear and vengeance. National character was played out in scenarios of heroics, sacrifice, suffering, marketing, and spending. Patriotic responses to the attacks were joined with commercialism and pleas for donations as well as support for an ill-defined and nebulous "war on terrorism" that referred to an idea as well as a tactic or method. Building on a foundation of fear, citizens who saw the repetitive visuals of the World Trade Center attacks generously followed governmental directives to donate blood, supplies, and money to the immediate victims of the attacks. They were also urged to travel, purchase items, and engage in numerous patriotic rituals, while civil liberties were compromised and critics warned by the attorney general to not "give ammunition to America's enemies."

The commercial response was immediate and immense as collective grief was marketed and products were cast as opportunities for Americans to stand tall, be united, and help "move forward" or, as General Motors advertisements put it, "Keep America Rolling." Membership and participation was thereby expanded to include "good deals" such as "zero-interest financing" as well as a willingness to support massive increases in military expenditures that would be necessary to conduct a war on terrorism around the world. Ironically, the specific demonization of Osama bin Laden as the "mastermind" and the target of military action helped transform symbolically the quest to defeat a diffuse international terrorism that could be found in dozens of countries.

A new foreign policy, born nine months after the attacks of 9/11, was skillfully implanted in a fertile womb of fear and victimization. Avowed

social unanimity of agreement was a strategic tool for expanding commensurate reaction to the attacks. Patriotic rituals continued months after
zero-percent financing of cars disappeared. News reports reminded audiences of the "long struggle" ahead, and the repeated "accidental bombing" of civilians in Afghanistan was cast as part of the struggle against terrorism and the ongoing stand against evil. The circle was completed when
advertising and public service announcements connected evil drug use
with the support of terrorism. Consistent with symbolic commensuration,
attacking one was attacking the other. And we could do it together.

NOTES

1. I thank Arthur J. Vidich for calling this important article to my attention and
for his incisive suggestions about the context of national/international politics for
managing public opinion.

2. Ogilvy and Mather has offices in fifty-six countries, and guided by such slogans as "One Agency Indivisible" and "We Work for Brands," it produces ads for
Miller beer, Coca-Cola, Nestlé, and others. The Interfaith Center on Corporate Responsibility condemned Nestlé's marketing of "infant formula" in Third World
countries in the late 1980s that violated the World Health Organization's infant
formula marketing code. See www.essential.org/monitor/hyper/issues/1989/
12/mm1289_05.html.

6

Terrorism and the Politics of Fear

Al Qaeda is to terror what the Mafia is to crime.

—George W. Bush

Previous chapters have set forth the concept of the politics of fear and provided explanations and examples of its logic and how it is connected to the mass media and popular culture. I also examined how the context of crime reporting by an increasingly entertainment-oriented mass media contributed to the expansion of media logic throughout social life. Increasingly it seems that what people experience as audiences of popular culture is reflected in their experiences with social institutions, especially agents of social control. The preceding chapter argued that the war on terrorism was enmeshed in this same politics of fear but greatly extended it by drawing analogies with crime and the drug war and even suggesting that dissent at home was aiding the enemy. A number of examples were given about how social life changed to accommodate this newest politics of fear, particularly the intrusiveness of social control and surveillance into more of our lives. This chapter examines another aspect of the politics of fear: language. The argument is that changing the meanings and definitions of words and symbols of everyday life to reflect fear and social control is a very powerful way to connect social changes with social consciousness.

This chapter examines how fear as a topic was presented in news reports about terrorism and victimization. The news media's use of these terms is tied to a long-standing linkage of fear and victimization with crime that has been fueled by government and police officials who serve as dominant news sources and therefore are significant actors in defining problems and setting political agendas (Chiricos, Padgett, and Gertz 2000; Kappeler, Blumberg, and Potter 1999; Surette 1998). As noted several times in previous chapters, propaganda research shows that decision makers who serve as key news sources can shape perceptions of mass audiences and promote acquiescence to state control measures (Ellenius and European Science Foundation 1998; Gerth 1992; Jackall 1994). An expansive use of the word "fear" in news reports has been documented (Altheide 2002b; Altheide and Michalowski 1999; Furedi 1997; Glassner 1999). Indeed, the extensive use of fear to highlight crime news has produced a discourse of fear that may be defined as the pervasive communication, symbolic awareness, and expectation that danger and risk are a central feature of the effective environment, or the physical and symbolic environment as people define and experience it in everyday life. Journalistic accounts about terrorism reflect news organizations' reliance on official news sources to provide entertaining reports compatible with long-established symbols of fear, crime, and victimization about threats to individuals and the United States in the "fight against terrorism." I argue that tying terrorism coverage to an expansive discourse of fear has contributed to the emergence of the politics of fear, or decision makers' promotion and use of audience beliefs and assumptions about danger, risk, and fear in order to achieve certain goals. This chapter examines how news reports about terrorism in five nationally prominent newspapers reflect the terms and discourse associated with the politics of fear. I wish to examine the conceptual and empirical support for the politics-of-fear thesis, which may be stated as follows: the terms "crime," "victim," and "fear" are joined with news reports about terrorism to construct public discourse that reflects symbolic relationships about order, danger, and threat that may be exploited by political decision makers.

An overview of the discourse of fear will be followed by an elaboration of the politics of fear and a discussion of the materials and content analysis of news reports. Data about the emerging politics of fear and how it is manifested in news coverage involving fear, victimization, terrorism, and crime will then be presented.

NEWS AND THE DISCOURSE OF FEAR

As noted already, the common thread for most scholarly and popular analysis of fear in American society is crime and victimization. Social constructionist approaches to the study of social problems and emergent social movements stress how mass-media accounts of crime, violence, and victimization are simplistic and often decontextualize rather complex events in order to reflect narratives that demonize and offer simplistic explanations (Best 1995, 1999; Ericson, Baranek, and Chan 1991; Fishman and Cavender 1998; Johnson 1995) that often involve state intervention while adding to the growing list of victims.

To reiterate a previous point, the discourse of fear has been constructed through news and popular-culture accounts. The main focus of the discourse of fear in the United States for the past thirty years or so has been crime. News reports about crime and fear have contributed to the approach taken by many social scientists in studying how crime is linked with fear. Numerous researchers link crime, the mass media, and fear (Chiricos, Eschholz, and Gertz 1997; Ericson 1995; Ferraro 1995; Garland 1997; Pearson 1983; Shirlow and Pain 2003). There is also an impressive literature on crime, victimization, and fear (Baer and Chambliss 1997; Chiricos et al. 1997; Ferraro 1995; Warr 1987, 1990, 1992). Other researchers have examined the nature and consequences of fear in connection with crime but also in relationship to political symbols and theories of social control (Altheide 2002b; Furedi 1997; Garland 1997; Glassner 1999; Massumi 1993; Moehle and Levitt 1991; Naphy and Roberts 1997; Russell 1998).

Crime and terrorism discourses are artfully produced. The most pervasive aspect of this "victim" perspective is crime. Criminal victimization, including numerous crime myths (e.g., predators, stranger danger, and random violence) (Best 1999), contributed to the cultural foundation of the politics of fear, particularly the belief that we were all actual or potential victims and needed to be protected from the source of fear—criminals or terrorists (Garland 2001). Politicians and state control agencies, working with news media as "news sources," have done much to capitalize on this concern and to promote a sense of insecurity and reliance on formal agents of social control—and related businesses—to provide surveillance, protection, revenge, and punishment to protect us, to save us (Chiricos et al. 1997; Ericson et al. 1991; Surette 1992).

The mass media and popular culture are best conceived of as key elements of our symbolic environment rather than as independent causes and effects. News does not merely set agendas (Iyengar and Kinder 1987; Shaw and McCombs 1977); rather, consistent with symbolic interaction theory, news that relies on certain symbols and promotes particular relationships between words, deeds, and issues also guides the perspectives, frameworks, language, and discourse that we use in relating to certain problems as well as related issues. My focus in this chapter is on news that guides discourse.

Social meanings are constructed through news reports by associating words with certain problems and issues. Repeated use of certain terms is linked to public discourse (Altheide and Michalowski 1999; Beckett 1996;

Ekecrantz 1998; Fowler 1991; Gamson et al. 1992; Potter and Wetherell 1987; van Dijk 1988; Zhondang and Kosicki 1993). Tracking the emergence of new "connections" over a period of time is one way to assess the process of the social construction of reality. Research documents how fear and crime have been joined. Crime and threats to the public order—and therefore all good citizens—are part of the focus of fear, but the topics change over time. As noted in Chapter 4, what they all have in common is pointing to the "other," the outsider, the nonmember, the alien.

Fear, crime, terrorism, and victimization are experienced and known vicariously through the mass media by audience members. Information technology, entertainment programming, and perspectives are incorporated into a media logic that is part of the everyday life of audience members. Media logic is defined as a form of communication and the process through which media transmit and communicate information. Elements of this form include the distinctive features of each medium and the formats used by these media for the organization, the style in which it is presented, the focus or emphasis on particular characteristics of behavior, and the grammar of media communication (Altheide and Snow 1979; Snow 1983). This logic or the rationale, emphasis, and orientation promoted by media production, processes, and messages tends to be evocative, encapsulated, highly thematic, familiar to audiences, and easy to use.

News formats, or the way of selecting, organizing, and presenting information, shape audience assumptions and preferences for certain kinds of information. The mass media are important in shaping public agendas by influencing what people think about and how events and issues are packaged and presented. Certain news forms have been developed as packages or "frames" for transforming some experience into reports that will be recognized and accepted by the audience as "news." Previous research has shown how the "problem frame" was encouraged by communication formats and in turn has promoted the use of "fear" throughout American society (Altheide 1997). Other work has demonstrated that the linkage of crime with fear has promoted a discourse of fear, or the pervasive communication, symbolic awareness, and expectation that danger and risk are a central feature of everyday life (Altheide 1997, 2002a; Altheide and Michalowski 1999; Ericson and Haggerty 1997).

It was noted earlier that crime hoaxes abound, but so do false terrorism reports. I have more in mind than the hundreds of false reports of anthrax that followed 9/11 attacks. When people "pretend" that they have been assaulted, abducted, or in some way harmed by strangers, they are acting out a morality play that has become part of a discourse of fear, or the notion that fear and danger are pervasive. Indeed, a student's project in New York city involved placing black boxes in the subway in order to elicit citizens' concerns:

At the same time it turned out that those 37 black boxes with the word "Fear" on them, which mysteriously turned up attached to girders and walls in the Union Square subway station last Wednesday, were, as you may have guessed from the start, an art project. The boxes, which spread panic and caused the police to shut the station for hours and call in the bomb squad, turned out to be the work of Clinton Boisvert, a 25-year-old freshman at the School of Visual Arts in Manhattan, who surrendered Monday to the Manhattan district attorney's office, which intends to prosecute him on charges of reckless endangerment. (Kimmelman 2002)

NEWS SOURCES AND THE POLITICS OF FEAR

A politics of fear rests on the discourse of fear. The politics of fear serves as a conceptual linkage for power, propaganda, news and popular culture, and an array of intimidating symbols and experiences such as crime and terrorism. The politics of fear resides not in an immediate threat from an individual leader (e.g., Senator Joseph McCarthy [Griffith 1987]) but rather in the public discourse that characterizes social life as dangerous, fearful, and filled with actual or potential victims. This symbolic order invites protection, policing, and intervention to prevent further victimization. A public discourse of fear invites the politics of fear. It is not fear per se that is important in social life but rather how fear is defined and realized in everyday social interaction. The role of the news media is very important in carrying selective news sources' messages. News sources are claims makers, and studies of crime news show that government and police officials dominate how crime is framed (Ericson, Baranek, and Chan 1987, 1989; Surette 1992). Likewise, government and military officials also dominated news reports about terrorism and fear:

> But how men and women interpret and respond to their fear—these are more than unconscious, personal reactions to imagined or even real dangers. They are also choices made under the influence of belief and ideology, in the shadow of elites and powerful institutions. There is, then, a politics of fear. Since September 11, that politics has followed two distinct tracks: First, state officials and media pundits have defined and interpreted the objects of Americans' fears—Islamic fundamentalism and terrorism—in anti-political or non-political terms, which has raised the level of popular nervousness; and, second, these same elites have generated a fear of speaking out not only against the war and US foreign policy but also against a whole range of established institutions. (Robin 2002)

Newspapers as well as television network news relied heavily on administration sources that directed the focus and language of news coverage. This was particularly apparent with those persons interviewed. A study by the *Columbia Journalism Review* documented this trend:

> It exacerbates our tendency to rely on official sources, which is the easiest, quickest way to get both the "he said" and the "she said," and, thus, "balance." According to numbers from the media analyst Andrew Tyndall, of the 414 stories on Iraq broadcast on NBC, ABC, and CBS from last September to February, all but thirty-four originated at the White House, Pentagon, and State Department. So we end up with too much.

An analysis by Fairness and Accuracy in Reporting (FAIR) of network news interviewees one week before and one week after Secretary of State Colin Powell addressed the United Nations about Iraq's alleged possession of weapons of mass destruction found that two-thirds of the guests were from the United States, with 75 percent of these being current or former government or military officials, while only one—Senator Kennedy—expressed skepticism or opposition to the impending war with Iraq. Even newsmagazines like *Newsweek* concurred that the news was being managed:

> News management is at the heart of the administration's shake-up of Iraq policy. The National Security Council recently created four new committees to handle the situation in Iraq. One is devoted entirely to media coordination—stopping the bad news from overwhelming the good. (*Newsweek*, October 27, 2003)

Very dramatically, journalists cried on camera, wore flag lapels, and often referred to those involved in planning and fighting the Afghanistan and Iraq wars as "we." Moreover, they invoked routinely the claim that the "world is different," that security and safety can no longer be taken for granted, and that many sacrifices would have to be made (Altheide 2004). Numerous observers raised serious questions about the role that journalism played in covering the attacks, the wars with Afghanistan and Iraq that followed, and the increased surveillance and control of United States citizens:

> The major media fully ignored gangbuster stories reported exhaustively overseas. Among them were: (1). a manifesto that described the invasion of Iraq and pacification of the Mideast penned in 1998 by a think tank whose board included a raft of current administration hawks. . . .
> In a rare case of breaking ranks, one news "celeb," NBC correspondent Ashleigh Banfield, took her industry to task in a speech at Kansas State University April, averring that it had painted a "glorious, wonderful picture" of war that "wasn't journalism."
> Quoting Robert McChesney (Professor of Communications at the University of Illinois) "If the Soviet Union cited reasons like this in their invasion of Afghanistan and Pravda reported nothing but what the government said, we

would've dismissed it out of hand. Our press hasn't been much better. That sends a lot of Americans maybe not consciously but intuitively, looking for something our media is not offering." (Grimm 2003, p. 37)

The collective identity of victim of terrorist attacks was promoted by news reports stressing communal suffering as well as opportunities to participate in helping survivors and in defeating terrorism. More traditional and culturally resonant narratives about crime, drugs, and evil were transformed into the "terror story." Sorrow, suffering, empathy, and pain were merged with fear and vengeance. National character was played out in scenarios of heroics, sacrifice, suffering, marketing, and spending. This was the context for constructing the politics of fear.

The remainder of the chapter presents some material about how words of fear have become incorporated into news reports. First, I will explain how I studied the discourse of fear. Data will then be presented about news media coverage of fear, crime, victimization, and terrorism. Second, I will examine how the nature and extent of news coverage about fear, crime, terrorism, and victimization became more closely linked after the 9/11 attacks. Third, the linkage between the discourse of fear and the politics of fear will be presented. A graduate seminar undertook the challenge to build on research about the discourse of fear by examining the relationship and changing connections between fear, crime, and victims. That work focused on the various meanings of victim in news reports from several countries (Altheide et al. 2001). We wanted to understand whether and to what extent terrorism would "challenge" crime for "ownership" of fear and victim. The next project took place within days of the 9/11 attacks. The general focus was to investigate news themes about victims, patriotism, and consumption. This project was inspired by the extraordinary amount of coverage given to terrorism after the 9/11 attacks (Altheide 2004).

The aim in this study was to compare coverage of terrorism with crime and victim and note how these may be related to use of the word "fear." Accordingly, the research design called for comparing newspaper coverage of fear, crime, terrorism, and victim (in headlines and reports) at two eighteen-month time periods: time 1 was from March 1, 2000, to September 10, 2001, and time 2 was from September 12, 2001, to April 1, 2003. The first newspaper examined was the *Los Angeles Times*. Subsequently, students in a seminar project obtained data from the *New York Times*, the *Washington Post*, the *San Francisco Chronicle*, and *USA Today*. News reports were selected using Lexis/Nexis materials. News reports were selected according to the following search criteria:

1. Reports with "fear" in headlines and "victim" in report.
2. Reports with "fear" in headlines and "crime" in report.

  3. Reports with "fear" in headlines and "terrorism" in report.
  4. Reports with "fear" in headlines and "crime" and "terrorism" in report.
  5. Reports with "victim" and "fear" in headlines.
  6. Reports with "crime," "terrorism," and "fear" in headlines.
  7. Reports about "victim" within two words of "fear."
  8. Reports about "crime" within two words of "fear."
  9. Reports about "terrorism" within two words of "fear."
 10. Reports dealing with "crime," "terrorism," and "victim."

A qualitative content analysis study of news coverage sought to examine the politics of fear and terrorism. The emphasis in this chapter is on the changing pattern of fear, terrorism, and victimization in news reports. The politics-of-fear thesis can be demonstrated by examining the nature and extent of news coverage of fear, crime, terrorism, and victim before and after the attacks of 9/11. The discourse of fear is considered to be expanded to incorporate the politics of fear if terrorism and victimization appear closely associated with fear in a substantial number of news reports after 9/11 (time 2). Following the steps outlined in previous work (Altheide 1996), additional qualitative data were collected with a protocol to check from a theoretical sample of reports. An initial protocol was constructed to include the relevant categories (e.g., date, page length, topic, focus, and sources). Data were recorded primarily as text, although frequencies were also noted. Coding, analysis, and comparisons were carried out with the aid of word processors and NUD*IST 4 qualitative analysis software. While some qualitative materials will be presented, the emphasis is on the changes in the extent of coverage in news reports linking fear with terrorism and victimization that occurred after 9/11.

NEWS AND THE POLITICS OF FEAR

A central argument of previous research (Altheide 2002b) is that "fear" is cumulatively integrated into topics over time and, indeed, becomes so strongly associated with certain topics that, on repetition, it is joined with that term—as with an invisible hyphen—and eventually the term "fear" is no longer stated but is simply implied. Examples from previous work include "gangs," "drugs," and, in some cases, even "crime," although "crime" continues to be heavily associated with fear (Altheide 2002b). My aim here is to show the continuity between major events—the attacks of 9/11—and a history of crime reporting emphasizing fear and social control. Victim and victimization are common to each.

The key questions for this project concerned the comparisons between time 1 and time 2. The changes in coverage were considerable although varied. Building on previous work, I was interested in whether fear and terrorism were strongly associated with articles featuring "fear" in headlines. Of course, they were but to varying degrees. Tracking changes in the use of "fear," "crime," "terrorism," and "victim" in several newspapers eighteen months before and after 9/11 reveals the following changes:

1. There was a dramatic increase in linking terrorism to fear.
2. Coverage of crime and fear persisted but at a very low rate.
3. There was a large increase in linking terrorism to victim.

First, as figure 6.1 shows, the five newspapers that provided data for this project varied considerably in the increases of "fear" in headlines and "crime" in report. The *Angeles Times*, which already had a strong "base" in crime reporting at time 1, showed the least increase during time 2 (32 percent), while *USA Today* (73 percent), the *New York Times* (85 percent), and the *Washington Post* (116 percent) all trailed the most massive increase in crime reporting by the *San Francisco Chronicle*, from fifteen to forty-five reports, for an increase of 181 percent, although about a third of these reports also dealt with terrorism. (It should be noted that the *San Francisco Chronicle* had the smallest number of reports with "fear" in the headline and "crime" in report at time 1.) The relevance of terrorism and sensitivity to crime can be illustrated by an editorial in the *San Francisco Chronicle* on October 15, 2002, about the "Tarot Card" serial killer, who was shooting people, seemingly at random. In this and subsequent reports by other news media, shooting people is linked to terrorism, and the shooters are labeled as terrorists:

This inexplicable string of murders has triggered yet another disappointing overreaction from the media. But this is different from the Chandra Levy or O.J. Simpson overreactions. We are a different country from the one that weathered those stories. We feel more vulnerable to terrorism, and no matter how you cut it, this killer is a terrorist. His purpose, or at least one of them, is to spread terror. And the media playing right into his hands, as if Sept. 11 never happened.

"We may be entering a time when what has been ghetto-ized in Israel and the Middle East breaks its boundaries," says UC Berkeley dean of journalism Orville Schell, referring to suicide bombers and other acts of terrorism. "The unspoken thought is, 'What if this guy is a Muslim?' The media is feeding this most paranoid fear of all but without acknowledging it. . . .

The national climate of fear, energized by this psycho sniper, demands that the media examine its decisions more critically than ever. What kind of coverage serves the public interest? What information helps, and more important what harms?" (Ryan 2002, p. A23)

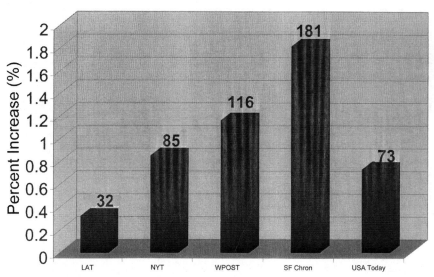

Figure 6.1.   Percentage Increase of "Fear" in Headlines and "Crime" in Reports for Five Newspapers after 9/11/01

Next, figure 6.2 shows the massive increase in reports that associated fear with terrorism. Fear in headlines and terrorism in news reports greatly exceeded the increases in fear and crime. Each of the newspapers increased the linkage of fear with terrorism by more than 1,000 percent, with the *San Francisco Chronicle* exceeding 4,500 percent (having pub-

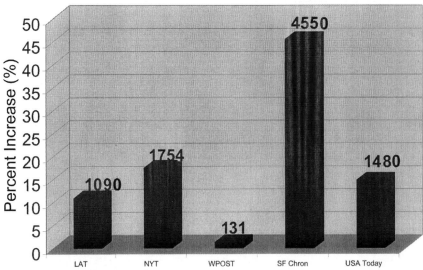

Figure 6.2.   Percentage Increase of "Fear" in Headlines and "Terrorism" in Reports for Five Newspapers after 9/11/01

lished only two reports of this nature before 9/11) at time 1. Clearly, terrorism was a relatively new and bold connection for fear. This included a few articles that were critical of the government's use of fear to exact more social control, but the overwhelming majority demonstrated that terrorism was bonded to the discourse of fear.

A context of crime reporting proved to be consequential for the seemingly easy public acceptance of governmental proposals to expand surveillance and social control. The resulting measures reflected a foundational politics of fear that promoted a new public discourse and justification for altering everyday life and social interaction. While the following discussion is informed by insights of others about social context and change (Shapiro 1992; Thiele 1993) and various studies about fear and the media (Furedi 1997; Glassner 1999) and especially fear and crime (Chiricos et al. 1997; Ferraro 1995), my focus is on political action that utilizes widespread audience perceptions about fear as a feature of crime, violence, deviance, terrorism, and other dimensions of social disorder.

The politics of fear is buffered by news and popular culture stressing fear and threat as features of entertainment that increasingly are shaping public and private life as mass-mediated experience has become a standard frame of reference for audiences, claims makers, and individual actors (Best 1995). Similar to propaganda, messages about fear are repetitious and stereotypical of outside "threats" and especially suspect and "evil others." These messages also resonate moral panics, with the implication that action must be taken to not only defeat a specific enemy but also save civilization. Since so much is at stake, it follows that drastic measures must be taken—that compromises with individual liberty and even perspectives about "rights," the limits of law, and ethics must be "qualified" and held in abeyance in view of the threat.

In addition to propaganda effects, the constant use of fear pervades crises and normal times; it becomes part of the taken-for-granted word of "how things are," and one consequence is that it begins to influence how we perceive and talk about everyday life, including mundane as well as significant events. Tracking this discourse shows that fear pervades our popular culture and is influencing how we view events and experience. This is particularly relevant for the use of victims and victimization, particularly in the context of 9/11.

Still another consequence of the emphasis on "fear" that foretells the emerging politics of fear is the rise of victimization. Entertaining news emphasizes "fear" and institutionalizes "victim" as an acceptable identity. Other work has shown that "fear" and "victim" are informed by perceived membership (Altheide et al. 2001).

While news reports strengthened the connection between terrorism and fear, a critical symbol in the politics of fear is "victim and victimization."

Figure 6.3 shows the relationship of "fear," "crime," and "victim." This figure demonstrates that there was a much larger increase in the eighteen months after 9/11 in reports with "fear" within two words of "victim" than there was "fear" within two words of "crime." Most striking for our argument about the expanded focus of "fear" and "victim" beyond crime after 9/11 was the clear increases in "fear" within two words of "victim" across the span of nationally prominent newspapers. *USA Today* increased reports with "fear" within two words of "victim" by 280 percent, while the *Los Angeles Times*, the *New York Times*, and the *Washington Post*, often regarded as among the nation's most prestigious newspapers, saw increases of nearly 100 percent. Examining the five newspapers shows that each greatly increased reports with "fear" within two words of "victim" at time 2: *Los Angeles Times*: 108 percent; *New York Times*: 89 percent; *Washington Post*: 91 percent; *San Francisco Chronicle*: 33 percent; and *USA Today*: 280 percent. Moreover, three of the five newspapers published fewer reports with "fear" within two words of "crime" during the eighteen months after 9/11. Indeed, all newspapers had either very little increase or a decrease in reports of "fear" within two words of "crime" at time 2. For example, *USA Today* showed a 20 percent increase and the *New York Times* a 10 percent increase, while the *Los Angeles Times* (–25 percent), the *Washington Post* (–8 percent), and the *San Francisco Chronicle* (–13 percent) presented less coverage about "fear" within two words of "crime" than they did prior to 9/11. Another way to illustrate the magnitude of change in these newspapers' reports about "fear" within two words of "victim" compared to "fear" and "crime" is to add the percentage increases in the former and the total change (increases minus decreases) in reports about "fear" and "crime." The five newspapers' cumulative increase from time 1 to time 2 in reports with "fear" within two words of "victim" was 493

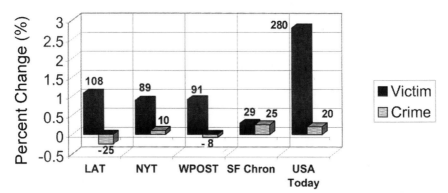

Figure 6.3. Percent Changes in Report with "Fear" within Two Words of "Victim" and "Fear" after 9/11

percent, with a cumulative decrease of -16 percent in reports showing "fear" within two words of "crime." This means that "fear" and "victim" became more closely linked at time 2 across these major news media.

The world of popular culture and news stressing crime and victimization promotes the pervasive awareness of "victimage" that is easily cultivated by officials who respond to terrorist acts. Victims abound in American life. Victims are but the personal side of crisis; a crisis is where victims reside. A personal crisis may affect "one victim," but more generally "crisis" refers to "social crisis," involving numerous people. All take place in a time of fear. All of this requires that citizens have information and constant reminders of the pitfalls and hazards of life, whether potential or realized (Ericson and Haggerty 1997). News reports, talk shows, newsmagazine shows, and a host of police and reality crime dramas seem to proclaim that everybody is a victim of something even though they may not know it. The notion that "life is hard" and that things don't always work out the way we'd like seems to be lost on popular-culture audiences who clamor for "justice," "revenge," and, of course, redemption, often in the form of monetary rewards. And it is not just in the United States:

> It is in the USA that victimhood is most developed as an institution in its own right. . . . Victimhood is one of the central categories of the culture of abuse. . . . Celebrities vie with one another to confess in graphic detail the painful abuse they suffered as children. The highly acclaimed BBC interview with Princess Diana symbolized this era of the victim. (Furedi 1997, p. 95)

Just as our culture has become obsessed with fear, it has also become accepting of victim and victimization. My analysis of news and popular culture indicates that these two terms are linked. We even use the term "victim": when we don't have a victim, as in "victimless crime," although reports are far more likely to stress the "victim" status. And certain domestic violence "presumptive arrest" policies define people as "crime victims" even though they do not perceive themselves as such and refuse to press charges. We even have "indirect victim."

Patriotism was connected with an expansive fear of terrorism and enemies of the United States. The term "terrorism" was used to encompass an idea as well as a tactic or method. The waging of the "war on terrorism" focused on the "idea" and the "method," depending on the context of discussion and justification. The very broad definition of terrorism served the central authorities' purposes while also justifying action of others (e.g., Israel) in their own conflicts.

Figure 6.4 provides another important piece to the conceptual argument about the politics of fear. These data show that each of the newspapers substantially increased the number of reports with fear within two

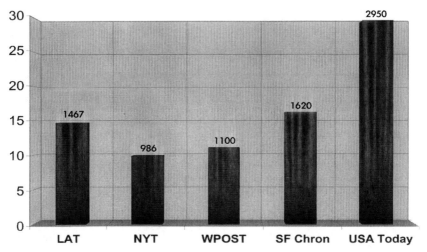

Figure 6.4.   Changes (%) in Reports with "Fear" within Two Words of "Terrorism," after 9/11/01

words of "terrorism" after 9/11: *Los Angeles Times*: 1,467 percent; *New York Times*: 986 percent; *Washington Post*: 1,100 percent; *San Francisco Chronicle*: 1,620 percent; and *USA Today*: 2,950 percent. Clearly, terrorism was strongly linked to the discourse of fear.

DISCUSSION

A brief recap of the argument is that claims makers' accounts of the attacks of 9/11 contributed to an expanding use of "fear" with "victim" and "victimization" that increased much faster than an already established tradition of reports linking "fear" and "crime." "Victim" and "terrorism" did not replace "crime" but simply expanded the "fear" and "victim" connection that has long been associated with "crime." And it is this expansion that is consistent with the politics of fear. The point can be further illustrated. A closer "internal" look at variations in the *Los Angeles Times* indicates that the emphasis on crime decreased when compared to more attention given to terrorism. Examining other data (not provided here) shows that at time 1 (eighteen months prior to 9/11), only 1 percent of stories with "fear" in the headlines had "crime" and "terrorism" in the report. This increased to 8 percent at time 2. Most striking is the headline changes. There was a 1,600 percent increase in reports with "terrorism" and "fear" in the headlines at time 2.

The upshot is that "terrorism" and "victim" have been more closely joined with "fear" at time 2, while time 1 reporting was more likely to associate "fear" and "victim" with "crime." "Victim" continued to "grow" from "crime" at time 2, but it was engorged by "fear." While "crime" and "terrorism" do coexist and can expand together, "terrorism" became more strongly associated with "victim."

The discourse of fear now includes terrorism as well as victimization and crime. Terrorism and fear have been joined through victimization. Crime established a solid baseline in its association with fear, and it continues to grow, but it is terrorism that now occupies the most news space. The primary reason for this, as noted previously in the discussion of news sources, is that government officials dominate the sources relied on by journalists. When journalists rely heavily on government and military officials not only to discuss an immediate war or military campaign but also for information about the security of the country, rationale for more surveillance of citizens, and comments about related domestic and international issues, then the body politic is symbolically cultivated to plant more reports and symbols about the politics of fear. This is particularly true during periods of war, such as the ongoing war with Iraq. Messages that the war on terrorism and the importance of homeland security, including periodic elevated "terror alerts," will not end soon lead journalists to turn to administration news sources for information about the most recent casualties, operations, and reactions to counterattacks as well as the omnipresent reports about soldiers who have perished and those who are still in peril. In this sense, news updates from authoritative sources quickly merge with orchestrated propaganda efforts.

Terrorism plays well with audiences accustomed to the discourse of fear as well as political leadership oriented to social policy geared to protecting those audiences from crime. I am proposing, then, that the discourse of fear is a key element of social fears involving crime and other dreaded outcomes in the postmodern world. As rhetoricians have noted, terrorism is easily included within this perspective:

> Terrorism, then, is first and foremost discourse. There is a sense in which the terrorist event must be reported by the media in order for it to have transpired at all. (Zulaika and Douglass 1996, p. 14)

The pervasive threat of terrorism is given credibility by events that are interpreted as part of an unfolding and very uncertain schema for the future:

> Terrorism discourse singles out and removes from the larger historical and political context a psychological trait (terror), an organizational structure (the

terrorist network), and a category (terrorism) in order to invent an autonomous and aberrant realm of gratuitous evil that defies any understanding. The ironic dimension of terrorism discourse derives from its furthering
the very thing it abominates. (Zulaika and Douglass 1996, p. 22)

Terrorism is more than a narrative, but its essence is the definition of the
situation, one that extends beyond the present into a distal future, gray
but known. The forebodingness of events (e.g., the 9/11 attacks) is cast as
a terrible trend inevitability, but the power comes from the uncertainty of
"when" and "where." Like the prospective victims of crime in the future,
citizens will be made terrorist victims in the future.

Terrorism—and especially the attacks of 9/11—enabled political actors
to expand the definition of the situation to all Americans as "victims."
Moreover, all those fighting to protect actual and potential victims should
be permitted to do their work, unimpeded by any concerns about civil liberties or adding context and complexity to the simple analysis that was offered: evil people were attacking good people, and evil had to be destroyed:

> Victimhood has also been expanded through the concept of the indirect vic
> tim. For example, people who witness a crime or who are simply aware that
> something untoward has happened to someone they know are potential in
> direct victims. . . . With the concept of the indirect victim, the numbers be
> come tremendously augmented. Anyone who has witnessed something un
> pleasant or who has heard of such an experience becomes a suitable
> candidate for the status of indirect victim. (Furedi 1997, p. 97)

Victims are a by-product of fear and the discourse of fear. I contend that
"fear" and "victim" are linked through social power, responsibility, and
identity. The linkage involves concerns about safety and perceptions of
risk. Thus, President Bush was relying on more than skilled speechwriters in connecting the mafia and terrorism; he was also relying on audiences' acceptance of mythical mafia "dons" and "godfathers" depicted in
entertainment to grease the conceptual slide of terrorism as a similar
threat. What audiences were presumed to share, then, was the sense that
terrorism, like crime (especially "Mafia Crime"), was a monstrous black
hand that was invisible, omnipresent, and all powerful and that could be
stopped only by a stronger force if ordinary Americans were to survive. I
refer specifically to the "role and identity of victim," as held by numerous
audiences who expect victims to perform certain activities, speak a certain
language, and in general follow a cultural script of "dependence," "lacking," and "powerlessness" while relying on state-sponsored social institutions to save and support them (Garland 2001). Clearly, the terrorists,
like their criminal predecessors, had put us all at risk:

The precondition for the emergence of the victim identity was the consolidation of the consciousness of risk. In the UK and the USA, the growing fear of crime and the growing perception of risks have contributed to the sentiment that everyone is a potential victim. However, crime and the fear of crime are only the most striking manifestations of the kind of insecurity that strengthens the belief that everyone is at risk. (Furedi 1997, p. 100)

Recall that the politics of fear refers to decision makers' promotion and use of audience beliefs and assumptions about danger, risk, and fear in order to achieve certain goals. The politics of fear promotes attacking a target (e.g., crime or terrorism), anticipates further victimization, curtails civil liberties, and stifles dissent as being unresponsive to citizen needs or even "unpatriotic." The Homeland Security Office advised the American people to buy duct tape and plastic sheeting as a barrier to terrorism. This advisory had little to do with "chemical protection" and much to do with the politics of fear. As one observer noted,

Since September 11, that politics has followed two distinct tracks: First, state officials and media pundits have defined and interpreted the objects of Americans' fears—Islamic fundamentalism and terrorism—in anti-political or non-political terms, which has raised the level of popular nervousness; and, second, these same elites have generated a fear of speaking out not only against the war and US foreign policy but also against a whole range of established institutions. (Robin 2002)

This argument has no counterproposal because of the symbolic links that are made between an event, a threat, and the avowed character and purpose of the terrorists, who, like criminals, are construed as lacking any reason, moral foundation, or purpose except to kill and terrify. Not likely to be ravaged by childhood diseases or workplace injuries, postindustrial citizens are prime potential victims, viewing mass-mediated scenarios of crime, mayhem, and destruction; they have no option but to believe and wait:

The most typical mode of terrorism discourse in the United States has been, indeed, one of Waiting for Terror. . . . That which captivates every mind is something so meaningless that it may never happen, yet we are forced to compulsively talk about it while awaiting its arrival. In the theater of the absurd, "no significance" becomes the only significance. . . . When something does happen, after decades during which the absent horror has been omnipresent through the theater of waiting, the vent becomes anecdotal evidence to corroborate what has intuited all along—the by-now permanent catastrophe of autonomous Terror consisting of the waiting for terror. (Zulaika and Douglass 1996, p. 26)

There can be no fear without actual victims or potential victims. In the postmodern age, victim is a status and representation and not merely a person or someone who has suffered as a result of some personal, social, or physical calamity. Massive and concerted efforts by moral entrepreneurs to have their causes adopted and legitimated as "core social issues" worthy of attention have led to the wholesale adaptation and refinement of the use of the problem frame to promote victimization (Best 1995). Often couching their "causes" as battles for "justice," moral entrepreneurs seek to promote new social definitions of right and wrong (Johnson 1995; Spector and Kitsuse 1977). As suggested previously with the examples of hoaxes, victims are entertaining, and that is why they abound. They are evocative, bringing forth tears, joy, and vicarious emotional experience. But victim is more. Victim is now a status, a position that is open to all people who live in a symbolic environment marked by the discourse of fear. We are all potential victims, often vying for official recognition and legitimacy.

CONCLUSION

I suggest that the politics of fear is a dominant motif for news and popular culture. Moreover, within this framework, news reporting about crime and terrorism are linked with "victimization" narratives that make crime, danger, and fear very relevant to everyday life experiences. The social construction of social problems, as Best (1999) noted, is an ongoing process, building from previous experience. However, the politics of fear as public discourse represents an emergent feature of the symbolic environment: moral entrepreneurs' claims making is easier to market to audiences anchored in fear and victimization as features of crime and terrorism. The politics of fear can be theoretically useful in understanding the relevance of mass-mediated fear in contemporary popular culture and political life. This concept is useful for clarifying the closer ties between entertainment-oriented news and popular culture on the one hand and media-savvy state officials on the other. Consider an example of a news report about a dispute in Phoenix, Arizona, over regulating "low-rider" cruising. An attorney for the low-riders stated,

> Unfortunately this bill might be considered by some Hispanics as a form of state-sponsored terrorism through vague local ordinances. (*Arizona Republic*, April 21, 2004, p. B1)

On the one hand, the politics of fear is consistent with entertainment-oriented news and mass media, particularly its resonance with "victim" and victimization. On the other hand, the politics of fear helps political decision makers as news sources and as political actors define social life as dangerous and requiring formal social control and state intervention.

The politics of fear joined crime with victimization through the "drug war," interdiction and surveillance policies, and grand narratives that reflected numerous cultural myths about moral and social "disorder." We are in the midst of an emerging politics of fear that discourages criticism and promotes caution and reliance on careful procedures to "not be hasty," to "cover oneself," to "not be misunderstood." The politics of fear promotes extensive use of disclaimers, those linguistic devices that excuse a comment to follow by providing an explanation to not "take it the wrong way," usually taking the form of "I am not unpatriotic, but . . ." or "I support our troops as much as anyone, but . . .". Very few politicians will stand up to the politics of fear because it is the defining bulwark of legitimacy.

Skillful propaganda and the cooperation of the most powerful news media enabled simple lies to explain complex events. Like entertaining crime reporting, anticipation of wars, attacks, and the constant vigilance to be on guard is gratifying for most citizens who are seeking protection within the symbolic order of the politics of fear. The skillful use of heightened "terrorist alerts" to demand attention to the task at hand is critical in avoiding any detractor. And that is the key point: an otherwise sensible or cautionary remark that signals that one is aware, rational, and weighing alternatives marks one as a detractor, someone who is "against the United States."

The rituals of control are easier to accept as they become more pervasive and institutionalized. Fear is perceived as crime and terrorism, while police and military forces are symbolically joined as protectors. The politics of fear with a national or international justification is more symbolically compelling than "mere crime in the streets." Accompanying heightened terror alerts are routine frisks, intrusive surveillance, and the pervasive voyeuristic camera, scanning the environment for all suspicious activity. The next chapter discusses how the politics of fear has been extended to control of the Internet.

7

The Control Narrative
of the Internet

Filters are workable. We'd rather err on the side of caution instead of being too liberal.

—American Family Association spokesperson

The FBI must draw proactively on all lawful sources of information to identify terrorist threats.

—John Ashcroft, U.S. attorney general

Both the lanternist and the film projectionist have relied on the "persistence of vision"—the fact that the human eye cannot see the gaps between pictures if they're shown fast enough. . . . To the Victorian who had never seen projected pictures before, the sense of expectation when wondering what would happen next must have been considerable.

—"The Magic Lantern"

The politics of fear is a form of social control in modern societies. I noted in chapter 1 that the politics of fear results in policies and procedures affecting many aspects of our lives. Chapter 6 argued that regulating words and meanings in public discourse begins to affect how we talk and discuss things and ultimately how we see the world. This chapter is about the expansion of control and surveillance to the Internet. There are two contexts that reappear throughout this chapter: first, the concern with crime, particularly sexual predators preying on young children but also the growing concern about "identity theft" on the Internet, and, second, threats to national security by terrorists and others who might obtain information via the Internet but also use this "electronic superhighway" to communicate with coconspirators in planning future attacks.

The pages to follow show that the Internet opens up possibilities for people, including escaping certain bounds of social control (e.g., the ease with which pornography can be viewed, contraband merchandise purchased, and so on). The aim of social control is to have people regulate themselves by avoiding activities that could get them into trouble with authorities. The process that makes this work, however, is that social actors will be concerned that they will be found out if they do something "wrong." Thus, even if someone is not watching you, if you think they are, you might not do certain things. Surveillance has greatly expanded under the politics of fear. The argument now is that "things are crazy," so we need to be careful, and "if you have nothing to hide, then you shouldn't mind being watched." The Internet is the new playground of surveillance.

We celebrate the increased freedom and opportunities that accompany computers and the Internet while demanding more control, protection, and surveillance of our use. I will address the increase in computer and Internet surveillance, monitoring, and control by the users, the state, and business as features of mediated interaction. I think that this is a large part of the culture and story of the Internet. I suggest that the visual communication of the Internet exemplifies surveillance culture and that a control narrative is becoming the story of the Internet. The control narrative refers to the relevance for the communication process of actors' awareness and expectation that symbolic meanings may be monitored and used by diverse audiences for various purposes. Control is implicated in rules, prescriptions, and proscriptions involving access, presentation, and use of the Internet. Nuances and intentions can be monitored and objectified by "traces" or the record of use (Beniger 1986). Born of the "risk society," the control narrative reflects the sanctioning process of mediated communication, including perceived and actual preparation, precautions, and consequences (e.g., being "warned" or fired about communicative behavior). The technology of the Internet can "track" or "profile" at the same time, and the communication format of the Internet—the logic of its operation and use—permits users to "search" and allows others to control. A supporter of Attorney General John Ashcroft's call for more Internet authority stated, "In the 1970s, maintaining a clip file on someone was a big deal. Now, Google does it for you," referring to the popular Internet search engine (Savage 2002a, p. 22). Formal agents of social control do act as "Big Brother" on the Internet, but the control narrative operates apart from Big Brother's actions. The control narrative is consistent with Staples's (2000) notion of "meticulous rituals of power" partly because "cyberspace is deeply mired in consumerism surveillance and voyeurism" (Staples 2000, p. 130). In this chapter, I will address how particular features that mediate interaction on the Internet inform the control narrative, including the format features of the Internet, visual character, private/public audiences, the societal context of fear, and control. I will illustrate the control narrative with an overview of Internet security and the paradox of privacy and violation.

The control narrative is made up of the communication format of the Internet, described by Surratt (2001) as "net logic" that must be considered in trying to understand the place of the Internet in the lives of those who use it and the social relationships that are informed by it: "The Internet is unique not because 'it conquers space and time,' but because it is the first strategy that operates according to a many-to-many (one-to-one) communications pattern or logic" (Surratt 2001, p. 42). The visual character of the Internet and the ease with which communication can be seen suggests that on the one hand Internet users are exhibitionists—in the sense that they communicate to be seen—while on the other they are voyeurs, aiming to see others' communications (Denzin 1995). "Surfing the Net" is a surveillance activity. I suggest that an adequate understanding of Internet communication should include analysis of all mediating influences on the Internet and clarify how actors' awareness and use of surveillance and monitoring informs their communicative acts.

Computer technology in general and the use of the Internet in particular is one of many forms of mediating communication and interaction between people. I suggest that these new forms of communication have arisen during a period of heightened expectations of freedom and opportunity within a massive campaign to promote fear of the "other" and especially crime. Indeed, the expansion of surveillance throughout social order (Marx 1988) involves much more than crime; rather, the tools and perspectives of "policing" against crime have been extended as a format of control to "policing" society more generally. Ironically, it is the knowledge we have that is now being used as a foundation for more control, regulation, and surveillance. The preoccupation with protecting us from what is a potential threat has been referred to as "policing the risk society" by Ericson and Haggerty (1997) and others who contend that postindustrial society is marked by an expanding body of knowledge about risks:

> Risk communication systems are entwined with privacy and trust. The more that foreboding and fear lead people to withdraw from public involvement, the more they value privacy and withdraw into privatized lifestyles. The greater the privacy, the greater the need for surveillance mechanisms to produce the knowledge necessary to trust people in otherwise anonymous institutional

transactions. Paradoxically, these mechanisms intrude on privacy and are a constant reminder of the uncertainties of trust. Yet it is only in a framework of trust that patterns of risk can be adequately institutionalized and forms the basis of decisions. Privacy, trust, surveillance, and risk management go hand in hand in policing the probabilities and possibilities of action. (Ericson and Haggerty 1997, p. 6)

The possibility of quick and easily accessible communication with others is paradoxically linked to the fear and control of others to us and our children (Altheide 2002b). As Lyon (2001) notes,

Surveillance today is a means of sorting and classifying populations and not just of invading personal space or violating the privacy of individuals. In postmodernizing contexts surveillance is an increasingly powerful means of reinforcing social divisions, as the superpanoptic sort relentlessly screens, monitors and classifies to determine eligibility and access, to include and to exclude. . . Surveillance has become an indirect but potent means of affecting life chances and social destinies. (p. 151)

As Staples (2000) suggested, Internet surveillance by formal authorities and by everyday users is a microtechnology of surveillance performed millions of times each day as users perform surveillance ceremonies as they surf the Internet and thereby enact meticulous rituals of power.

The challenge is to identify how mediation and control operate in cyberspace. I will focus mainly on the expansion of Internet surveillance and particularly the use of "Internet stings" by formal agents of social control. My argument is that surveillance and control are expanding in everyday communication on the Internet and that it is becoming more acceptable to compromise privacy. Indeed, the nature of privacy is changing because of this surveillance. The awareness of monitoring and surveillance informs all Internet communication. Moreover, other social effects, not addressed in this chapter, are likely to follow as users engage in deceptive practices (e.g., using false names, multiple e-mail addresses, and so on) to protect their privacy.

Investigating the nature, extent, and social consequences of mediated communication should consider the relevant dimensions that contribute to the meaning and significance of this use. I intend for the following remarks to help us grasp a bit more completely the structures, formats, and meanings of various mediating factors. My focus will be on a small segment of Internet use that may be characterized as state control and surveillance. I choose this because the state structure is closely related to the organization, licensing, monitoring, access, and control of information technology like computers and the Internet links that enable citizens to "interact" with one another and engage in various forms of sociation. Simply stated, my major aim is to draw our attention to a translucent veil of control and surveillance that informs use of the Internet, including actors' perceptions, communication styles and content, reading, interpretation, and use. Following some introductory remarks, I will focus on recent developments pertaining to surveillance, deception, and entrapment by formal agents of social control in the name of protecting children from predators and pedophiles.

A THEORETICAL RATIONALE FOR MEDIATED INTERACTION

The politics of fear rides on social meanings and taken-for-granted assumptions about threats to social order and ways of avoiding such threats. Symbolic communication and the processes that produce it mediate all interaction. An entire theoretical orientation to the study of social life, symbolic interaction, along with multiple versions of other "social psychologies," incorporate (albeit in different ways) the "communication process." So basic are many of these precepts to any understanding of social life—including all its "macro" forms—that David Maines (2001) finds an increasing trend toward the widespread use by general sociology of standard concepts and propositions once held almost solely by pragmatists and interactionists. I will touch on only a few components of this process in order to move on to a discussion of mediated interaction and the Internet.

The elements of the process involve the definition of the situation and identity and what Schutz (1967) termed "typification," or typical course of action. Each of these, along with information technologies, mediates interaction. The communication process involves an actor taking into account an audience by "taking the role of the other" outlined by Mead and Morris (1962) and articulated by Blumer (1962). As Surratt (2001) observes, the key to this process is the actor's identity, or that part of the self by which he is known to others: "Defining the self and the generalized other in a meaningful way becomes one of the key problems of social order in the highly modern world" (p. 218).

These in turn reflexively join the communicative act with the definition of the situation that is also influenced by a broader context of meaning, memories, and history. For example, work on the changing nature and conceptions of identity suggests that broader social changes, including information technology and popular culture, can affect the emerging conceptions of self within an altered communications order (Altheide 2000; Cerulo 1997). Most of these elements that are involved in computer-mediated communication were not present throughout most of human history:

> The information/communications revolution creates a vast and mysterious electronic landscape of new relationships, roles, identities, networks, and communities, while it undermines that cherished luxury of the modern self— privacy. (Anderson 1997, quoted in Surratt 2001, p. 209)

Each element that influences social interaction can be regarded as a potential contributor or mediator to interaction. For example, the visual and temporal nature of computer interfaces mediates the communicative act. Actors must develop sophisticated understandings, skills, styles, and even rhythm for operation of these "interfaces" in order to run a computer as well as "operate" online (Altheide 1985). Moreover, the equipment, skills, and social capital essential for online participations are differentially accessible because of social and economic considerations (Pew Charitable Trusts 2002).

A unique feature that the Internet shares with cell phone use is that communication is visible (Altheide 2002c). The increasing visual nature of the Internet is consistent with a trend in all media:

> "There is so much media around," said Mr. Wenner, who retains the title of editor. "Back when *Rolling Stone* was publishing these 7,000-word stories, there was no CNN, no Internet. And now you can travel instantaneously around the globe, and you don't need these long stories to get up to speed."
>
> "All the great media adventures of the 20th century have been visual," said Mr. Needham, 37, who grew up in Cambridge, England. "Television, movies, the Internet, they're all visual mediums, and I don't think people have time to sit down and read. The gaps in people's time keep getting smaller and smaller, and the competition is getting more intense. It's one of the facts of media life." (Carr 2002, p. 5C)

The public and visual nature of one-to-one communication on the Internet invites surveillance and control. The paradox of Internet security is that it requires violation and surveillance: on the one hand, consumer transactions require privacy and confidence in security, but, on the other, users want protection from "hackers" and others who may exploit commerce or national security or use the publicly available access to defraud, intimidate, harass, and commit crimes. As media become more visual, they are more visible, less private, and more susceptible to deception by users who may use multiple identities for different purposes and websites. Deceptive communication breaches trust and legitimacy and contributes to an expansion of social control and surveillance. Efforts to monitor and regulate social behavior have reached the Internet (Lyon 2001; Staples 1997). Part of Internet logic includes awareness and anticipation by many that there may be unintended consequences of their actions because of surveillance and control by agents seeking to take advantage of their activity. These external controls, monitors, and surveillance can mediate interaction insofar as an actor takes them into account in defining a situation. For example, surveys indicate that 17 percent of Internet users know someone who has lost a job because of computer infractions (Pew Charitable Trusts 2002):

> The AMA's [American Management Association] survey of major U.S. firms found that 77.7% now record and review some sort of employee communications and activities on the job.
>
> For example, Internet connections were monitored by 63% of the more than 1,600 companies responding to the survey. Telephone use was tracked by 43%. Computer use such as time logged on or keystroke counts was monitored by 19%. Video surveillance for security purposes was used by 38%. (*USA Today* 2001)

Internet security and surveillance are now linked to provide privacy as well as protection and control:

> Similarly, Americans are just as likely to approve of FBI or law enforcement surveillance of criminal suspects' phone calls and postal mail as they are to approve of surveillance of suspects' email. Fully 56% of all Americans approve of the FBI or law enforcement agencies intercepting telephone calls to and from people suspected of criminal activities; 55% of all Americans approve of the FBI or law enforcement agencies intercepting letters and packages sent by mail to and from people suspected of criminal activities; 54% of all Americans approve of the FBI or law enforcement agencies intercepting email over the Internet sent to and from people suspected of criminal activities. (Pew Charitable Trusts 2002)

Consumer transactions and protection from "hackers" require monitoring and surveillance to achieve various goals. Numerous computer and security publications report thousands of attempts to breach computer "security" by domestic and international hackers. The latter has implications for national security, but the biggest concern is commerce. As a spokesperson for one computer security company put it,

> "You need security, privacy and trust to get to the real electronic wallet," said Christiansen. "You need a high degree of confidence, not that you won't be ripped off, but that someone isn't tracking your interactions—that it will be a trusted connection with the party you intended." (Fox 2001)

Adult Internet users are about split between those who are more or less trusting of Internet interaction. Survey data suggest that they take various measures to "protect" themselves, including engaging in deception:

> 63.1 percent of generalized trusters say that they use their real names on the web, compared to 55.7 percent of mistrusters. . . . We see similar effects for ever used a fake ID on the web and replied to an e-mail from strangers—and slightly larger ones for using a credit card on the phone, and receiving an offensive e-mail from strangers. (Uslaner 2000)

Children tend to be more trusting of Internet communications than adults and are more likely to provide personal and identifying information (Electronic Privacy Information Center 2002).

The context of use and format of computer and Internet mediation produces the conundrum that surveillance and privacy violations are justified in order for users to have confidence in the privacy of communication and transactions. It is the context and the power to define situations of use as "legitimate" or not that produces the contradiction. It is as though whoever controls a server and/or rules of use controls intrusion and surveillance rights. Thus, we have seen that employers essentially have been sanctioned to intrude on employees, while businesses can now monitor critics with "snoop tools":

> Beware the public relations person with a modem. Now corporate spinmeisters, too, can go online to track customers—especially the disgruntled ones who vent their spleen in cyberspace. . . . To me, there's something very troubling about cyberspinning. Good public-relations personnel can quell panic and remind people of their company's side of the story in the heat of a crisis. But personalized spin campaigns? The potential for abuse seems too high, and the idea sounds ominous to those who cherish free speech without risk of punishment. (Stepanek 2000)

Government and security experts are authorized and paid to intrude on hackers and "nonauthorized" parties, and formal agents of social control are authorized to engage in surveillance of all. Not surprisingly, there is also a good deal of countersurveillance going on in cyberspace as hackers and corporate security experts do battle, as government snoops combat "nonauthorized" parties from other countries, as citizen watchdogs and formal agents of social control monitor clandestine activities, and as private citizens are monitored by those formal agents of social control.

American citizens expect privacy and want this secured. Numerous opinion polls indicate that they do not approve of having information about them collected or sold without their permission (Pew Charitable Trusts 2002).

In other areas, 87 percent of Americans say they are concerned about credit card theft online, 82 percent are concerned about how organized terrorists can wreak havoc with Internet tools, 80 percent fear that the Internet can be used to commit wide-scale fraud, 78 percent fear hackers getting access to government computer networks, 76 percent fear hackers getting access to business networks, and 70 percent are anxious about criminals or pranksters sending out computer viruses that alter or wipe out personal computer files.

These concerns may be a factor in the public's support of the right of the FBI and other law enforcement agencies to intercept criminal suspects' e-mail. Some 54 percent of Americans approve of the idea of FBI monitoring of suspects' e-mail, while 34 percent disapprove. There is equal public support of the FBI monitoring of e-mail, phone calls, and postal mail (Pew Charitable Trusts 2002).

Moreover, Internet users do not approve of "Web tracking," and are suspicious of private and governmental surveillance, although most citizens are not aware of the range of electronic tracking methods (Electronic Privacy Information Center 2002). However, Americans are willing to trade some liberty for security, particularly in times of crisis. After the 9/11 attacks, initial support increased for government surveillance and even the call for a "national ID," but this declined rather rapidly:

> A study conducted in November 2001 for the *Washington Post* found that only 44% of Americans supported national ID. A poll released in March 2002 by the Gartner Group found that 26% of Americans favored a national ID, and that 41% opposed the idea. Popular support for other surveillance technologies has declined as well. (Electronic Privacy Information Center 2002)

INTERNET SURVEILLANCE AND THE LAW

While U.S. citizens are aware that social control of the Internet can influence constitutional rights to free speech, perceived threats to safety of oneself, children, and, more recently, national security have promoted various efforts to regulate and monitor Internet use. The knowledge and use of Internet surveillance is inconsistent, with huge gaps separating legality from what is done in practice. Formal agents of social control have long sought more regulation of information technology such as the Internet, although the courts have not supported such efforts. For example, regulating "private use" of computers was dealt a blow when the Supreme Court opposed a law in 1997 that made putting "indecent" material on the Internet a crime, and in 2002 the Court ruled against rules aimed at keeping minors away from commercial pornography on the World Wide Web (Savage 2002b). The U.S. Court of Appeals for the Third

Circuit sustained public use of Internet technology when it ruled that legislation that requires libraries to screen Internet communications is unconstitutional:

> The judges, who heard eight days of testimony, concluded that software programs designed to filter out such material are flawed and ineffective. Although the law sought to block access to "visual depictions" of sex, the software scanned for words, not images. Students researching breast cancer or sexual orientations were blocked, while some pornography slipped through.
>
> The law "requires [librarians] to violate the 1st Amendment rights of their patrons," said Chief Judge Edward R. Becker of the U.S. 3rd Circuit Court of Appeals. "The filtering programs bar access to a substantial amount of speech on the Internet that is clearly constitutionally protected for adults and minors." (Savage 2002b, p. 12)

Justices' concerns about Internet surveillance were dramatized in May 2001, when federal judges in the U.S. Court of Appeals for the Ninth Circuit disabled software that had been set up by the Administrative Offices of the Court to detect downloading of streaming video, music, and pornography (Lewis 2001). Notwithstanding the American Management Association's finding that 63 percent of companies monitored employees' communications, the Ninth Circuit workers—and their judicial bosses—were not impressed and disconnected the surveillance equipment. Chief Judge Mary Schroeder wrote that the rationale to monitor the court was objectionable because it was not based on concerns about overloading the system but rather "content detection":

> Many employees had been disciplined, she noted, because the software turned up evidence of such things as viewing pornography, although they had not been given any clear notice of the court's computer use policy. Moreover, she wrote, the judiciary may have violated the law. "We are concerned about the propriety and even the legality of monitoring Internet usage," she wrote. Her memorandum said that the judiciary could be liable to lawsuits and damages because the software might have violated the Electronic Communications Privacy Act of 1986, which imposes civil and criminal liability on any person who intentionally intercepts "any wire, oral or electronic communication."
>
> She noted that the Ninth Circuit had ruled just this year that the law was violated when an employer accessed an employee Web site. In fact, the issues of what is permissible by employers have produced a patchwork of legal rulings and the matter has never been addressed directly by the Supreme Court. (Lewis 2001)

Prior to the justices' actions, it had been agreed that the Judicial Conference of the United States would discuss the software surveillance issue on September 11, 2001. Notwithstanding the heightened concern with surveillance after the 9/11 attacks, the Judicial Conference supported the actions by the

Ninth Circuit justice when they ruled on September 19, 2001, that employees did not lose all rights to privacy concerning e-mail and Internet use:

> The proposed policy, which explicitly stated that court employees had no expectation of privacy "at any time" while online at work, was withdrawn last week before a scheduled vote by the Judicial Conference of the United States, the policymaking body for the courts. Yesterday, the 27-judge panel approved a revised version, which permits no monitoring of e-mail and only limited tracking of Web-surfing. The judicial retreat from unrestricted monitoring will have an immediate impact on the 14 million U.S. workers who, according to a recent Privacy Foundation study, are subject to continuous monitoring while online. This rejection of unrestrained monitoring is particularly important, given the calls for increased Internet security in the past week. (Gordon 2002, p. B7)

Until this "precedent" is extended to private and public workplaces, the monitoring of employee e-mail and Internet activity will continue. Those planning the nation's response to "security threats" paid little heed to the action.

The 9/11 attacks boosted the momentum of authorities to expand surveillance of the Internet even though it would reduce civil liberties and give the FBI more unbridled surveillance of citizens and potential terrorists. Despite cautions raised by civil rights advocates, the "war on terror" resurrected the spectacle of FBI domestic spying and surveillance:

> In tandem with the perception of the Net as a technology that is difficult to control is a pessimistic view of humanity that assumes the worst about people's intentions. The darkest elements of humanity are seen as finding a home on the Net to pursue their anti-social and destructive ends. Combined with the panic of the potential damage a borderless medium can do to the authority of the State, the Net is seen by Western governments as a potential source of destabilisation.
>
> The anxieties expressed by Western elites about their direction and purpose have attached themselves to the Net—a new medium that represents the unknown. It used to be that the unknown was viewed as a potential opportunity to be explored and exploited to aid social and material progress. Now the unknown, regardless of its real potential is viewed as a risk that has to be contained and managed so it inflicts as little disruption and harm as possible. (Amis 2002)

The USA Patriot Act (USAPA) was passed on October 26, 2001. This act expanded governmental authority to engage in surveillance and challenge limits to civil liberties:

> The civil liberties of ordinary Americans have taken a tremendous blow with this law, especially the right to privacy in our online communications and

activities. Yet there is no evidence that our previous civil liberties posed a barrier to the effective tracking or prosecution of terrorists. In fact, in asking for these broad new powers, the government made no showing that the previous powers of law enforcement and intelligence agencies to spy on US citizens were insufficient to allow them to investigate and prosecute acts of terrorism. The process leading to the passage of the bill did little to ease these concerns. To the contrary, they are amplified by the inclusion of so many provisions that, instead of aimed at terrorism, are aimed at nonviolent, domestic computer crime. In addition, although many of the provisions facially appear aimed at terrorism, the Government made no showing that the reasons they failed to detect the planning of the recent attacks or any other terrorist attacks were the civil liberties compromised with the passage of USAPA. . . .

The USAPA removes many of the checks and balances that prevented both police and the foreign intelligence agencies from improperly conducting surveillance on US citizens who are not involved in criminal or terrorist activity. For Internet users, it opens the door for widespread surveillance of web surfing, e-mails and peer to peer systems. In addition, the protections against the misuse of these authorities—by the foreign intelligence agencies to spy on US citizens and by law enforcement to use foreign intelligence authority to exceed their domestic surveillance authority—have been greatly reduced. (Electronic Frontier Foundation 2001)

These changes opened a floodgate for subpoenas to investigate numerous groups and activities:

"The amount of subpoenas that carriers receive today is roughly doubling every month—we're talking about hundreds of thousands of subpoenas for customer records—stuff that used to require a judge's approval," said Albert Gidari, a Seattle-based expert in privacy and security law who represents numerous technology companies. (Benson 2002)

As noted, several major changes were contained in the USA Patriot Act, but other changes were forthcoming as well:

President Bush and Attorney General John Ashcroft said the changes are needed to boost the FBI's arsenal against terrorism. But civil libertarians and others complained that the FBI is being rewarded for its investigative lapses before the Sept. 11 terrorist attacks.

"We intend to honor the Constitution and respect the freedoms that we hold so dear," Bush assured.

Added Ashcroft: "Our objective today is not to sift through the rubble after another terrorist attack."

The changes will enable FBI agents to do such things as monitor mosques, churches and synagogues, listen in on Internet chat rooms, watch library or supermarket card use, or even photograph or make lists of people attending political or other public gatherings without first providing any evidence of criminal activity.

"As we have heard recently, FBI men and women in the field are frustrated because many of our own internal restrictions have hampered our ability to fight terrorism," Ashcroft said at a news conference. (House 2002)

Ashcroft's announcement Thursday changed the government's guidelines to encourage agents to gather more information, even when they have no evidence of a crime in progress.
"The FBI must draw proactively on all lawful sources of information to identify terrorist threats," Ashcroft said. (Savage 2002a, p. 22)

A related issue that has been raised is the "career of information," or what happens to the massive amount of material being collected. Government agencies have not been particularly successful at protecting the information for one specific purpose and are less likely to do so now that interagency cooperation essentially has been mandated:

Prosecutors, acting under the authority of grand jury investigations, may issue subpoenas without prior approval of a judge. Critics complain that the Patriot Act makes it possible for CIA agents working with law enforcement officers to jointly draw up subpoenas, obtain information, and never have to appear in court to explain how the information was used. (Benson 2002)

Part of the context of this new information access and use is that most Americans are unaware that the FBI and CIA, for example, have not openly shared information in recent years in order to protect civil rights and to prevent the kind of witch hunts that occurred previously in American history, particularly the civil rights era. As one observer stated,

In the '60s and '70s, the FBI ran a massive program called COINTELPRO that included secret investigations, surveillance, infiltration and disruption of political activist groups that were not engaged in illegal conduct, including the civil rights movement, anti-war protesters and feminists. . . .
"Consumers should know that the information they give to America Online or Microsoft may very well wind up at the IRS or the FBI," said Jeffrey A. Eisenach, president of the Progress & Freedom Foundation, a think tank that studies technology and public policy. "Security is not costless." (Benson 2002)

Government agencies, along with commercial interests armed with cyber-snooping technology, are entering what one critic called the "Golden Age of Wiretapping" (Benson 2002). Today the information access and monitoring of the Internet as well as cell phone messages is more insidious because it is about control and making money. Business and formal agents of social control not only have interests in security and surveillance but also are often partners in a complex dance of communication and control.

Consider the development of two computer snooping programs, Carnivore and Magic Lantern. Essentially, both are designed to monitor computer keystrokes and messages (MSNBC 2001). The first one was Carnivore. After news organizations broke the story about this software that could "snoop" on one's e-mail and Internet use, the FBI addressed their work on the project:

> Two weeks ago, the *Wall Street Journal* published an article entitled "FBI's system to covertly search E-mail raises privacy, legal issues." This story was immediately followed by a number of similar reports in the press and other media depicting our Carnivore system as something ominous and raising concerns about the possibility of its potential to snoop, without a court order, into the private E-mails of American citizens. . . .
>
> In response to a critical need for tools to implement complex court orders, the FBI developed a number of capabilities including the software program called "Carnivore." Carnivore is a very specialized network analyzer or "sniffer" which runs as an application program on a normal personal computer under the Microsoft Windows operating system. It works by "sniffing" the proper portions of network packets and copying and storing only those packets which match a finely defined filter set programmed in conformity with the court order. This filter set can be extremely complex, and this provides the FBI with an ability to collect transmissions which comply with pen register court orders, trap & trace court orders, Title III interception orders, etc. (Kerr 2000)

American citizens were about evenly divided on whether this software would be used appropriately by the FBI (Pew Charitable Trusts 2002). Carnivore requires access to a user's computer in order to be installed, but Magic Lantern does not. This is a virus that can be sent to individual computers to monitor keystrokes and send the information to the FBI (earlier versions sent information to hackers). Magic Lantern, which would be an extension of the Carnivore Internet surveillance program, takes the idea one step further by enabling agents to place a trojan on a target's computer without having to gain physical access (Leyden 2001).

However, the virus detection programs available on most computer systems can detect them if the software is programmed to find them. Ironically, the confidence and trust of software manufacturers could be compromised if word got out that they had cooperated with the FBI in installing a virus:

> Prior to the FBI's official disclosure, several major antivirus companies told news sources earlier this week that they would not aid the FBI in allowing its viruses any special advantage over other viruses and worms, saying that selective virus interception would diminish public confidence in the effectiveness of their security products. (Weisman 2001)

> "If it was under the control of the FBI, with appropriate technical safeguards in place to prevent possible misuse, and nobody else used it—we wouldn't

detect it," said Chien. "However we would detect modified versions that might be used by hackers."

Graham Cluley, senior technology consultant at Sophos, disagrees. He says it is wrong to deliberately refrain from detecting the virus, because its customers outside the US would expect protection against the Trojan. Such a move also creates an awkward precedent. (Leyden 2001)

The pervasiveness of the politics of fear is partly due to the acceptance of certain programs by people throughout social life, especially certain key organizations and industries. For example, if the military and law enforcement organizations enact certain policies, this can have widespread consequences. By the same token, when computer and Internet companies accept the principle that computers should be made to comply with government surveillance, that is also consequential. When this occurs, the government oversight is no longer just the government's; it is society-wide. In fact, this has happened with the computer industry. The Associated Press reported that the FBI was no longer going to use Carnivore but instead would rely on surveillance by Internet providers (*Arizona Republic*, January 19, 2005, p. A3). Instead, the FBI said it has switched to unspecified commercial software to eavesdrop on computer traffic during such investigations and has increasingly asked Internet providers to conduct wiretaps on targeted customers on the government's behalf, reimbursing companies for their costs. This means that the use and logic of communication using the computer also is based on a format of control that permits surveillance. To communicate is to be observed. The politics of fear is essentially an integral feature of computer hardware and software. But this is only half the story.

The other half of the story is that the CIA and FBI are in conflict about surveillance and control. While the FBI's interest has been in developing Magic Lantern to monitor computer use, the CIA has developed software to avoid this surveillance. The CIA has had a hand in developing more software that will override Carnivore and Magic Lantern. A CIA-backed software company, Safe Web, created Triangle Boy, which enables people in "tyrannical" countries (e.g., China) to get access to blocked Internet sites:

Yet, as the FBI struggles to introduce its new system to monitor the Internet, the CIA is working to develop a software program that thwarts government monitoring. The CIA is a major sponsor of SafeWeb, a company that distributes a free program called Triangle Boy. Triangle Boy allows users to surf the Web anonymously. Citizens inside dictatorships are using the program to avoid monitoring by the oppressive regimes.

Triangle Boy operates much like a mail forwarding service. Each user request to view a Web page is scrambled and randomly sent to another machine, which actually performs the request, returning the data to the original user. Triangle Boy is very popular inside China, and the Chinese government is working hard on ways to counter secure access to the Internet. (Smith 2001)

A potential problem is that terrorists could use Triangle Boy to avoid detection by the FBI's Magic Lantern (although officials deny that this is likely):

> Ironically, many inside the computer security field declined to describe ways to stop Triangle Boy—not for technical reasons but for political reasons. Software experts are usually anxious to publish flaws inside Microsoft operating systems or other major software packages. Yet this is not the case for Triangle Boy. "Normally, I'm all for publishing flaws in software, but on this one I have to vote against," stated one computer security expert located in the Netherlands.
> "The Chinese finally have access to the Internet. The flaws could be used by the Chinese government to block the Internet once again." (Smith 2001)

At this point I should stress what the foregoing has implied: it is now official that anyone who uses the Internet is legally subject to surveillance and monitoring by formal agents of social control. As one observer cautioned,

> The bottom line here is that companies and individuals will be responsible for protecting themselves from both cyberterrorism and the government's response to it. (Weisman 2001)

It is clear, then, that the Internet mediates interaction in several ways. On the one hand, certain monitoring is not new to Internet users, most of whom simply take it for granted that various businesses, organizations, and universities collect information from them and sell parts of their "social identity" for marketing and cash. On the other hand, the mediation of Internet interaction goes well beyond "buyer beware": it extends to the communicative foundations of trust that may be utilized to "trick" and deceive actors.

INTERNET STINGS

Surveillance takes on a different meaning with new technology. Virtually everyone who uses a "search engine" is gathering information that is available in public, so formal agents of social control reason that anyone should be able to do so. A law professor who did not regard the new FBI Internet surveillance as unconstitutional added, "Still, if sleazy credit card companies can look up our supermarket or other purchases, then I see nothing wrong at first blush with letting the FBI agents do the same thing" (House 2002). Many Americans share this sentiment, particularly when it comes to preventing crime and protecting their children from pornography.

The concern with "sleazy" surveillance extends beyond credit card companies and FBI agents to the monitoring and deception by law enforcement officials in setting up "Internet stings." Internet stings have been conducted by formal agents of social control on topics ranging from prostitution and escort services, gay chat rooms, drugs (including Viagra), computer software, stolen goods, stolen credit cards, fraudulent IDs, satellite dish cards, animal videos, stock Internet scams, and child pornography.

The use of Internet stings to police deviance and risk is a technological fix to what are clearly diverse interests and perspectives on many facets of social life, including sexuality. But deviance in the risk society relies less on moral persuasion that is absent because of a lack of consensus and more on technology:

> Risk communication systems turn the moral discourse of deviance into a utilitarian morality of probability calculus. The systems make up people more according to the former's internally referential systems of rationality than in terms of extrinsic moral questions of deviance. People are panoptically sorted according to utilitarian criteria—a more or less stable, bright, strong, efficient, useful, and so on—creating the "transmission society" of risk career tracks. Gutter of moral wrongdoing, deviance is treated as a normal accident. That is, deviance is treated as a contingency for which there are risk technologies to spread the loss and prevent recurrence. Deviance becomes a technical problem that requires an administrative solution, rather than an occasion for expressing collective sentiments and moral solidarity, which are relegated to mass media morality plays through which people remember values that are increasingly at odds with those of other institutions. (Ericson and Haggerty 1997, p. 448)

Stings are commonly used in order to "protect children" from online predators and pedophiles. These stings tend to focus on (1) participants in chat rooms and Web pages where "sex tours" or traveling (across town or around the world) to meet children for sex or pornographic purposes are advertised, and (2) websites where information and materials are exchanged about child pornography as well as child or adult prostitution.

Like all stings, the intent is to create a false scenario and opportunity for a crime to be committed, such as undercover police officers acting as prostitutes. Internet stings involve providing information about any regulated "bait," which may be merchandise, activities, or opportunities, such as stolen goods, credit cards, cell phone numbers, pirated video cards for cable reception, drugs, escort services and prostitution, pornography, drugs, child pornography, and pedophilia. Typically, police officers (but also citizen vigilantes) using a deceptive and false identity will broadcast via the Internet that they have certain goods or services. This is done very aggressively, using role playing, typical scenarios, presentations of self, and relevant discourse and terminology in order to draw the interest of potential customers/buyers who will be treated as offenders. Many Internet stings bait a "suspect" to buy something (e.g., drugs) or "meet" someone for some deviant/illegal purpose. The provider of the service, who is usually a police officer, will show up to "sell" a product or "meet" the suspect, who will typically be arrested after money is exchanged—or some other incriminating information is provided to represent "intent."

Undercover sting operations appear to have increased dramatically over the past forty years (Marx 1988) and particularly since the mid-1990s. Virtually every major city in the United States—and several smaller ones—have used the Internet for sting operations. Sting operations are easy to sell to audiences consuming popular culture and the discourse of fear—the pervasive communication, symbolic awareness, and expectation that danger and risk are a central feature of everyday life (Altheide 2002b). Particularly popular are stings that target corrupters of children such as "child pornographers" and pedophiles.

"Americans are deeply worried about criminal activity on the Internet, and their revulsion at child pornography is by far their biggest fear. Some 92 percent of Americans say they are concerned about child pornography on the Internet, and 50 percent of Americans cite child porn as the single most heinous crime that takes place online" (Pew Charitable Trusts 2002). As one federal prosecutor put it, "There are only two ways to do these cases. . . . A sting operation or wait till a kid gets hurt" (Stern 2002, p. 1).

The concern with protecting children is a feature of the discourse of fear that calls for more control (Altheide 2002a). While officials estimate that a very small fraction of sexual abuse victims began their relationships on the Internet (five of 4,000 in Chicago [Miller 1999]), public perception is that it is rampant. Moral entrepreneurs promoting sensational news reports have prompted officials to spring into action and get involved. Operating under various names (e.g., Operation Landslide and Innocent Images), federal and state police increasingly are in the sting business. Even before the terrorist attacks cemented the perception that everyday life is dangerous and that "evil" predators are lurking everywhere, formal agents of social control were given substantial support to "crack down" on child molesters and perverts. Innocent Images, for example, is an annual $10 million FBI operation that sprang from the 1995 Innocent Images National Initiative. Its purposes are the following:

- To identify, investigate, and prosecute sexual predators who use the Internet and online services to sexually exploit children

- To establish a law enforcement presence on the Internet as a deterrent to subjects that use it to exploit children
- To identify and rescue witting and unwitting child victims (www .fbi.gov/hq/cid/cac/innocent.htm)

One of the first FBI operations under Innocent Images was Operation Candyland, which was named after an E-group Web page oriented to posting messages and images about children. The FBI pursued some 7,000 e-mail addresses, 4,600 in the United States. As of March, 2002, 231 searches of computers had been conducted, and eighty-six individuals were charged in twenty-six states (www.fbi.gov/pressrel/candyman/ candymanhome.htm).

Like the undercover police officers studied by Marx (1988) who were often spying on other undercover police officers, Internet police are often "talking to themselves":

> Agents posing as teens almost certainly outnumber actual teens in many of the Internet's seedier chat rooms these days. And though would-be sexual predators are surely aware of this ploy, the number of them stepping into these digital traps continues to soar. . . . "It's probably overkill," said Shari Steele, director of legal services for the Electronic Frontier Foundation. "At least half the 13-year-old girls in chat rooms are probably policemen." (Miller 1999, p. AI)

This is how one Arizona "sex tour" sting worked: U.S. Customs Service agents placed an ad in an Internet newsgroup promoting a "sex tour." They did this by encouraging "visitors" to provide age, preferred activities, fantasies, and ages of sex playmates. A Customs agent feigning to be a "child sex purveyor" played to the men's "darkest desires, offering to make nearly any illegal fantasy come true on the sex tour" (Stern 2002, p. 1). Ten men sent payments and traveled to Yuma, Arizona, where undercover officers met them in a hotel room. No one was actually victimized by these people, but it is against federal law to "travel with intent to engage in a sexual act with a juvenile" (Stern 2002, p. 1). Eight men pleaded guilty, and most have been sentenced. One man who claimed that he had been molested by his priest said that the agent encouraged his fantasies: "I felt like this guy understood what I was going through. . . . They kind of normalized it for me" (Stern 2002, p. 1). Another man, Glyn Harrod, flew to Arizona from Australia. The mine worker had never had sex with children, although he admitted that he had viewed pornography. Australian authorities cooperated with U.S. formal agents of social control and raided his home in Australia, where they confiscated his computer containing pornographic materials. He served thirty-two months of a thirty-seven-month sentence in jail (Toohey 1999). On his release some three years later, a journalist interviewed Harrod about his experiences and perceptions. The formal agents of social control, Harrod explained, provided a survey for the potential sex tour customers to state their preferences:

> Harrod told the *Centralian Advocate*: "I'd seen child pornography on the internet but it didn't bother me, it didn't offend me, but I was sort of curious.
> "That curiosity is what led me to getting wrapped up in the internet sting.
> "They sent me an e-mail questionnaire asking things like 'what would you like to do sexually?'
> "There was a list of about 10 different things you could do.
> "Things like bondage and discipline and sado masochism.
> "I deleted a lot of stuff off it and left three things—vaginal, oral and anal sex.
> "I'm obviously guilty of something, but I don't think that I would have gone through with having sex with the girls." (Wilton 2002, p. 5)

There have been other Internet stings where the focus is on belonging to an illegal Web page. Supported by the FBI's Innocent Images cyberpatrol, New Jersey police closed down a pornographic website and arrested its operators. Formal agents of social control restarted it within two months using the same domain and explained to "surfers" that the site had been down but was now open for business. They invited prospective subscribers to join for a $19.99 membership fee and to share their materials of prepubescent males. Law enforcement officials throughout the world seized computers in sixteen nations and twenty-nine states. The suspects included a teacher, a principal, a police officer, and a firefighter (Wire Services 2002).

Another Web page sting trapped journalist Larry Matthews, who had published several reports on pedophiles and was conducting research on pedophilia. Matthews joined a website and frequented chat rooms that traded child pornography because he felt that it was a better method of doing quality journalism:

> He told prosecutors that conventional research methods for his latest project, like posing questions as a journalist in open chat rooms, were unsuccessful and that to delve deeper, he needed to assume the persona of a trader in child pornographic images. (Janofsky 1999, p. A17)

In a bizarre twist of events, Matthews himself was arrested as a result of the FBI's Innocent Images program in Baltimore, Maryland, where agents had adopted a similar strategy of frequenting anonymous chat rooms to catch adults who solicit minors and exchange child porn (Burton 2002). He was not permitted to use a conventional journalistic defense of First Amendment rights and was convicted and sentenced to eighteen months.

The surveillance is very real in Internet stings, although the characters are just that: usually caricatures of stereotypes of "child molesters" and pedophiles. While laws were established to protect "real persons" from those intending to harm them, the mediated nature of the Internet warrants presentation of identity as one thing when, in fact, it may be something else—it may be a middle-aged formal agent of social control rather than a thirteen-year-old girl or boy.

This point was made in a case in Wisconsin when the accused's attorney argued that no crime could have occurred since the intended victim was "virtual" and not real, although he did travel to a hotel room where he believed that an encounter would follow. The defense attorney argued that one may have also had a change of heart because of guilt, shame, remorse, or fear of getting caught. Attorneys claimed that the law should be overturned:

> Department of Justice spokesman Randy Romanski said that if the law is overturned, it will shake up the way the agency's Internet Crimes Against Children Task Force does business. "It would be unfortunate if it was decided that those investigators could not continue operating the way they are," Romanski said, noting that since 1999 the task force has arrested 72 people—including 57 men who traveled to meet "children" who were actually undercover agents. (Chaptman 2002, p. 1A)

Regardless, the prosecution claimed that what matters before the law is clear intent, and that is where most cases seem to reside. As the prosecution wrote,

> Sound public policy . . . supports identifying those who would inflict such harm on children and preventing them from doing so, rather than waiting for real children to be victimized. (Chaptman 2002, p. 1A)

Then there is the case of Mark Poehlman, an Air Force veteran who was ordered released from Lompoc prison as a result of a zealous police Internet sting. Poehlman was a "cross-dresser" and was trying to meet a single woman on the Internet. FBI officials posing as "Sharon" posted an ad on an Internet site for people with "alternative" sexual habits as part of their Sexual Assault Felony Enforcement Team. "Sharon," via e-mail, prodded him to also be involved with three fictional daughters. He said that he would try to raise them properly and give them moral guidance, but this wasn't what the feds had in mind. "Sharon" insisted that he agree to have sex with them if he wanted to be involved with her. When he finally agreed to do so, he traveled from Florida to Long Beach, California, where he was busted. A federal appeals court freed Poehlman and rebuked the formal agents of social control who troll the Internet:

> "There is surely enough real crime in our society that it is unnecessary for our law enforcement officials to spend months luring an obviously lonely and confused individual to cross the line between fantasy and criminality," wrote Judge Alex Kozinski. (Rosenzweig 2000, p. B1)

The massive news reports about threats to children have spurred some citizens to set up their own Internet sites and pose as available victims. Thirty-seven-year-old Julie Posey, a Colorado grandmother, regularly signs on to various Internet sites as Kendra, a fourteen-year-old girl who is looking for a good time. When strangers bite, she entices them, sets up a meeting, and alerts police, who move in for the bust. She has done this nearly two dozen times and joins forces with other individuals and groups around the United States, such as Predator-Hunter, Soc-Um, and Cyberarmy Pedophilia Fighters. One of the largest groups is Cyber-Angels. This spin-off of the Guardian Angels boasts nearly 10,000 members. As the reach of the Internet grows, Posey counts herself among a handful of private citizens who have assumed the role of online crime fighters, hoping to smoke out sexual predators and traders in kiddie porn. They say they fill the gap that many local police departments leave because of meager resources (Leonard and Morin 2002).

Police officers may decry such cybervigilantism, but they enlist the help of the public routinely. Posey offers seminars to teach officers about computer enticements. Described as a "bulldog" by a child abuse investigator whose office provided her with an award, Posey pursues her cyber-sleuthing calling with gusto without leaving her house:

> It's there that Posey spends about 40 hours a week trolling the Net. When the chat rooms are silent, she turns to her Web site, www.pedowatch.org, a one-woman watchdog operation that has passed hundreds of tips to police. She finances her detective work through banner ads on the site, which have brought in as much as $1,000 a month. (Leonard and Morin 2002, p. A1)

CONCLUSION

This chapter addressed some issues about mediated interaction and the relevance of communication processes on the Internet for surveillance practices by formal agents of social control and others. I suggested that a control narrative is implicated in numerous attempts and logics to monitor and regulate Internet use. The control narrative refers to actors' awareness and expectation that symbolic meanings may be monitored and used by diverse audiences for various purposes. The control narrative is tied to the discourse of fear—the pervasive communication, symbolic awareness, and expectation that danger and risk are a central feature of everyday life. Far more is involved than efforts to restrict access and use of information technology as fear and control are reflexively joined to virtual communication.

A society may be known by its control narratives and logics, particularly their reach across institutions and into everyday life (Marx 1988; Naphy and

Roberts 1997; Staples 2000). During the Victorian era, the Magic Lantern provided entertainment and awe for audiences who were unfamiliar with technology that made images "move." The illusion is a feature of the physiology (nature's technology) of the eye that cannot detect gaps between "still" pictures. Slowing the process down shows the illusion for what it is. Today, millions of actors use the Internet to produce messages and images that may be seen by some people who sell or buy and by others who would censor, trick, and punish messengers. The constant is the potential for, the practice of, and, increasingly, the awareness of policing. While "Big Brother" continues to be implicated in surveillance, Internet policing has been internalized and integrated with virtually all aspects of its use.

In a risk society, governance is privatized and dispersed across myriad fragmented institutions. The onus is placed on organizations and individuals to be more self-sufficient, to look after their own risk management needs. This emphasis on self-governance is underpinned by the interconnected discourses of morality, rights, responsibility, and accountability (Ericson and Haggerty 1997).

I have suggested that Internet users are voyeurs and exhibitionists; we watch others, are seen watching others, and want to be seen. Ours is a society that relies on "dataveillance," or the widespread mining and sharing of consumer information (Staples 2000). Even as I write this, my "computer jar" fills with "cookies" sent by technological voyeurs to monitor and track. What will we "get back" from a message sent, who will see it and for what purpose, and will there be consequences?

Internet technology, formats, and the push to police risks in a societal context grounded in fear mediate interaction on the Internet (and elsewhere). While the existence of the Internet may be unimaginable without extensive security, it is security that has produced some of the paradoxes addressed here. One paradox of Internet security is that it requires violation and surveillance. Policing the risk society has created additional risks of not only compromising privacy, stifling curiosity and adventure on the Internet for fear of detection, and causing embarrassment—what Marx (1988) termed "auto surveillance"—but also routinizing deception as people create false identities for specific audiences at certain sites. Ultimately, people are helping to normalize communicative control. "Crises of the day" (e.g., terrorist attacks and the control of children) are treated with an Internet twist. Similar to the "concern about television" in an earlier time, parents are instructed to "watch their children" and use "Internet filters" to keep them away from inappropriate sites, and formal agents of social control want to monitor the Internet, control its use, and engage in the surveillance of everyone.

Numerous research questions accompany the casting of Internet communications as part of an ecology of communication and control. Applying a mediated interaction perspective to Internet use suggests questions such as the following: How do Internet users perceive and account for surveillance and control by friends, businesses, and formal agents of social control? What are organizational consequences of such surveillance and control? How does such control inform actors' efforts to manipulate their own and others' identities? Over what aspects of Internet and electronic communication is this control—and adjustments to it—manifested? How do users resist and even subvert the control narrative and logic? How is other communication influenced by actors' awareness and use of the control narrative? And how is Internet surveillance tied to other aspects of social, economic, and political action and policy? These and many other questions should be addressed using a variety of research methods, including field and case studies, if social scientists hope to understand the social relevance of the Internet. The next chapter examines how the Internet provided some contrary information to the propaganda onslaught to sell the Iraq War to the American people.

8

The Propaganda Project
and the Iraq War

The success of "Bush's PR War" . . . was largely dependent on a compliant press that uncritically repeated almost every fraudulent administration claim about the threat posed to America by Saddam Hussein.

—MacArthur (2003, p. 62)

Propaganda dominates the politics of fear. This is most apparent in time of war. This chapter examines how propaganda and fear were combined in selling a war against terrorism. I contend that the Iraq War was presented to U.S. and international audiences as a war program, although foreign audiences interpreted the visuals and official narratives much differently since they did not share the ideologically embedded accounts of previously broadcast U.S. wars. This chapter documents how the Project for a New American Century (PNAC), the Iraq propaganda campaign, and a compliant news media developed, sold, enacted, and justified a war with Iraq that has resulted at this writing (October 2005) in more than 10,000 dead and wounded American soldiers, plus numerous contract workers (not including mercenaries), as well as an estimated 100,000 Iraqi civilians (Cooney 2004), and 10,000 Iraqi soldiers who defended their country. I report on certain features of the propaganda campaign that contributed to the policy planning and "implementation" in the guise of the Iraq War and raise several key theoretical questions about a refined approach to the study of propaganda in a mass-mediated age that has produced war programming.

This chapter has three major objectives. The first is to show how the PNAC shaped the most massive propaganda campaign since World War

II and engaged in a public conspiracy that laid the groundwork for the United States to invade Iraq on March 20, 2003. By public conspiracy, we mean that available but not widely publicized documents show that a well-organized group of individuals reshaped defense and foreign policy and then became active political officials. The second objective is to describe and clarify why the PNAC's plans for Iraq and for an imperialist foreign policy received very little news media coverage. In general, we argue that this plan was not publicized by the major news media because it fell outside the focus of the Bush administration's propaganda campaign to demonize Iraq and its leader, Saddam Hussein.

The third objective of this chapter is to set forth a theoretical argument for analyzing modern propaganda campaigns as a feature of mass-mediated discourse crafted by media logic, defined as a form of communication, and the process through which media transmit and communicate information (Altheide and Johnson 1980). Elements of this form include the distinctive features of each medium and the formats used by these media for the organization, the style in which it is presented, the focus or emphasis on particular characteristics of behavior, and the grammar of media communication (Altheide and Snow 1979; Snow 1983). Another feature of media logic is that audience experiences through media accumulate and blend with certain symbols and images; stereotypes are reinforced, and simplistic divisions between friends and foes become reified. This logic will be examined while testing a model of war programming that was developed through previous analysis of war planning and coverage (Altheide 1995).

The theoretical argument may be summed up as follows. Students of propaganda and American journalism have long noted that the press capitulates to the government during times of war (Der Derian 2002; Ellenius and Foundation 1998; Gerth 1992; Herman and Chomsky 2002; Jackall 1994, 1999; Kellner 1992, 2003; Shapiro 1992). Typically, scholars, journalists, and others reflect on the "poor coverage" after a conflict (see step 4 later in this chapter). My intent is different. While I will discuss the lax news coverage that was part of the propaganda drive to conduct the Iraq War, we include our critique within a model of media logic and war programming (Altheide 1995): no critiques are given until after the propaganda preparation, the war, and the attendant slaughter. I continue with an overview of war programming.

WAR PROGRAMMING

Sociological theory suggests that social actors' definitions of situations are informed by previous experiences and meanings (Altheide 1987;

Blumer 1962, 1969; Couch et al. 1986; Denzin 2003; Hall 2003; Hewitt 1991; Nash 2003; Perinbanayagam 1986; Stone and Farberman 1970). This process holds true for audiences, politicians, and journalists (Shapiro 1997). The irony, of course, is that each new "war situation" is presented by producers as something unique and novel, while the informational and emotional context for relating to it is historically embedded in previous wars, often experienced mainly through the mass media. Analysis of news media coverage of previous wars indicates that each "current" war is greatly informed by the images, symbols, language, and experience associated of "previous" wars, including the demonization of the enemy, the virtues and necessity of waging war, and the social and political benefits of doing so. Thus, we draw on war programming, an ordered sequence of activities:

1. Reportage and visual reports of the most recent war (or two)
2. Anticipation, planning, and preparing the audiences for the impending war, including "demonizing" certain individual leaders (e.g., Noriega or Hussein)
3. Coverage of the subsegments of the current war, using the best visuals available to capture the basic scenes and themes involving the battle lines, the home front, the media coverage, the international reaction, and anticipation of the war's aftermath
4. Following the war, journalists' reaction and reflection on various governmental restrictions and suggestions for the future (which are seldom implemented)
5. Journalists' and academics' diaries, biographies, exposés, critiques, and studies about the war and increasingly the media coverage
6. Media reports about such studies, which are often cast negatively and often lead to the widespread conclusion that perhaps the war was unnecessary, other options were available, and that the price was too high (all this will be useful for the coverage of the next war)
7. For the next war, return to step 1

Each of these phases has been verified empirically with other U.S. wars and will not be repeated here (Altheide 1995). The aim is to apply this model to the Iraq War and make conceptual adjustments in order to enhance our theoretical capacity to explain modern propaganda.

As war programming indicates, a game-like structure has emerged for joining action and critique sequentially. The challenge of the Iraq War is that while it officially ended on May 2, 2003, with Bush's dramatic photo-op landing on an aircraft carrier—"major combat operations in Iraq have ended"—the war has continued a year later, and troops are likely to remain in combat for many months. Nevertheless, critiques (steps 4 and 5) are forthcoming. (Indeed, this chapter itself falls within step 5.) This model is different from conventional propaganda analyses because war programming builds in critique as part of the narrative and script of promotion.

I argue that the current structure of policy and critique is now institutionalized and, essentially, connects criticism and "challenge" within the action as a war program. The scope of the action is so immense that it precludes and preempts its critique. I contend that a new approach is needed to offer critique before the event. This can be accomplished by theorizing as praxis or stating by drawing on previous experiences how an action's planning, execution, successes, and failures will produce social consequences. That this has already been anticipated is apparent from certain websites that forewarned journalists to avoid making mistakes and promoting propaganda. For example, in an open letter to "editor, publisher, producer, reporter" dated March 4, 2003, two weeks before Baghdad was bombed, a list of academics, journalists, politicians, and celebrities besieged "media people" to avoid common mistakes:

> We are writing to convey a level of heightened expectation in your forthcoming coverage of the U.S.-Iraq situation.
>
> War coverage, and coverage of the period preceding war, test the reliability of our news media. Access to truly independent sources of information is essential, given the government's control of knowledge, data, pictures and other information during this period. The media's display of all significant points of view is especially important because of the tendency of our top officials to equate patriotism with uncritical support of official policy. Precisely for this reason, the public expects its media to meet this challenge by maintaining its independence for the good of the country. It is your professional duty and your obligation to our democratic ideals.
>
> Unfortunately, objectivity and critical questioning of official sources, which is a measure of your separation from officialdom, have not been true in war-time reporting during Gulf War I and during the present proposals for Gulf War II. (www.essential.org/features/mediacoverage.html)

The signees then listed common propaganda errors, such as the horse race theme, simplifying problems and the "evidence" to justify war, overlooking the importance of oil, disregarding how American firms had actually contributed to Hussein's stock of biological weapons, and so on. All indications are that these warnings—indeed, pleadings—had little if any impact on media reports that followed. The problem, then, is not simply lack of "knowledge" and information on the part of the press. The argument is that an alternative format to the current sequence of action-then-research/critique of social policy, particularly war making, is essential.

PREPARING FOR WAR

The propaganda campaign in the Iraq War consisted of what was omitted from presentation to the public as well as what was selected for coverage and the way in which information was managed. The United States was well on its way to justifying the attack of Iraq in 1992 when Secretary of Defense Dick Cheney and others, who would occupy positions in the Bush administration eight years later, drafted the Defense Planning Guidance document. The thrust of the message was to act unilaterally and to use military force freely, with preemptive strikes if necessary. Making a pitch for a threatened military budget in 1992, Chairman of the Joint Chiefs of Staff Colin Powell told the House Armed Services Committee that the United States required "sufficient power" to "deter any challenger from ever dreaming of challenging us on the world stage." To emphasize the point, he cast the United States in the role of street thug. "I want to be the bully on the block," he said, implanting in the mind of potential opponents that "there is no future in trying to challenge the armed forces of the United States" (Armstrong 2002, p. 78). The plan was carried forth by the PNAC. The plan, with revisions, was promoted repeatedly during the next decade, even though some members were out of office for eight years, and was in full swing one month before the 9/11 attacks.

This message was not widely publicized to the American people. Indeed, we located eighteen reports (discussed later in this chapter) about this endeavor by public officials and a conservative think tank to alter fundamentally U.S. foreign policy and attack sovereign nations before missiles hit Baghdad. The major television networks were practically silent about the commitment to attack Iraq even though many members and "signees" of the PNAC were in control of the Bush administration's foreign policy, and a revealing magazine article (Armstrong 2002) was read into the *Congressional Record* on October 8, 2002, as part of the Spratt-Moran resolution to support UN guidelines some six months before the "official" bombing began. Not a single regular evening network newscast mentioned this public conspiracy prior to the start of the war. We offer an account of the role that the news media played in the construction of the Iraq War and some of its consequences.

MASS-MEDIA WAR

Administration news sources provided a compliant news media with ample material and conjecture about both of the claims that linked Iraq and Hussein with the terrorist attacks of 9/11. Prior to the invasion (as well as after the president triumphantly declared from the deck of an aircraft carrier that victory had been won), the Bush administration insisted that Hussein had supported the terrorists and had weapons of mass destruction that he planned to use. Even though no one in the administration directly stated that Iraq was involved, the innuendo, tone, and slant of numerous reports stressed this relationship before, during, and after the invasion of Iraq. Indeed, it was not until October 2003 that President Bush acknowledged that Hussein and Iraq were not involved in the 9/11 attacks, but even then Vice President Cheney was reported to still believe that Hussein was implicated:

> The propaganda campaign to "sell the Iraq War" emphasized Iraq's connections with Al Qaeda and development of "weapons of mass destruction" (WMD), including chemical, biological, and nuclear weapons.
> As The Associated Press put it: "The implication from Bush on down was that Saddam supported Osama bin Laden's network. Iraq and the Sept. 11 attacks frequently were mentioned in the same sentence, even though officials have no good evidence of such a link." Not only was there no good evidence: according to *The New York Times*, captured leaders of Al Qaeda explicitly told the C.I.A. that they had not been working with Saddam. (Krugman 2003, p. 29)

Public opinion surveys provide one way to assess how public support could be influenced by information about Iraq. Several opinion polls tracked public perceptions of administration claims, especially after the invasion of Iraq. The results make it clear that when the public has more information about critical issues, they are less supportive and, moreover, actually prefer, when asked, more information from the administration. In April 2003, 58 percent of those polled were "somewhat or very concerned that U.S. troops have not yet found any weapons of mass destruction." Two months later (June), the Harris Poll reported that while the majority of Americans continued to believe that Iraq had weapons of mass destruction, 40 percent also believed that the "U.S. government deliberately exaggerated the reports of weapons of mass destruction in Iraq in order to increase support for war."

The doubts about the Bush administration's justification for the war with Iraq have gradually increased over time, as more press information has been forthcoming about the elusive weapons of mass destruction as well as much stronger evidence that Hussein was not directly involved with those who flew planes into the buildings on 9/11. The strongest data for the chipping away of credibility are provided by a *Newsweek* report in October 2003 on the gradual but consistent erosion of support by a public that is better informed about the information management of the war. Citizens were asked the following question: "Before the Iraq War, the Bush administration said it had intelligence reports indicating that Iraq was hiding banned chemical or biological weapons from United Nations weapons inspectors. So far, however, no such banned weapons have been found in Iraq. Do you think the Bush administration misinterpreted or misanalyzed the intelligence reports they said indicated Iraq had banned weapons?"

	Yes	No	Don't Know
	%	%	%
October 23–24, 2003	50	39	11
October 9–10, 2003	49	39	12
August 21–22, 2003	44	47	9
July 24–25, 2003	41	49	10
July 10–11, 2003	45	41	14
May 29–30, 2003	36	54	10

"Purposely misled the public about evidence that Iraq had banned weapons in order to build support for war?"

	Yes	No	Don't Know
	%	%	%
October 23–24, 2003	42	49	9
October 9–10, 2003	45	45	10
August 21–22, 2003	43	51	6
July 24–25, 2003	39	56	5
July 10–11, 2003	38	53	9
May 29–30, 2003	36	57	7

These data show that the credibility of the "evidence for the war" gradually declined, as 42 percent of the public indicated that the administration had "purposely misled the public," while another 8 percent (50 percent total) was more charitable, accepting the wording that the administration had "misinterpreted or misanalyzed the intelligence reports they said indicated Iraq had banned weapons."

The documents and plans to topple Iraq were known about but were not widely covered by the major news media for the decade preceding the Iraq invasion, nor were they covered by network television in the months preceding the Iraq War. Publicizing these materials for the American people may have made a difference in public support for the Iraq War and an emerging foreign policy that included "preemptive strikes" and bypassing the United Nations and international agreements about aggression. However, previous conflicts and wars provided experiences and a context that prepared audiences for what would follow. We turn briefly to this context.

Chapter 8

THE POLITICAL CONTEXT FOR PROPAGANDA

Ideas about world domination existed in popular-culture accounts of outlaw nations and rulers such as Nazi Germany and imperial Japan and even back as far as Genghis Khan. Not the United States. Only conspiracy theorists and a few ardent Marxists would claim, until recently, that the United States had imperialist intentions. This all changed during the Reagan administration and was exacerbated several years later when a conservative "think tank" gained the ear of key national staff members and indeed recruited them among its ranks. This is the PNAC, a major lobbying and influential cadre of ideologists dedicated to the proposition that the world had changed after the fall of the Soviet Union and that the United States was now not only a "superpower" but a hegemon that needed to lead and dominate. Its members have been active in conservative politics—including serving under Presidents Reagan, George H. W. Bush, and George W. Bush—and publishing magazines and newspaper editorials and serving as television commentators for two decades. All this was done under the guise of a "new defense policy" for the United States. Indeed, Robert McGovern, a veteran CIA analyst of twenty-seven years, who represented a group of former intelligence officers (Veteran Intelligence Officers for Sanity), noted that Hitler's hegemonic horrors were set forth in his book *Mein Kampf*. McGovern told CNN's Jonathan Mann that the PNAC provided Bush's imperialistic game plan:

> Well, all you need do is look at "Mein Kampf." The U.S. "Mein Kampf." You probably remember that "Mein Kampf" laid down the framework for Hitler's campaigns and for his strategy. Well, there's a "Mein Kampf" for the U.S. scene, and it's called the "Project for a New American Century." Download it from its Web site and you'll see the documents going back to 1992, which outline everything that is intended by this crew that's running Iraqi policy. (Mann 2003)

Indeed, two prominent members of the Bush administration, Paul H. O'Neill and Richard A. Clarke, claimed that war with Iraq was a forgone conclusion. The Bush administration's willingness to carry out the PNAC's commitment to attack Iraq without further provocation was made clear several months after the war began. O'Neill, longtime Republican stalwart and President Bush's former treasury secretary, stated in an interview on CBS's *60 Minutes*, "From the very beginning, there was a conviction that Saddam Hussein was a bad person and that he needed to go" (*New York Times*, January 12, 2004, p. A11). Regarding the claim that war would uncover and destroy threatening the destruction of weapons of mass destruction, O'Neill told *Time* magazine,

> In the 23 months I was there, I never saw anything that I would characterize as evidence of weapons of mass destruction. I never saw anything in the intelligence that I would characterize as real evidence. (*New York Times*, January 12, 2004, p. A11)

O'Neill was joined in his criticism of the rush to war with Iraq by former White House counterterrorism chief Richard A. Clarke, who, in a book and subsequent press interviews, stated that there was pressure to find an immediate link between Al Qaeda, Iraq, and the 9/11 attacks that was not warranted by evidence from the intelligence community. Clarke claimed that

> while neither president [Clinton and Bush] did enough to prevent the attacks of Sept. 11, 2001, the Bush administration has undermined American national security by using the 9/11 attacks for political advantage and ignoring the threat of Al Qaeda in order to invade Iraq. (*New York Times*, March 22, 2004, p. A18)

There was an important context for defining this situation as war worthy and consistent with war programming.

DEFINING THE SITUATION

The general public derives most of its understanding of international affairs and foreign policy from news and particularly television news (Adams 1981, 1982; Alali and Byrd 1994; Aldridge and Hewitt 1994; Altheide 1997, 2003; Barson and Heller 2001; Bennett 1988; Best 1999; Chiricos 2000; Comstock and Scharrer 1999; Douglas 1970; Doyle 2001; Edelman 1985; Graber 1984; Hall 1988; Hertog 1995; Hunt 1999; Jackall 1994; Margolis 1996; Shaw and McCombs 1977; Wasburn 2002). The American public's window on the world of foreign affairs is framed by what is presented on the nightly newscasts of ABC, NBC, CBS, and CNN. This does not mean that the only source of foreign affairs news is television but that it is the most consistent and widely used source of information for the American public. Public understanding of issues, particularly those involving non-Western cultures, is filtered through the daily information and visual images. Moreover, public perceptions are greatly informed by the repetition of certain themes, slogans, and symbolic representations of problems and issues:

> War stories are told with the flourish of explicit moral discourse. Trade stories are told with the patient repetition of words suggesting, but not directly stating, that the rival nation is unreasonable and unfair. (Wasburn 2002, p. 125)

Our argument is that the American news media, and especially network television news organizations, chose not to present important contextual and background information about the Middle East and especially Iraq because it was not consistent with other news themes, nor was it as entertaining. The dominant "story" since the attacks of 9/11 was the "war on terrorism." This broad story included U.S. retaliation, the hunt for al Qaeda leaders (e.g., Osama bin Laden), and plans to attack countries and "outlaw regimes" that supported or harbored terrorists. Implementing these programs involved invading Afghanistan and expanding the U.S. military presence throughout the world. Other adjustments were made in foreign policy, military budgets, domestic surveillance, and attacks on civil liberties. Threats to invade other countries (the "axis of evil") that included Iraq were part of an effort to "defend" the United States from future attacks. It is hard to believe that the American people would not have been interested in carefully presented reports about systematic efforts to undermine international treaties, destroy the United Nations, expand the military, and engage in more military attacks, including preemptive first strikes.

THE NEWS MEDIA CONTEXT FOR PROPAGANDA

We have argued that the PNAC was critical in managing information for a compliant U.S. press in order to sell its "claims" about Iraq without making it widely known that a small but very influential group of officials had been working to change foreign policy in general and attack Iraq in particular for about a decade. The neglect of these issues reflects major organizational shifts in the production and presentation of news. Nowhere is this more apparent than with network television news. The infotainment urge to "pander" to the audience in order to gain viewers would soon become the networks' established way of doing business.

Other analyses have documented how the climate and organization of network news changed over the past two decades. Changes in technology and marketing approaches helped "normalize" infotainment, particularly the expansion of the entertainment for network television news. Former *CBS Evening News* anchor Dan Rather's reluctance to embrace infotainment was gradually eroded by increased competition with traditional rivals as well as CNN and Fox. Research on network trends shows that between 1977 and 1997, "hard news" declined from 67.3 to 41.3 percent, while celebrity news tripled, from 2 percent in 1977 to 7 percent in 1997, and "soft" lifestyle news doubled during the same time period, from 13.5 percent to nearly 25 percent, or one-fourth of all network news offerings. Network news time was increasingly devoted to celebrity news, and the "morning news" shows emphasized more commercial and product advertising to promote the conglomerates that owned them.

In June 2001, network morning news programs had become, in significant part, a way of selling things, often lifestyle products, books, movies, television shows, cookbooks, products for the home, and the like. Excluding commercials and inserts for local news, 33 percent of the news time on these programs was devoted to selling some product.

The challenge of censorship and credibility became even more acute after the first Gulf War in 1991 as military officials joined news organizations, often as reporters. That war followed "photo-op" combat footage from Grenada (1983) and Panama (1989) and bridged the military–media divide that had engulfed the Vietnam debacle. The military expanded its arsenal of savvy media consciousness. "Today, when you get an opportunity to stand up and represent your command, you've got to hit a home run," Army Major Bob Hastings told the students in his public affairs course (Vogel 1998, p. 6). This contributed to the expansion of the "military–media complex" which refers to the cooperative alliance between the military and news organizations in sharing personnel (generals and other military spokespersons become reporters or consultants) to promote public relations campaigns and provide entertaining coverage of various crises and conflicts (Altheide 1999).

THE PROPAGANDA SAGA

The PNAC received very little news media coverage prior to the invasion of Iraq even though it was part of the "public record" in government documents and had been briefly mentioned in several newspaper and radio reports in the late 1990s (see table 8.1). The most detailed coverage of the history of the PNAC and its role in shaping U.S. foreign policy was David Armstrong's essay in *Harper's Magazine* in October 2002:

> The plan is for the United States to rule the world. The overt theme is unilateralism, but it is ultimately a story of domination. It calls for the United States to maintain its overwhelming military superiority and prevent new rivals from rising up to challenge it on the world stage. It calls for dominion over friends and enemies alike. It says not that the united States must be more powerful, or most powerful, but that it must be absolutely powerful. (Armstrong 2002, p. 76)

Only a few newspaper articles dealt with PNAC six months before the United States attacked Iraq on March 20. No reports appeared on the major television networks' regular evening newscasts during this time, although *Nightline* did examine the "conspiracy claims" and interview William Kristol,

Table 8.1.   Partial Chronology of News Reports about the Project for a New American Century and Plans to Invade Iraq

January 26, 1998	National Public Radio, *All Things Considered*
August 4, 2001	National Public Radio, *Weekend Edition Saturday*
August 11, 2001	*New York Times*, Jane Perlez, "Bombing Iraq and Mission Change"
August 21, 2001	*Washington Post*, Thomas Ricks, "Empire or Not: A Quiet Debate over U.S. Role"
September 10, 2001	NPR, *Talk of the Nation*
September 23, 2001	NBC, *Meet the Press* (Colin Powell), PNAC letter to president mentioned
December 3, 2001	*New York Times*, excerpts from 1998 PNAC letter to President Clinton
December 9, 2001	*New York Times*, article about PNAC position
September 10, 2002	National Public Radio, *Talk of the Nation*
October 2002	*Harper's Magazine*, David Armstrong, "Dick Cheney's Song of America"
January 12, 2003	*Los Angeles Times*, Chalmers Johnson, about Rumsfeld and the urge to attack Iraq
February 1, 2003	*New York Times*, Todd Purdum, "The 'Brains' behind Bush's Foreign Policy" (on same day Bush says that he no longer supports containment)
March 4, 2003	Soviet journalist, monitored by BBC
March 5, 2003	ABC, *Nightline*
March 11, 2003	*New York Times*, David Carr, article about PNAC and Kristol's *Weekly Standard* influence on Bush and foreign policy
March 16, 2003	CBS, *Sunday Morning*
	Guardian newspaper (and others, Toronto)
MARCH 20, 2003	WAR WITH IRAQ BEGINS
March 23, 2003	NBC, *Meet the Press* (Rumsfeld)
	Los Angeles Times, Gary Schmitt (PNAC) writes article
	New York Times, Steven R. Weisman, article about history of PNAC influence
March 27, 2003	Paul Wolfowitz's denial to Senator Dick Durbin about his authorship of pre-PNAC 1992 document and preemptive bombing
April 6, 2003	*Chicago Sun Times* (Lynn Sweet) refers to Wolfowitz's denial (see Senate meeting)
April 21, 2003	National Public Radio, *Talk of the Nation*
May 9, 2003	National Public Radio, *All Things Considered*
June 5, 2003	National Public Radio, *All Things Considered*

chairman of the PNAC, on March 5. Reporter Ted Koppel dismissed the conspiratorial charges by several foreign newspapers. He framed it in terms of what could be called "it depends on how you look at it":

They did what former government officials and politicians frequently do when they're out of power, they began formulating a strategy, in this case, a foreign policy strategy, that might bring influence to bear on the Administration then in power, headed by President Clinton. Or failing that, on a new Administration that might someday come to power. They were pushing for the elimination of Saddam Hussein. And proposing the establishment of a strong US military presence in the Persian Gulf, linked to a willingness to use force to protect vital American interests in the Gulf. (ABC News 2003)

When reporter Jackie Judd asked Gary Schmitt, a long-time PNAC architect, if they were fanatics or conspirators, Schmitt replied,

Well, I think there's a lot of folks that are unhappy with the, with the change in the Administration's policy and the American policy at large. And in the absence of actually addressing the concerns directly, they'd rather think that it's some sort of conspiracy.

[Judd, voice-over]: Some critics compare the Project to the group of men who helped lead America into Vietnam and came to be known as "the best and the brightest." Kristol dismisses the comparison. Still, he says, as America seems poised to go to war, there is a degree of accountability he will feel when the first bomb drops.

[William Kristol]: Of course I'll feel some sense of responsibility. The only point I would also make, though, is one also has to take responsibility, would also have to take responsibility if one advocated doing nothing and then if something terrible happens. And, and I worry. I worry, not because I'm going to look bad, I worry because people could die and will die in this war.

Both newspaper and electronic media paid more attention to the PNAC and its role in shaping the Bush foreign policy after the war began. This was particularly true of the foreign press, which tended to be far more critical of the PNAC and American foreign policy. This is partly because the United States is the most covered country in the world (Wu 2000).

News organizations explicitly and implicitly editorialize through their use of news sources for certain issues. The major news agencies in the United States and particularly the television networks limited their coverage of the role the PNAC played in shaping the Iraq War. These propaganda efforts occurred as the various PNAC members served as routine news sources, primarily in television network news accounts oriented to infotainment. Table 8.2 illustrates how the *New York Times* used a handful of PNAC spokespersons and "fellow travelers" to shape national reporting about the context and issues that led to the Iraq War.

Our analysis of Iraq War coverage by the *New York Times* and other news organs revealed that several individuals were closely associated with PNAC over the past decade: Thomas Donnelly, Andrew Bacevich, William Kristol, Richard Perle, Marc Gerecht, Gary Schmitt, and Robert Kagan. Other individuals, such as Paul Wolfowitz, Secretary of Defense Donald Rumsfeld, and Dick Cheney, were heavily involved with supporting

**Table 8.2.   Supporters and Critics of the Project for a
New American Century Appearing in the *New York Times*
before and after 9/11**

	Before 9/11	After 9/11
Supporters	N = 72	N = 133
Thomas Donnelly	1	3
William Kristol	42	48
Richard Perle	21	61
Marc Gerecht	7	9
Gary Schmitt	3	1
Robert Kagan	7	35*
Critics	N = 5	N = 8
Joseph Nye	4	7
Chalmers Johnson	1	1

*Twenty of Kagan's post-9/11 interviews involved book reviews.

PNAC, but they and other PNAC supporters who were in the Bush administration were not included in this analysis. We compared the coverage they received in the *New York Times* as news sources six months before and after 9/11. We did the same with four individuals that our review of news reports identified as critics of the PNAC proposal and plans to invade Iraq.

The results are clear. The pro-PNAC sources were used seventy-two times before 9/11 and 133 times within six months after 9/11, an increase of 85 percent. Only five references appear for the anti-PNAC sources (four refer to Joseph Nye), and eight appear after 9/11 (seven refer to Nye).

The meaning of these large differences is more complex. First, it is important to note that the PNAC sources were used quite often by the *New York Times* prior to 9/11. This is particularly noteworthy for William Kristol ($N = 42$), former chief of staff for Vice President Dan Quayle and publisher and editor of the conservative *The Weekly Standard*, and Richard Perle ($N = 21$), former assistant secretary of defense and member of the Defense Policy Board, which advises Donald Rumsfeld. These are prominent Washington sources that are called on to discuss a range of foreign and domestic policy issues. The circulation of Kristol's publication is small, but the media play that he gets from his numerous references extends his influence:

> The circulation of *The Weekly Standard*, which was founded by the News Corporation in 1995, is only 55,000. *The Nation*, a liberal beacon, has 127,000. The *New Republic* has 85,000, and *National Review*, long a maypole for conservatives, counts 154,000 readers. But the numbers are misleading in a digital age

in which thought and opinion are frequently untethered from print and reiterated thousands of times on Web sites, list servers and e-mail in-boxes. . . .

"Look, these guys made up their own minds," he [Kristol] said. "I would hope that we have induced some of them to think about these things in a new way. We have a lot of writers who have independently articulated a version of how we deal with this new world we live in that has been read by Dick Cheney, Condi Rice and Donald Rumsfeld. Hopefully it had some effect." (Carr 2003, p. 1)

AN ANALYSIS OF PNAC DISCOURSE

While it is clear that journalism did not "stand out" in its coverage, this has been a recurring trend. It is partly for this reason that the concept of war programming was offered because journalism, in general, does not operate independently of power and those who are the main news sources. Nevertheless, an alarmingly limited discourse exists in the mainstream print and television news media addressing the PNAC's influence on American foreign policy. Of those articles that do address the apparent influence of PNAC and its founders, several key terms are inexorably linked with the discussions, including "empire," "imperial," "propaganda," and "conspiracy." A review of these terms and their relationship to media coverage of current American foreign policy supports the argument that members of PNAC were able to influence substantial foreign policy changes under very little scrutiny from any of the major news outlets. Because of the relatively little attention paid by the mainstream media to the ambitions of PNAC and its founders, the following analysis is limited to a small number of news articles and programs.

A review of the media's coverage (or lack thereof) of the emerging role of the United States as a modern-day empire supports the argument that the popular media have done little to draw attention to the policy agenda advanced by the neoconservative think tank PNAC. Only eleven articles or news programs specifically address the apparent shift in American foreign policy since the beginning of the current Bush administration toward that of embracing the advancement of a new American empire bent on global domination. Of these eleven articles or programs, four are critical or cautionary, five are descriptive, and two are supportive of PNAC policy recommendations. Discourse surrounding the use of the word "empire" as part of the current U.S. foreign policy agenda involves primarily a twofold debate: first, debate regarding whether the United States is indeed acting in a manner as if to pursue imperialistic pursuits, and, second, whether the debate is simply one of semantics and whether the United States as a world leader should be utilizing the extant power at its hands to disseminate American values to the rest of the world. The former argument rests mainly with activists and others critical of U.S. actions, while the latter group is represented primarily by current and former members of PNAC. For example, in a July 2003 article in *In These Times* titled "Seize the Time," Arundhati Roy, who clearly opposes the U.S. emerging empire, states,

> But when a country ceases to be merely a country and becomes an empire, then the scale of operations changes dramatically. So may I clarify that I speak as a subject of the American Empire? I speak as a slave who presumes to criticize her king. . . . I don't care what the facts are. What a perfect maxim for the New American Empire. Perhaps a slight variation on the theme would be more appropriate: The facts can be whatever we want them to be. . . . So here we are, the people of the world, confronted with an empire armed with a mandate from heaven (and, as added insurance, the most formidable arsenal of weapons of mass destruction in history). . . . Here we are, confronted with an empire that has conferred upon itself the right to go to war at will, and the right to deliver people from corrupting ideologies, from religious fundamentalists, dictators, sexism, and poverty by the age-old, tried-and-tested practice of extermination. (Roy 2003, p. 14)

An article published in the *New York Times* in 2001 and many subsequent articles found in *The Weekly Standard* and reproduced in more mainstream media provide the PNAC response to these and similar criticisms. Then deputy executive director of the PNAC Thomas Donnelly argues,

> We had better get used to seeing ourselves as others see us. . . . It doesn't matter if we don't consider ourselves an empire. Others see us as impinging on their lives, their space, their way of life. If we are going to protect our enduring interests, in the Middle East and elsewhere, then we have to do something about it. . . . The fundamental difference between America and other, past empires is that we don't issue writs in Washington that we expect others to follow. . . . We have seen the spread of liberty in our own country as our power spreads, as well as around the world. . . . As we have grown more powerful, we have extended rights to women, to racial minorities, to everyone. (Baker 2001, sec. 6, p. 53)

One of PNAC's fundamental criticisms of those who challenge the think tank's ideologies is that supporters of a more aggressive foreign policy agenda do not hold territorial ambitions, therefore creating a distinction between the United States and previous historical examples of world empires. Two of the articles critical of PNAC and its political ambitions were released within months of the beginning of the U.S. war against Iraq, while the other two critiques were published just days before the U.S. invasion. Both articles supporting the U.S. role as an empire cite Donnelly, a senior fellow at the PNAC. According to Donnelly, who denies an implicit agenda to transform U.S. foreign policy into one with imperialistic ambitions, "The United States is an empire of democracy or liberty" (Ricks 2001, p. A01). In a separate article, Donnelly states, "Our new manifest destiny is to disseminate our values" (Baker 2001, sec. 6, p. 53).

An analysis of the occurrence of the word "imperial" in mainstream news articles and programming yielded similar results: twelve articles or news programs link American imperialism to the ideas advanced by the PNAC, with six articles presenting a critical or cautionary tone, three being predominantly neutral or descriptive, and four being supportive of American imperial ambitions. Kristol makes no apologies for the connection being made between PNAC policy recommendations and the appearance that the United States is advancing imperial ambitions. Kristol stated, "We need to err on the side of being strong. . . . And if people want to say we're an imperial power, fine" (Atlas 2003, sec. 4, p. 1). Perhaps this public statement was a response to an article published one month earlier in the *New York Times*. The April 2003 *New York Times* article stated,

> Imperialism—a concept that existed outside of the realm of acceptable American political discourse for a great deal of the 20th century or, when it did appear, a term that was more likely than not wielded by leftist critics of US foreign policy—is now comfortably embedded in contemporary political and popular thought. Fueled by the Bush administration's war on terrorism, boldly outlined in the administration's National Security Directive, and actively backed by the conservative Project for the New American Century, this vision of an American empire boldly proclaims the centrality of the United States as the world's only superpower without a shred of bashfulness or reservation. (Traub 2003, sec. 6, p. 50)

Editorials were more likely to link the PNAC think tank with a veiled conspiracy to alter American foreign policy. Of the seven articles or news programs discussing the possibility that U.S. foreign policy is being manipulated, three of these conspiracy allegations were made in the editorial sections of newspapers. All but one of the occurrences of the word "conspiracy" in conjunction with PNAC were blatantly critical of the organization's policy recommendations and seemingly secret agenda, with such words as "deception" and "racism" used to describe PNAC policy.

The PNAC's conspiratorial influence on the Bush administration is blamed for the administration's decision to go to war against Iraq. In six instances, the term "propaganda" was utilized in articles discussing how the Bush administration misled the American public into believing that Iraq posed an immediate threat, even though an invasion of Iraq was part of a previously existing PNAC recommendation that had been made available even before the 9/11 attacks. From a June 2003 article that addressed the debate regarding whether the Bush administration is being

controlled by a secret group of conspirators who dictate the foreign policy agenda, James J. Natsis (2003) writes, "It is neither a conspiracy nor a
secret—check the Project for the New American Century Web site to see
for yourself. If these people stay in power, our young men and women in
military service will be in the Middle East indefinitely" (p. 5A).

Fourteen articles or news programs discuss the Bush administration's
claims that Iraq had weapons of mass destruction and therefore that the
United States was justified in going to war against Iraq. The majority of
articles (ten) present the argument that the media are either directly responsible for enabling false information to be distributed so rampantly or
neglectful of disclosing hidden policy agendas. The mainstream media
are criticized for failing to present the most important facts behind the
U.S. decision to go to war against Iraq:

> If you want to understand the true motivations behind the war in Iraq and
> the subsequent nation-building and saber-rattling, forget about the noise and
> nonsense on TV and in most of the mainstream media. You first need to
> know something about the Project for the New American Century. (Ashwill
> 2003, p. H5)

Mainstream media are also referred to as the "neoconservative media"
(Buchanan 2001, p. 15A). American foreign policy is linked to an "ugly ca-
bal, half-Pentagon, half-media" (Gold 2002, p. 21), with news coverage
provided by a "sympathetic media" (Lobe 2003) or a "compliant media"
(Pilger 2003). Ten articles examine the media's role in advancing the
PNAC's and subsequently the Bush administration's secret foreign policy
agenda; an editorial goes so far as to criticize the American media for being "mouthpieces for the Bush administration" (Renmore 2003, p. 3).

In sum, this plan was not publicized by the major news media because
it fell outside the focus of the Bush administration's propaganda campaign. The evidence suggests that mainstream media failed to bring important ideological shifts and the people behind them to the attention of
the general public. Prior to the U.S. war against Iraq, the American news
media neglected to publicize the PNAC's agenda, which illustrates that
aggression against Iraq had been planned long before the 9/11 attacks. It
also neglected to bring to the forefront crucial information regarding similar policy recommendations from PNAC that were in existence prior to
9/11. The evidence indicates that the media are indirectly responsible for
encouraging the public's support of the war against Iraq through their
acts of omission and/or compliance.

There were several pieces to the Iraq propaganda campaign, and journalists and others differ on when it started. MacArthur's (2003) analysis of
columnist Ellen Goodman's reflections on the administration's "misinformation" argues that the propaganda campaign began on September 7, 2002:

But nowhere in her nationally syndicated column did she state the obvious—that the success of "Bush's PR War" (the headline on the piece) was largely dependent on a compliant press that uncritically repeated almost every fraudulent administration claim about the threat posed to America by Saddam Hussein. (p. 62)

Late as she was, Goodman was better than most in even recognizing that there *was* a disinformation campaign aimed at the people and Congress. Just a few columnists seriously challenged the White House advertising assault. Looking back over the debris of half-truths and lies, I can't help but ask my own question of Goodman: Where was she—indeed, where was the American press—on September 7, 2002, a day when we were sorely in need of reporters?

It was then that the White House propaganda drive began in earnest, with the appearance before television cameras of President Bush and British Prime Minister Tony Blair at Camp David. Between them, the two politicians cited a "new" report from the UN International Atomic Energy Agency (IAEA) that allegedly stated that Iraq was "six months away" from building a nuclear weapon. "I don't know what more evidence we need," declared the president.

President Bush's statement was false and deceptive. The IAEA had never issued such a report, but the compliant press did not check out the claim. According to MacArthur (2003),

Only one newspaper story straightforwardly countered the White House nuclear threat propaganda; it appeared, of all places, in the right-wing, Sun Myung Moon-owned *Washington Times*. . . . Indeed, when IAEA inspectors pulled out of Iraq in December 1998, spokesman Mark Gwozdecky told [reporter] Curl, "We had concluded that we had neutralized their nuclear-weapons program. We had confiscated their fissile material. We had destroyed all their key buildings and equipment." (MacArthur 2003, p. 63)

Others argue that the campaign began much earlier. A British journalist, John Pilger, documents an early discussion about using the 9/11 attacks as a pretext for invading Iraq:

On the morning of September 12, 2001, without any evidence of who the hijackers were, Rumsfeld demanded that the US attack Iraq.

According to Woodward, Rumsfeld told a cabinet meeting that Iraq should be "a principal target of the first round in the war against terrorism."

Iraq was temporarily spared only because US Secretary of State Colin Powell persuaded Bush that *"public opinion has to be prepared before a move against Iraq is possible. . . ."*

In last April's *New Yorker*, investigative reporter Nicholas Lemann wrote that Bush's most senior adviser Condoleezza Rice told him that she had called together senior members of the National Security Council and asked

them "to think about 'how do you capitalise on these opportunities,'" which
she compared with those of "1945 to 1947"—the start of the cold war. (Pilger
2002, p. 19; emphasis added)

According to Pilger (2002), several advisers in the administration—
including those who were associated with the PNAC—had been seeking
a catastrophic event, a new "Pearl Harbor," that could be used as a cata-
lyst to adopt a more aggressive foreign policy: the attacks of 9/11 provided the new Pearl Harbor, described as "the opportunity of ages." The
next eighteen months were spent "preparing" public opinion for the invasion of Iraq on March 20, 2003.

ORGANIZATIONAL REASONS FOR PROPAGANDA

Our argument is that the lack of reporting about the PNAC's success at
planning the Iraq War illustrates embedded propaganda as a feature of institutionalized news sources and media formats. While there were detractors in editorial pages, the Internet, and the foreign news media, the major television networks were tightly aligned with the war scenario. We
wish to stress the critical contribution of news formats and the emerging
common definition of the situation—that the nation had to act, that audiences supported action against enemies, and that simplistic emotionally
tinged messages would carry the day. Key to the Bush administration's
success was journalists' penchant to get on the "war" bandwagon not
only for patriotic purposes but also because that was what "people were
interested in" and that's "where the story was." Network television
played to the administration.

Most of the Gulf War coverage originated from the White House and
the federal government. Journalists now acknowledged that they did not
cover many aspects of the impending war with Iraq. A veteran producer
for a major network television news program indicated that the story was
about the preparation for war. In his words, things were set in motion for
over a year, and the "rock was rolling downhill." That's where the story
was (interview notes).

That other network news producers must have surely agreed with this
position is suggested by a dearth of network television news coverage of
virtually any congressional opposition to the impending war, including
Senator Robert Byrd's impassioned speech on the floor of the Senate on
February 12, 2003, just weeks before Baghdad was bombed, in which he
referred to the drastic changes in foreign policy. While there was some
discussion in newspaper editorial pages, Senator Byrd noted that there
had been little in the Senate:

We stand passively mute in the United States Senate, paralyzed by our own uncertainty, seemingly stunned by the sheer turmoil of events. . . .

This nation is about to embark upon the first test of a revolutionary doctrine applied in an extraordinary way at an unfortunate time. The doctrine of preemption—the idea that the United States or any other nation can legitimately attack a nation that is not imminently threatening but may be threatening in the future—is a radical new twist on the traditional idea of self defense. It appears to be in contravention of international law and the UN Charter. (*Pittsburgh Post-Gazette*, February 23, 2003, p. E2)

Network news shows were quite consistent with guests who supported the war. An analysis by Fairness and Accuracy in Reporting (FAIR) of network news interviewees one week before and one week after Secretary of State Powell addressed the United Nations about Iraq's alleged possession of weapons of mass destruction found that two-thirds of the guests were from the United States, with 75 percent of these being current or former government or military officials, while only one—Senator Edward Kennedy—expressed skepticism or opposition to the impending war with Iraq (FAIR 2003).

Journalists did not present this very important story for various reasons. Studies of news rules and news values support Snow's (1983) observations that the news media, like much of popular culture, tend to support and reflect "ideal norms," or preferred ways of living, feeling, and behaving. Likewise, research on "news decision making" suggests that commercial news organizations tend to select items and events for news reporting that can be told in narratives that express ethnocentrism, altruistic democracy, responsible capitalism, small-town pastoralism, individualism, moderatism, social order, and national leadership (Gans 1979; Wasburn 2002). In other words, reports are favored that sustain the worldviews of news audiences about social order and legitimacy. This includes the conduct of their leaders. Thus, reports will be less favorable or "sensible" to audiences if they suggest that the institution of government has failed, that the process of selecting leaders is corrupt, and that decisions about life and death, such as declaring war, are not made with the national interest in mind and with the well-being of citizens as a priority. Network television news relied on the administration for news and, in the spirit of objectivity, seldom challenged statements from such high sources. This approach to journalism produced untruths and major distortions:

It exacerbates our tendency to rely on official sources, which is the easiest, quickest way to get both the "he said" and the "she said," and, thus, "balance." According to numbers from the media analyst Andrew Tyndall, of the 414 stories on Iraq broadcast on NBC, ABC, and CBS from last September to February, all but thirty-four originated at the White House, Pentagon, and

State Department. So we end up with too much of the "official" truth. (Cunningham 2003, p. 24)

Still another factor was that challenging sources would not be popular with administration officials and the ever-dominant PNAC news sources, who were closely tied to the Bush administration. This was not American journalism's finest hour. Bush administration officials had their way with the major television networks, offering their interpretations, plans, and rationales for domestic and international policies that would follow. Major network television journalists, wearing American flag pins on their lapels, occasionally crying on camera, and offering constant moral support to an expanding network audience, offered very little perspective and understanding of the 9/11 events, seldom asking the most basic questions of administration officials who were pushing draconian legislation to limit civil rights through Congress while military appropriations were increasing drastically in pursuit of an emerging ambiguous war plan to attack Iraq. Clearly the pressure was on journalists to conform and not rock the boat, to not challenge those who were protecting us against evil and terror. This involved the "snubbing" of veteran United Press International correspondent Helen Thomas, whose critical reports resulted in President Bush breaking decades of tradition and not permitting her to ask the first—or any—question during a news conference. A few months prior, Thomas remarked that Mr. Bush "is the worst president in all of American history" (Mike Allen of the *Washington Post* was also excluded from questioning at the same press conference.) (Curl 2003).

The coverage of the war was clearly influenced by such pressure, along with the availability of "visuals" that permitted "live" shots of advancing tanks, Marines, gunfire, and explosions. Other journalists covering the Iraq War reported censorship and intimidation. The management of the Coalition Media Center at the Saliyah military base in Doha, Qatar, which "handled" the press requests and assigned the more than 500 "embedded journalists" who rotated through various units, kept a tight grip on information and questioning decorum by journalists. Massing (2003) suggests that veterans of this campaign likened the information control to the infamous "Five O'Clock Follies" of the Vietnam War, a briefing scenario that became a ludicrous joke by all respected journalists covering that war.

REFLECTIONS ON PROPAGANDA

News coverage of the Iraq War—and particularly the PNAC—reflects how the nature and timing of journalistic critique and alternative interpretations of official directives lags behind critical events but eventually appears as though it is part of a narrative script for war programming. The organizational and format limitations of war programming misdirected journalists from major topics. Moreover, as our model suggests, news organizations began to reflect on "what went wrong" in their coverage of Iraq, including missing the PNAC influence. A *Columbia Journalism Review* "debate" between a foreign editor, Leonard Doyle, for the British newspaper *The Independent* and ombudsman Michael Getler for the *Washington Post* illustrates this awareness:

> Getler: Any analysis of how the American press performed in the run-up to the war in Iraq is a complex task. And it is also vulnerable to the easy cheap shot. So much that was forecast by the Bush administration in the strongest possible terms and imagery has turned out, as of this writing, to be wrong. So it is easy to say the press did not do its job. That is true, in part. But it was a very hard job. . . .
>
> How did this happen? One factor, in my view, was a failure by editors, a lack of alertness on their part, to present stories that challenged the administration's line in a consistent way and that would have some impact on the public. That's why, I believe, so many of those public events were played inside newspapers rather than on page one. . . .
>
> Doyle: Mike Getler accepts that the press fell down on the job, that it was outflanked by the Bush administration. Surely it is now time for a fundamental reappraisal of the way the press operated. Because, like it or not, the media were co-conspirators in America's rush into this illegal war. How badly we needed—before the war—solid reporting that explained how a kitchen cabinet of neoconservatives and their bellicose friends were cooking up a war that has brought so much bloodshed to Iraq and danger to the world. Surely we need to reassess the whole concept of "embedded" reporting. Consider this conundrum: How could it be that Scott Ritter, the most famous U.S. inspector and the one person who got it right about Saddam Hussein's supposed arsenal of WMD [weapons of mass destruction], was treated with total suspicion? Meanwhile, dubious exiles with no inherent knowledge of WMD were treated with great respect by TV and newspapers. (*Columbia Journalism Review* Staff 2004, pp. 46–47)

The *New York Times* also acknowledged its systematic oversight and reliance on official news sources: "In some cases, information that was controversial then, and seems questionable now, was insufficiently qualified or allowed to stand unchallenged," the newspaper said. "Looking back, we wish we had been more aggressive in re-examining the claims as new evidence emerged or failed to emerge." The *Times* also said it had featured articles containing alarming claims about Iraq more prominently than follow-up stories that countered those claims. Many of the stories used information from Iraqi exiles and critics of Saddam Hussein (Associated Press in *Arizona Republic*, May 27, 2004, p. A1).

Consistent with war programming, other journalists joined in reflecting on the news coverage of the Iraq War:

> In the rush to war, how many Americans even heard about some of these possibilities [problems such as the forming of an Iraqi interim government and the recovery of health and water resources]? Of the 574 stories about Iraq that aired on NBC, ABC, and CBS evening news broadcasts between September 12 (when Bush addressed the UN) and March 7 (a week and a half before the war began), only twelve dealt primarily with the potential aftermath. (Cunningham 2003, p. 24)

CONCLUSION

The planning and selling of the war with Iraq is one of the most egregious propaganda campaigns in history. During the Nuremberg trials, Prosecutor Robert Jackson's closing speech, widely regarded as one of the most compelling statements about the planning of World War II by Hitler and his followers, stated,

> The dominant fact which stands out from all the thousands of pages of the record of this Trial is that the central crime of the whole group of Nazi crimes the attack on the peace of the world was clearly and deliberately planned. The beginning of these wars of aggression was not an unprepared and spontaneous springing to arms by a population excited by some current indignation. A week before the invasion of Poland Hitler told his military commanders: "I shall give a propagandist cause for starting war never mind whether it be plausible or not. The victor shall not be asked later on whether we told the truth or not. In starting and making a war, it is not the right that matters, but victory." (Jackson 1946)

Prosecutor Jackson explained how part of the provocation included dressing Polish concentration camp inmates in army uniforms in order to support a story that they had attacked a German radio station, thus justifying a retaliatory attack by Germany. Jackson then noted,

> Thus, the follow-up wars were planned before the first was launched. These were the most carefully plotted wars in all history. Scarcely a step in their terrifying succession and progress failed to move according to the master blueprint or the subsidiary schedules and timetables until long after the crimes of aggression were consummated. (Jackson 1946)

One can only wonder what Jackson would say about the U.S. propaganda campaign to wage war against Iraq. No weapons of mass destruction were found, and this was predicted by weapons inspectors as well as "intelligence reports" that were known to the Bush administration even before the 9/11 attacks. Yet President Bush insisted repeatedly that everyone thought Hussein had weapons, even his critics and opponents, including Democratic Senator John Kerry. In fact, that was not correct. There were clear statements to the contrary, and President Bush's advisers were well aware of this information because in some instances it came from their own staff members. Before 9/11 and prior to the U.S. invasion of Iraq, there were reports by governmental agencies that denied or cast serious doubt on Iraq's possession of weapons of mass destruction (Editorial 2004). While some reports indicated that Iraq may be motivated to develop such weapons, there was no evidence of their existence. These sources included the IAEA, the CIA, the Department of Energy, the defense intelligence, the State Department, the Air Force, and key White House cabinet members and advisers. In a press conference on February 4, 2001, Secretary of State Powell stated that Saddam Hussein "has not developed any significant capability with respect to weapons of mass destruction" (Editorial 2004). National Security Adviser Condoleezza Rice stated in a CNN interview on July 29, 2001, "Let's remember that [Saddam's] country is divided, in effect. He does not control the northern part of this country. We are able to keep arms from him. His military forces have not been rebuilt" (CNN 2001).

We have argued that the PNAC was the underlying force propelling the malleable President Bush to take decisive action and attack Iraq. But the American people were not aware of the story behind this push. The war story was told, but the PNAC story was not told. The dominant discourse and thematic emphasis was that Hussein was evil, that he was involved in the 9/11 attacks, that he supported terrorism, and that he planned to use weapons of mass destruction or give them to terrorists. Thus, there was a clear sense of urgency to intervene. The major news media presented virtually no strong disclaimers to this scenario; notwithstanding an occasional voice asking for patience and more information (e.g., Senators Byrd and Kennedy), all meaningful opposition to these claims was buried within the discursive framework of the war program.

Our analysis of the coverage of the Iraq War and the specific construction of the PNAC is consistent with the conceptual framework of war programming. The news media did not present much information about the PNAC for several reasons. Organization and planning were important factors. News agencies, like the military and other large organizations, must plan ahead. News media plan future coverage with broadly defined "themes" or "story lines" in order to anticipate staffing and logistical needs. Even though satellite technology makes "global coverage" more manageable, there are nevertheless complex logistics involved in covering a war halfway around the world. There is always a "game plan" for future news coverage, although certain events, such as natural catastrophes, may alter the plan. Moreover, the planning of news organizations often follows that of the relevant organization that will be involved in upcoming and anticipated events. Military planning is key for the conduct of war, but so too is media planning to cover that war. It is hardly surprising, then, that the news media tend to follow the military's lead in planning.

Analysis of numerous news reports suggests that key themes dominated much of the news coverage. The coverage of the Iraq War was shaped by themes of victims and suffering (including heroism and compensation), retaliation, the "war on terrorism," fear, homeland security and surveillance, and the conduct and preparation for the wars with Afghanistan and Iraq (Altheide 2004). These "forward-looking" themes were future and action oriented (except for the constant retrospective about the victims of 9/11). The news coverage was presented as a series of unfolding plans and events that often included scripted language to prepare audiences for future news, such as anticipating that the United Nations and all the allies may not support U.S. efforts, laying the foundation for preemptive strikes as a way to "defend ourselves," and attacking Iraq to prevent it from harming the United States with alleged weapons of mass destruction.

We have stressed that serious problems with the Bush administration's claims about weapons of mass destruction were known about well in advance of March 20, 2003, but these received very little attention because the story was about the coming war, which was the mantra of organizationally endowed legitimate claims makers. As expected with the war programming conception of war news discourse, criticism and reflection are expected to follow major military action. This did occur. After the war began, it became more appropriate to raise the troubling factual questions about the PNAC's planning, along with other issues, but these were largely echoes from foreign publications and did not receive a lot of attention.

The mass media play a part in the support of war. The mass media did not start the war with Iraq, but they shaped the context, the audience expectations, the discourse, and the production of symbolic meanings. We live in a postjournalism era when there is no longer a separation between event makers, event promoters, and event chroniclers (Altheide and Snow 1991). All rely on media logic and the sense about what will look good to relevant audiences, how to promote appropriate meanings, and, above all, how to market and sell it all as something desirable. We have seen that war programming is now a package; propaganda is joined to the news process when journalists and news sources operate with media logic, share in the construction and emotional performance of events, and limit the public forums for discussion, especially dissent. Opinion poll data show how public perceptions are informed by news reports. Public support of the Iraq War and trust in the Bush administration followed the more critical news reports; as more information about the PNAC and the elusive weapons of mass destruction became available, public approval for the war declined, as did trust in President Bush (Morin and Wilbank 2004). Indeed, another news theme emerged of "troublesome weapons of mass destruction," which in turn prompted pursuit of critical stories consistent with this theme. This change is consistent with step 5 in war programming.

Research and sociological theory suggests that war programming will continue unless we break format, or revise our methods and media for defining, selecting, organizing, and presenting information. This can occur but not easily. First, we must revise our understanding of propaganda and the role communication plays in setting the stage for conflict, carrying out the conflict, and making that conflict meaningful. Second, it must be recognized that the way in which modern wars have been covered is predictable and now is part of the planning for the conduct of war. The PNAC's claims makers knew that reframing policy could be easily connected with the tragedy of 9/11 and that messages and meanings could be easily shaped with exhaustive media support, particularly television visuals. Third, social scientists must work with journalists to provide theoretical understandings about how news practices are reflexive of power and war programming.

We have presented a picture of communication control. This will not be corrected by changing individual reporters, passing new codes of ethics, or revising journalism curricula. War programming is not unlike other mass-media scripts, such as crime reporting (Baer and Chambliss 1997; Surette 1998; Westfeldt 1998) and frames for presenting social reality. These problems are features of an ecology of communication, or the structure, organization, and accessibility of information technology, various forums, media, and channels of information (Altheide 1995). This approach to news and public information has emerged from information technology, cultural context, and communication formats.

The solution is to retreat from the position that the news media can be reformed in ways that will eliminate war programming. A fourth step in breaking format, then, is to remove it and replace it with an alternative model, one that, in time, may also have to be replaced or substituted for alternative media, including the Internet, that are more accessible, albeit perhaps less reliable. It is time to consider advocating partisan news media and programs that take political and social positions on the big questions of the day. War programming reflects the co-optation of news organs that avowedly are "objective" and impartial, but, as we have seen repeatedly, the actual practice of news work and reporting sustains powerful institutional actors, such as the PNAC and other key claims makers. This model must include the communication components essential for a free society, including access by multiple perspectives and voices and welcoming dissent and challenging basic assumptions, such as that powerful people are capable of hubris, deception and lying, and apocalyptically oriented action, and that they should be called to account. The media monopolies that now control much of print and broadcasting tend to be conservative in their approach, but their main allegiance is to economic gains that are presumed to follow from programming oriented to entertainment and audience appeal.

The Iraq War was brought to us by hundreds of news organizations, including the nation's powerful ones, essentially repeating what they had been told. Veteran journalists refer to this as stenography journalism, a way to be "objective" by simply stating the position of a claims maker rather than asking whether it is true, especially when there is clear evidence that it is not.

We may fault the leaders who propelled the country into war with Iraq, but that is not our focus here. Leaders throughout history have tried to have their way with the world. A key sociological question is why some zealots and conspiracies succeed and others fail. We agree with Mills's (1959) distinction between troubles and issues: the former are individually oriented, while the latter tend to be associated with social institutions. Certainly personal integrity and character matters, but it is not enough; social routines and expectations, including legitimate social scripts and cultural narratives, provide the general meanings from which individuals construct and define social situations. A dominant discourse, war programming, emerged and now essentially guides journalistic coverage of war in the United States. It was because of the success of this discourse that journalism failed to provide the important context, and particularly clear statements about the think tank that pushed for war so strongly, altered U.S. foreign policy, and challenged basic civil liberties. These were not relevant until later, after the war, and then they would be taken up, on schedule, as part of war programming.

This chapter must become what it is not: it falls into step 5 of war programming (studies and critiques about the media coverage), and if our argument remains in this framework, our reflections will simply reify the conceptual model that we would like to destroy. Is there no escape? We think there is. Media framing and formats must change if future wars, aided by propaganda, are to be avoided. Journalists cannot wait for events to occur before trying to cover and analyze or critique them because the news process (e.g., creating news sources, creating and developing visuals, and so on) will have taken place and the script written for the social construction of another episode of war programming. The next chapter examines how heroes are socially constructed to support the logic of war programming.

9

Constructing Pat Tillman

I want my son to be like Pat . . . Pat's the man I want to be.

—Sports talk show host Jim Rome at Pat Tillman's memorial service

He still lived & died a hero . . . :cool:.

—E-mail comment in discussion group

The military let him [Pat Tillman] down. The administration let him down. It was a sign of disrespect. The fact that he was the ultimate team player and he watched his own men kill him is absolutely heartbreaking and tragic. The fact that they lied about it afterward is disgusting.

—Pat Tillman's mother, Mary

The power of the politics of fear is that it pervades social institutions and influences social routines and social interaction. Previous chapters noted how politicians who rely on the politics of fear can promote it through controlling news sources that journalists rely on as well as other forms of propaganda to promote a view that the world is dangerous, that our lives are threatened by numerous sources of fear, and that we should be willing to sacrifice civil liberties and other freedoms in order to be secure. Sport is a great propaganda vehicle, and sports personalities are surefire sources of fan identification. This chapter tells the story of how an Arizona sports hero was used to promote patriotism and the politics of fear.

Advertisers have recognized the power of sports to sell toothpaste, beer, and cars; politicians often turn to sports in times of "crisis." Sports and nationalism are joined in popular culture through narratives, metaphors, language, and emotions. This is particularly true with wars. Audiences recognize and identify with individual athletes who are associated with familiar sports. Propagandists, such as government officials, seek to link athletes and others who are well known with values, causes, and justifications for a particular war. The positive link is forged through "heroism," as the dead individual(s) are deemed "heroes." Joining individuals to collective definitions of patriotism takes work. Like bridge construction, forging heroic identity for an audience takes creative work; unlike building bridges, social constructions rely on symbolic meanings of words and images. I offer an account of one such construction project, the death and significance of Pat Tillman, a promising twenty-seven-year-old professional football player who walked away from a multi-million-dollar contract with the Arizona Cardinals to join the Army and serve as a Ranger in Afghanistan, where he was killed by fellow Rangers on April 22, 2004.

This chapter examines how the meaning of his life and death were defined and interpreted by various agents. On the one hand, he was honored, given medals, and celebrated in several football arenas, and his collegiate jersey number (42) was retired and his professional jersey sold widely. A high school football stadium was named after him, and Arizona State University (ASU) started the Tillman Foundation. On the other hand, the meaning of his death was given different interpretations and sparked rancor and reprisals against those who "misused" his symbolic meaning.

Like all lives lost in war, Tillman's death was tragic, but he was given special significance for making such "sacrifice" and even becoming heroic. My reflections on the social construction of Tillman are informed by sociological theory and particularly symbolic interaction concepts and perspective about the mass media and popular culture. I draw on news media reports, informal interviews, and a colleague's participant observation at one memorial service in Tempe, Arizona.

The construction process provides a sociological glimpse into (1) organizations (e.g., the propaganda of the U.S. Army and the news media), (2) the political process in a mass-mediated age (e.g., how politicians link names and "faces" to international conflict as an emotional identifier for audiences—there is now a "face" to this war), (3) collective identity and symbolic commensuration (e.g., "he's still a hero" even if his own men shot him), (4) value-enriching morality plays (e.g., "be worthy of the sacrifice made on our behalf"), and (5) contemporary popular and political usage of "hero."

A sociological account of the celebration of Tillman's death and alleged heroics entails an overview of the general and specific contexts that provided central meanings to this young man as well as the propagandists—

particularly the military, politicians, and the National Football League (NFL)—and to the target audiences accustomed to consuming athletic feats, patriotic symbols, and in turn interacting with friends and colleagues to promote membership and identities.

VOCABULARIES OF MOTIVE AND PAT TILLMAN

Previous chapters focused on the importance of language in established public discourse that would resonate fear and control. Examining the language used in describing Tillman helps add some perspective and context for not only his death but also for the point of view of those who commented and their support of the values making up the sporting and military activities that defined Tillman. Mills (1940) and other students of symbolic meanings (Hewitt and Stokes 1975; Scott and Lyman 1968) argue that the language we use—and particularly the motives we attribute to others—reflects understandings and socially acceptable views about moral meanings and social order. Descriptions or adjectives of some act (e.g., "that was a patriotic act") ascribe motives to the actor. It is not important whether such characterizations are valid for the individual; what does matter is that these meanings are accepted by audiences as an adequate explanation or answer to the question, Why did he or she do that? Not surprisingly, then, certain motives (e.g., bravery) are associated with deeds that we value (e.g., fighting for one's country), while those acts that are less valued (e.g., assaulting a neighbor) are described in very negative terms. Thus, we would like to believe that a soldier died in order to protect his country and his compatriots because he or she was brave and resourceful rather than scared to death or accidentally fell on a grenade while attempting to flee the danger.

The audience is the key target of the ascription of motives and other linguistic accounts. It is the "truth of the matter" as it befalls an audience rather than some objective meaning that stands apart from audience assessments. Language establishes the identity of the person who is associated with the deed as well as the speaker and the audience. The language used in attributing motives to an act and actor also reflects on the agent who makes the assertion. If an audience approves the terms used, then the speaker is given more credibility and acceptance. From this perspective, leaders are those persons who are most capable of speaking and acting in ways that audiences prefer. Thus, President Reagan's popularity and his moniker "The Great Communicator" was due, in part, to his acting skill in portraying emotions valued by the audience.

Tillman was constructed through news reports to reflect dominant values about cultural symbols (e.g., patriotism and "God Bless America"), masculinity (e.g., sports), and the war with Iraq. Positive vocabularies of motive were attributed to Tillman by major sports organizations (e.g., the NFL) and publications (e.g., *Sports Illustrated*) and institutions (e.g., the military, the university, and government), including nationally prominent politicians (e.g., Arizona Senator John McCain). In addition, numerous audience members affirmed such constructions to associate their own identities with the values, legitimacy, and support of audiences while also linking their own identities and biographies to the communal celebration of higher values. However, not all comments about Tillman represented the dominant values and support for patriotism, God, and war. But most of these were published only in Internet chat and blog communications. I will present several of these here.

Many of the accounts about Tillman informed an emerging narrative about who he was, his individual character, and the principles for which he stood. Within hours after his death was reported, we were told by an ASU vice president that this "puts a face" to this war for us. Part of what the administrator meant is that this was the first ASU student killed in the conflict, but there was also a wider meaning. His was a preferred face and story. The celebration of Tillman's death around the United States and much of the world also reflected a strong urge for many Americans, especially supporters of the "war on terrorism," to find an example of outstanding character and valor to help elevate the legitimacy of the war. After all, volunteers and National Guard troops who, with exceptions, were drawn from the underclass and poor of American life were carrying out most of the fighting in the war. Young men from minority groups dominated the portraits of the Americans killed in Iraq who were presented on *Nightline*. Morale was reported to be horrible, especially among troops whose tour of duty was extended in Iraq as well as among National Guard troops, whose job, historically, has been to protect American soil and aid in national emergencies, including natural disasters. Indeed, the headlines in many newspapers reporting Tillman's death shared the front page with reports about the sexual abuse and torture of Iraqi prisoners by U.S. troops.

Tillman's face was a timely makeover for the war. Another Arizonan, Lori Piestewa, a Hopi mother of two who was actually killed by enemy troops in combat in Iraq in March 2003, was the previous "face" of the war for Arizona. Piestewa was "missing" on the same day (March 23, 2003) as Jessica Lynch, who would later be rescued and featured on numerous television shows for her heroism. One scholar believes that the "silence" that befalls dead heroes helps cement others' accounts and beliefs about them:

"Because (Pfc. Jessica Lynch, Piestewa's roommate who was rescued last week by special forces) is still alive, she can be flawed and can't be sanctified," De Pauw said. "Whereas, Piestewa is dead. She is never again going to say a wrong word. . . ." "It's hard to say," Laderman said. "But her ethnic-religious status as a marker of identity likely makes this something that will not just disappear. I imagine her name on mountains, streets and other kinds or forms of memorializations that will keep her in mind." (House and Shaffer 2003)

Partly because she was believed to be the first Native American woman killed in a foreign war, Lori was heralded as a hero, her family was feted, and highways and a mountain were named for her in Arizona. Very little was written about why a young single mother with two children would join the army. One account stressed her uniqueness:

Piestewa, 23, already has been the focus of spots on programs as varied as *Hardball With Chris Matthews* and *Good Morning America*. Dozens of other programs, from *Inside Edition* to the *Oprah Winfrey Show*, are pursuing interviews with family members. German- and Spanish-language television stations also want to tell her story. . . .

She came from the same environs that produced the famed Navajo Code Talkers of World War II, who have enjoyed a recent renaissance in the public spotlight because of last year's movie *Windtalkers*.

And, with the number of U.S. war dead in Iraq at just over 100, the media focus on the victims has been concentrated and intense, especially on those with unusual backgrounds like that of Piestewa. (House and Shaffer 2003)

Others saw her service, like that of many poor Americans, as an opportunity to obtain some income, escape the grinding poverty of reservation life, and have an opportunity for her children. But it had been some time since Piestewa was killed, and until her death, she was unknown outside her community.

Tillman was different; he was male, white, successful, and a rich professional athlete who had clear local reputation and a bit of a national identity as a professional football player. There were few like him in this war or any U.S. war of the past thirty years. He was a prime icon, and there was an essential story line waiting for him: a courageous, patriotic, strong, successful, wealthy professional athlete who put it all aside to defend his country while bravely defending his comrades. As we will see in this chapter, most of these points stuck, except for the disquieting discovery that he was killed by his own men.

Sociologists refer to how Tillman's story was put together as a "retrospective interpretation," which refers to how past events get reinterpreted in view of a more recent action. Tillman's story is a retrospective interpretation of many discrete events (Cicourel 1974; Garfinkel 1967; Schutz 1967) framed as an athlete-warrior with proper morals, values, and character as distinct from other selfish athletes who care about fame and fortune and put themselves above the welfare of others. The accounts also reflect the special organizational treatment of Tillman, who, like many high-profile college and professional athletes, was popularly regarded as exceptional. He was an intelligent, aggressive, outstanding football player at ASU. He was also white. Apparently, no one at ASU knew—or at least it was not mentioned—that he served thirty days in detention for a brutal beating he delivered outside a pizza parlor before coming to campus. He played football for four years at ASU, where he received numerous recognitions for his aggressive defense play and relentless perseverance. These traits contributed to the Arizona Cardinals' decision to draft him, where he competed well for four years despite being "undersized" and slower than most NFL defenders. (Indeed, a bona fide NFL starter was ridiculed when he opined that Tillman was not really top NFL material but that he could play for the Cardinals.) Rule violations that may have been treated as unacceptably deviant by another athlete—and certainly another student—apparently did not hinder Tillman's success at ASU. In addition to the violent beating he administered shortly before hitting campus, he was also given to climbing the 200-foot light towers at ASU's Sun Devil Stadium to "meditate" and reflect on things. Indeed, a photo of Tillman in a light tower accompanied several media reports about his death. The caption in a *Sports Illustrated* report read, "Solitude: When in need of his own space in college, Tillman climbed to the top of Sun Devil Stadium" (Smith 2004, p. 46). Nothing was said about this being a rule violation.

Tillman was said to be unlike other athletes, never really seeking the limelight, interested in ideas, and stating that life was just too easy. Following the hijackings and attacks on several buildings on 9/11, Tillman and his brother, Kevin, were reported to have been very upset. They joined the Army six months later, aiming for the Rangers, and Pat and Kevin Tillman gave up, respectively, a $3.6 million contract with the Arizona Cardinals and a minor league baseball career. This action was interpreted as turning away from fame and fortune in favor of patriotism and duty to country. The Tillman brothers received the Arthur Ashe Courage Award at the Espy Awards ceremony after their enlistment. While it was reported that Tillman also left his new bride of a few months to join the Rangers, the departure was told from his vantage point—listening to an "inner voice"—that she may or may not have shared. Thus, the sense of selflessness—forsaking fame and fortune and living with his wife—were part of the character and commitment statement that would be told about Tillman after his death. Several Internet writers would later comment that while they, too, had joined the military, they did not leave such a contract. As Tillman told an interviewer, playing football seemed "unimportant compared to everything that's taken place" (Smith 2004, p. 42). Senator John McCain proclaimed before an audience at a memorial service and on television,

There is in Pat Tillman's example, in his unexpected choice of duty to his country over the riches and other comforts of celebrity, and in his humility, such an inspiration to all of us to reclaim the essential public-spiritedness of Americans that many of us, in low moments, had worried was no longer our common distinguishing trait. (Smith 2004, p. 46)

The drive and character that led to his athletic successes included his intelligence and work as a student. Graduating in three and a half years with a 3.8 grade-point average in marketing, Tillman stood heads and shoulders above most ASU and major college football players, who seldom take academics seriously and fail to graduate. He was regarded as an iconoclast, a nonconformist who wore his hair long when it was popular to wear it short and vice versa. He was regarded as rebel who "listens to his inner voice."

Tillman was described in the most laudatory terms of hero, heroic, patriot, courageous, inspiring, selfless, and role model. A book was quickly published (Rand 2004), a song was distributed over the Internet, but it was in the laudatory statements by politicians, fans, and many Americans who widely commented that the dramatic presentation of character is perhaps most evident. Thousands of comments echo terms like patriot, athlete, hero, honor, character, true American, role model, and so on. Former ASU athletic director Kevin White stated,

Larger than life, one writer described him as an intense boy governed by a personal code of honor, a machismo that he defined and no one else, a Hemingway character out of the 1920s in Spain transplanted seven decades later to California soil that produced surfers and cyber-boomers and seekers of the next trend . . . Pat Tillman is without question the biggest hero of my lifetime. (Smith 2004, pp. 43, 46)

His stature as a professional football player was blended with his choice of the elite Rangers. Sports talk show host Jim Rome (master of ceremonies at Tillman's memorial service) stated, "Athletes today are referred to as heroes or warriors when in reality they are neither" (Rand 2004, p. 20). Tillman became a warrior. As New England Patriots owner Robert Kraft commented while the 2004 NFL draft was in progress,

When you consider all the qualities that make a football team great— courage, toughness, perseverance, hard work, and an almost noble sense of purpose—this guy embodied them all. In the end, he was the ultimate team player. I've been thinking about him all weekend, even in the draft room, because I don't think that we as a league can forget this guy. He was the kind of guy I'd want on my team—in any business. (Smith 2004, p. 24)

The military, like all organizations, promote themselves by providing dramatic performances of their members. The initial report was that Tillman and his Ranger patrol were ambushed and that Tillman showed initiative that saved the lives of several comrades. According to the Army report,

> Tillman's platoon was split into two sections for what officials called a ground assault convoy. Tillman led the lead group. The trailing group took fire, and because of the cavernous terrain the group had no room to maneuver out of the "kill zone."
>
> Tillman's group was already safely out of the area, but when the trailing group came under fire he ordered his men to get out of their vehicles and move up a hill toward the enemy.
>
> As Tillman crested the hill he returned fire with his lightweight machine gun. "Through the firing Tillman's voice was heard issuing fire commands to take the fight to the enemy on the dominating high ground," the award announcement said. "Only after his team engaged the well-armed enemy did it appear their fire diminished.
>
> "As a result of his leadership and his team's efforts, the platoon trail section was able to maneuver through the ambush to positions of safety without a single casualty," the announcement said. (Rand 2004, p. 10)

Numerous publications, including the quickly published book by Rand (2004), carried the Army's account of Tillman's death. One version from the *Arizona Republic* stated,

> As Tillman and other soldiers neared the hill's crest, the Army reported, Tillman directed his team into firing positions and was shot and killed as he sprayed enemy positions with fire from his automatic weapon. (House 2004, p. 1)

A *Sports Illustrated* account provided graphic details of his death:

> Dusk fell . . . the shadows twitched with treachery . . . the Rangers scrambled out of their vehicles as they came under ambush and charged the militants on foot. Suddenly Pat was down, Pat was dying. Two other US soldiers were wounded, and a coalition Afghan fighter was killed in a firefight that lasted 15 or 20 minutes before the jihadists melted away. (Smith 2004, pp. 42, 46)

For this action, Tillman was awarded a Silver Star and a Purple Heart and was posthumously promoted to corporal. This account would later be called into question.

The "production" quality of these allegedly factual descriptions became apparent, as I note later in this chapter, when they later turned out to not be true. But more important perhaps, the language is itself scripted and widespread. For example, the phrase "take the fight to the enemy" is very common and occurs in numerous news reports and accounts of valor and toughness—and propaganda of sport. One of the first recorded uses in the Lexis/Nexis information base is James's account of former Soviet leader Yuri Andropov's style:

The *London Sunday Times* summed up the Andropov style thus: "Grab the initiative. Take the fight to the enemy. Make 'em an offer they can't refuse. Dance like a butterfly. Sting like a bee." (James 1983)

To my knowledge, the Army never gave an account of how its initial false detailed descriptions of Tillman's death were constructed.

The politics of fear needs heroes to hold up to audience members as role models who not only do "heroic things" but, more important, support the political order without question, including dying for it. Heroes are propaganda products and reflect the mass-media construction process. This includes media logic and entertainment formats: numerous public statements, Tillman's two memorial services, local television specials about Tillman, and the ESPY Awards, including the tribute from Tom Cruise the year after the Tillman brothers received the Ashe Award. Amidst an athletic-celebrity celebration of fame and entertainment, Cruise's statement about Tillman was described on ESPN's Web page:

> Actor Tom Cruise—who stars with Jamie Foxx in the upcoming film "Collateral"—presented a tribute to the late Pat Tillman, recipient of the 2003 Arthur Ashe Courage Award. The Phoenix Cardinals standout left his NFL career following the events of September 11, 2001 to join the Army Rangers, and was killed in action in Afghanistan in April. "Pat Tillman surrendered a life of fame and security to set an example," Cruise said. "An example of something that we deeply value but so often take for granted—our freedom in this nation to choose our own destinies." (http://espn.go.com/espy2004/s/04attendees.html)

While the speakers at the ESPY Awards and memorial services (as well as other participants) may have been sincere, these performances were still guided by well-established media norms and guidelines. Recall the discussion in chapter 2 about media logic. An important part of this form of communication is the entertainment format. As suggested by Snow's (1983) analysis of "media culture," the entertainment format emphasizes, first, an absence of the ordinary; second, the openness of an adventure outside the boundaries of routine behavior, and, third, the audience member being willing to suspend disbelief. In addition, while the exact outcome may be in doubt, there is a clear and unambiguous point at which it will be resolved. Packaging such emphases within formats that are visual, brief, action oriented, and dramatic produces an exciting and familiar tempo to audiences. Clearly, Tillman provided a terrific opportunity for this. In addition to his media character and persona, there was a lot of file film and compelling visuals of his football prowess. These were continually replayed. Indeed, several Sun Devil football games were rebroadcast in his honor. There were also the accolades from former teammates who, as professional football players, commanded even more attention.

THE MILITARY PERFORMANCE: THE BIG LIE

The military construction of Tillman's death became, for all practical purposes, the official one that was restated at memorial services, that appeared in a book and in songs, and that was the most consistent with the notion of a hero. The important point here is that looking up to heroes carries with it veneration for their cause and their principles. The adjectives used to describe Tillman and the values and cause for which he stood clearly reflected military propaganda and the major themes pushed by the military in instructing soldiers how to communicate with loved ones as well as the press. The military, like most organizations, seeks to control information about its activities and members (Altheide and Johnson 1980; Gerth 1992; Jackall 1994). This now includes writing form letters for soldiers to send home, and these presumably may appear in the local press.

One such example was uncovered in October 2003. What amounts to a warmly worded form letter telling of open-armed welcomes and rebuilt infrastructure was printed by hometown newspapers in the mistaken belief that it was the individual composition of the undersigned soldier in Kirkuk, a relatively peaceful city in Iraq. According to the Gannett News Service, which uncovered the deception, one soldier said that his sergeant had distributed the letters to the squad, while another traced his to an Army public affairs officer.

The susceptibility of local editors to the letter, in which each "Private Everyman" describes Iraqi children "in their broken English shouting, 'Thank you, Mister,'" is understandable. But the misleading letter, uncovered by Gannett after it was published in eleven newspapers, coincides with the Bush administration's renewed program of defending the war in an ambitious speaking campaign across the nation (Staff of the *New York Times* 2003.

The military, ever mindful of its linkage to the mass media as a feature of the "military–media" complex (Altheide 1999), continues to pressure troops to stress certain themes in communication with the news media and others. The Idaho National Guard's public affairs officer prefaces specific themes to stress with the advisory:

> When answering media questions, it is very helpful to refer to current command themes in your responses. This adds continuity to the message we are portraying as a unit. The current approved themes are printed below. Please incorporate them in your communications with the media and others.

1. We are proud now to be part of our nation's active-duty Army.
2. We have come together from many states, communities and backgrounds to prepare to help stabilize Iraq and support the Iraqi people.
3. We look forward to unifying our combat power with that of other coalition forces in support of Operation Iraqi Freedom.

4. Our soldiers are among the best. They are smart and disciplined and training with state of the art equipment and facilities.
5. Our love, respect and deepest appreciation go out to our families and employers who continue to support us in this mission. (Hibbert 2004, p. 1)

Many of the testimonials about the meanings of Tillman reflected these
themes, particularly pride, quality soldiers, the mission and purpose, and
love and families.

There were other more creative and innovative constructions of Tillman. Numerous eulogies and testimonials of Tillman blended his athletic
prowess with a false account of his death. Virtually every athlete who was
asked about Tillman gave fairly stock answers. For example, Bob Feller,
renowned Major League Baseball Hall of Fame pitcher who was deco-
rated with eight battle stars for his service in World War II, told a crowd
at the Georgia Sports Hall of Fame,

> I'm no hero, I'm a survivor. There are two different types of soldiers: those who
> survive and the heroes. The survivors come here. The heroes don't. (Associated
> Press, *Arizona Republic*, May 17, 2004, p. C5; http://espn.go.com/espy2004/
> s/04attendees.html).

But not every detail supported an idealized version of Tillman. On the
one hand, over 3,000 people, including celebrities, athletes, and politicians, attended a memorial service, with ESPN's Jim Rome acting as
master of ceremonies, on May 3 in San Jose, California, Tillman's home.
Among the celebrities was Maria Shriver, President John F. Kennedy's
niece and wife of absent California Governor Arnold Schwarzenegger.
Shriver quoted both of these men, ending with an application of one of
her uncle's famous statements: "Ask not what your country can do for
you, ask what you can do for your country." "Pat," she said, "has lived
those words" (*Almaden Times*, May 6, 2004, http://espn.go.com/
espy2004/s/04attendees.html).

On the other hand, Tillman's brother and several others openly drank
Guinness as a statement of Pat's style. His younger brother, Rich, toasted
with beer, commented that his brother didn't have a religious bone in his
body, and proclaimed, "He's dead" (Bickley 2004, p. C1), "Spicing up his
brief comments with several obscenities of the kind Tillman himself was
known to let fly with abandon" (Flannery 2004, p. A1). Local television
stations carrying the event live quickly cut off broadcast. A station vice
president stated,

> We never imagined at a service like this, with Senator [John] McCain in at-
> tendance, Maria Shriver in attendance and other guests, that that kind of lan-
> guage would be used. . . . It just came to a point where we thought that our
> viewers should not be hearing that type of language on the air.
> (Goodykoontz 2004, p. A10)

A few days later, on May 8, some 800 people attended a service at Sun Devil Stadium. Attendees included fellow pro athletes, students, coaches, Governor Janet Napolitano, and ASU President Michael Crow, who, along with former coach Larry Marmie, quoted stories of Pericles about warfare and heroes. Marmie added that Tillman was "all about truth," and an elementary school teacher was reported to have said that second- and third-grade students have been writing narratives about Tillman (Collom 2004). Pat Tillman Sr. commented on the outpouring of support for his son in a letter to the *Arizona Republic*. He also commented on the reaction to statements made by another son, Richard:

> I understand that Richard, our youngest, stung a few ears during Pat's me-morial with his heart-felt rendition of "A World Without Pat." Tough; get over it, and don't go to any more funerals. To all others, he too sends his best regards. (Tillman 2004, p. B6)

Several weeks after the memorial services, a different story appeared. The facts that later emerged challenged the heroic tale of his death. The prob-lem was that most of the account was not true. Tillman and his Rangers were not ambushed; rather, a mine exploded, and in the confusion he, like numerous comrades in the last two U.S. wars, was shot by his own men. For some journalists, this was troubling.

> That everyone from George W. Bush to NFL commissioner Paul Tagliabue to we in the media—the player's likeness graced the cover of *Sports Illustrated* the week after his death—rushed to confer immortality after Tillman made the ul-timate sacrifice is understandable. As a nation we were eager to believe the army's official version of Tillman's tragic demise, which turns out to have been a fanciful illusion—sort of like Weapons of Mass Destruction. . . .
>
> Only six weeks later—after Tillman had been posthumously awarded the silver star and purple heart, been promoted to corporal, been lauded by Con-gress and had a plaza at the Cardinals' new stadium named in his honour—did the truth begin to emerge. Tillman wasn't killed by "enemy" fire, because there wasn't any enemy present. He was shot by his fellow soldiers . . . killed by what the army chooses to oxymoronically describe as "friendly fire." (Kimball 2004, p. 24)

Tillman's death had already been defined as heroic not only for the way he died but mainly, as suggested previously, for his sacrifice volunteering to serve his country. While most media accounts stressed that death by friendly fire should not diminish his heroism, having one of the nation's prime heroes killed by his own troops did tarnish the polish a bit, al-though not without controversy.

Many comments were made in the minor media, mainly the Internet, by the E-audience, those who communicate electronically throughout daily life via the Internet, cell phones, and even pagers. Like the more polished media performers, the E-audience's statements resonate identity competence and performance; they could relate to Tillman, often through values but also through unique biographical circumstances. Unlike the performative media logic that guided most of the presentations on television and at memorial services by featured speakers, the E-audience does not rehearse or write drafts of statements before speaking them; rather, they tend to make curt replies that blend routine communicative format and content with the "news of the day," in this case Tillman's death and its meaning. Most comments we've seen tend to be very supportive of Tillman's choices, resonating the applause and sentiments of the celebrities and others noted previously. A few critical comments appeared in the press, but they were less about Tillman and the construction process and more about context and the war. Interestingly, in the same *Sports Illustrated* issue in which Smith's (2004) dramatic—and largely incorrect— account of Tillman's death appeared, renowned writer Rick Reilly contrasted Tillman's interest in obscurity and being like everyone else with the death of another soldier, Todd Bates, an impoverished black athlete who wanted recognition but was able to join only the Ohio Army National Guard:

> Pat Tillman and Todd Bates were athletes and soldiers. Tillman wanted to be anonymous and became the face of this war. Bates wanted to be somebody and died faceless to most of the nation.
>
> Both did their duty for their country, but I wonder if their country did its duty for them. Tillman died in Afghanistan, a war with no end in sight and not enough troops to finish the job. Bates died in Iraq, a war that began with no just cause and continues with no just reason.
>
> Be proud that sports produce men like this.
>
> But I, for one, am furious that these wars keep taking them. (Reilly 2004, p. 80)

The mainstream press offered little reflection and context. The Internet was a different story. There were also many exceptions, gadflies perhaps, who raised other points, including such views as that Tillman was killed by the CIA and so on. The identity connections and emotions were found in a number of statements. Some writers commented on the waste of war:

> I feel bad that so many are being sent to kill and die, yet some are considered better than others for doing so. it falls into the "life isn't fair" category and it's a shame. i suppose i did mean a some denegration, which was rude mean and thoughtless of me, and for that, i apologise. It is better directed at the liars, thieves and cheats who convinced him to go, then lionised him in death. Another American dead Hero. the loss of Brother Tillman and all of the American and Coalition members civilian and military and Iraqi men women and children is a terrible waste of life, talent and spirituality. it brings us all down as members of the human race. (Internet notes; spelling as in the original)

I noted that the accurate account of Tillman's death was less than heroic; quite simply, he was mistakenly shot by his own men—friendly fire. Not everyone thought that learning about this was a good thing. One person did not think this was a good thing:

> The *Atlanta Journal-Constitution* demonstrated bad taste in choosing the day before Memorial Day to publish the article on the death of Pat Tillman. ("Ex-NFL Star Died from Friendly Fire," *News*, May 30)

> In war, people fight for their lives against other people fighting for theirs and the winner survives. But mistakes happen. Our artillery falls on our troops, or a soldier pops up for a better view during a firefight and gets shot from behind by a friend. There are many variables of this. Death by "friendly fire" hurts more than death by the enemy, and the armed forces usually pass it off as a combat loss so it will not seem as great a waste. Investigations typically are not publicized, but Tillman's status generated extraordinary examination. Articles such as the one that ran in the AJC will cause additional pain to his family. (Internet field notes)

> As for the other article, well, I guess it's a free country. But as a future lawyer, could I, if called upon, defend these people in a courtroom? Could I honestly look at a photo of Pat Tillman and, knowing what he did, defend these people's point of view? I don't know. . . . I don't care what you think of the situation overseas—right/wrong, good/bad, about oil/about something else— Pat Tillman and I both were at a point in our lives once where we had a decision to make: pursue a career or serve our country. I made one decision, he the other. I'm here, he's not. It's easy to pursue a career. It's much harder to step in front of a bullet so that the idiot behind you can make fun of you for doing it, all the while not realizing that, had you not done so, he never would have been able to speak freely.
> Perhaps those people need to get off their fat asses and see what life is like outside of their Play-Station-and-Computer-Porn lives. Maybe then they'd realize they have it pretty good. Maybe then they'd come to appreciate the magnitude of the sacrifices our men and women in the armed forces are making on our behalf. (Internet notes)

Not surprisingly, some of the most positive comments about Tillman's death came from those who had also served in the military:

> I'll grant you that not all men and women that serve in the Army adhere to that creed. I did. And I believe that Pat Tillman did as well. There are many more men and women like Pat Tillman that deserve respect and if that's too much for some people—a simple "thank you" will suffice. (Internet notes)

We found comments from people who interpreted news of Tillman's death by "friendly fire" as evidence of U.S. superiority as well as this generation's patriotism and unselfishness. This demographic identity was strong. One E-audience participant specifically disagreed that the World War II–era football players were more patriotic.

Another writer represents a perspective of being a "critical thinker" that considers views of cynical writers less sympathetic to the popular constructions of Tillman:

> Pat Tillman was too great of a warrior to be taken out by Taleban types. Only a fluke or mistake could bring him down. In my life I have heard a lot of trash about how today's pro atheletes do not measure up to say the ones drafted into WWII. Well Pat Tilman disproves all of that. No WWII era athelete gave up millions of dollars to fight for their country the way he did. Money meant nothing to him when it came to serving the American people. He would not bake down from death either. His life and dedication proved that. I will always remember Pat Tillman as a Great American Warrior. His spirit will touch us from the other side and inspire us on to crush the evil jihad now upon us. His fight continues with us. (Internet field notes; spelling as in the original)

The strong identity connection to writers addressing such an emotional story is quite noteworthy. Here are two examples, from an online "guest book" where people empathize through their own experiences:

> To the Family of Pat Tillman,
>   A man, an athlete, a hero. Those are the 3 best words to describe Pat Tillman. My sincere condolences go out to the family of Pat Tillman. I know how you must feel w/ all of the "I'm sorry's," but in the long run it will make you so much stronger. I know that that is how I felt when my sister was killed on April 10, 2004 in a car accident. I just wanted to let you know that Pat Tillman will always be in out thoughts and his family will you always be in our prayers. We will ALWAYS love you miss Pat Tillman. It will get easier, I promise.

And another:

> Pat Tillman's story has made me a better person. It has reminded me to not waist my days, live hard, and to do my best at everything I do. I am a elementary school PE teacher, and I will tell his story to my students for then next 26 years. (both at www.legacy.com/bostonglobe/Guestbook.asp?Page=Guest Book&PersonId=2163592&GuestPage=10; spelling as in the original)

ANOTHER VOICE FROM THE TILLMAN POSTER

The politics of fear is a discourse that can be loaded, aimed, and fired. It is the meaning of the attacks that is crucial. The politics of fear renders all attacks defensive. The target is justified in defense of a protected domain, but it is the overall narrative that gives the attack its appeal. The meaning and ownership of Tillman is illustrated by the defense of a counterclaim. Tillman was sacrificed to the God of War. His was a self-sacrifice; after all, he did join up of his own accord. The problem was how to make his life meaningful to us all, the audience. His family and fiancée certainly did not need that; they knew he was an exceptional individual, unique and free-spirited. They did not need our support of them; they had each other, and like any family grieving for a soldier slain in war, they would have to sort out the raw emotions of pride that he volunteered to serve and defend the country while missing him sorely. After all the analysis of news reports and claims about what Tillman stood for, represented, and beckoned us all to do, who is he really? Clearly, he had become a face for the war in Iraq, a face that would serve war proponents well, a face that would enable social control agents in the mass media to proclaim his significance as a model or, perhaps more to the point, a command performance by which we should all be measured. The idea, of course, is that anyone who did not do what he did would not measure up. But the charge to the mass-media audience was not to actually enlist and become a Ranger (most would not be wanted by the military, anyway) but rather to avow symbolic support for the selflessness, the sacrifice, and the courage to, if not actually serve the country by going off to war, at least support the country. The United States of America looked like Tillman, and we were told that just as we were proud of him, he would be proud of us. The problem is that his parents and family members and friends did not control his meaning and his identity; this was taken up by the mass media for their entertainment purposes. Politicians and organizational leaders also took over Tillman and made him their own, to use for their purposes. They owned the image and the identity of Tillman, and they were jealous of their control. Their perspective on Tillman can be illustrated with a conflict that occurred over the meaning of Tillman.

John Leanos, a young Chicano studies art professor at ASU, constructed his own meaning of Tillman and invited audiences to examine the heroic discourse about him. He created a poster with Tillman's image in his military uniform, with the words, "Remember me? I was killed by my own Army Ranger platoon in Afghanistan on April 22nd, 2004. I am a hero to many of you. My death was tragic, my glory was short lived. Flawed perceptions of myself, my country and the war on terror resulted in the disastrous end to my life." He put the posters up around campus and on several buildings in Phoenix. "The idea was to open up a dialogue about Tillman's story—about Tillman's heroic nature," Leanos said. He said he designed the first-person message in the tradition of the Day of the Dead, a Latin American holiday that happened to be on Election Day, November 2, 2004. "We celebrate and remember our dead every year," Leanos said (James 2004).

The cultural significance of the Day of the Dead apparently was lost on many who commented on the poster. That meaning is contextualized and often contested was not an official option with Tillman. Many people objected to the poster, challenging his right to use the image (Saidi 2004). Responses included more than 300 negative e-mails, and letters were sent to the campus newspaper, to the head of the Arizona Board of Regents, to the president of ASU, and to many other officials. Most, from what we can tell, were negative, some being very critical, even calling for the firing of the young professor.

Critics seemed to imply that the poster was a misuse of Tillman and that it was using him for a purpose and a message that he would not have supported. Leanos's art challenged certain claims and uses of Tillman by the university and others.

"The University is using Tillman as a brand for marketing," Leanos said. "My whole issue is that Tillman is being used by the University and the right wing as a hero. He's being used as a hero figure to propose a pro-war, nationalistic stance" (Saidi 2004).

The president of the Board of Regents and ASU's president wrote letters criticizing the artist, decrying the effort at degrading and using our hero and even adding that apologies would be sent to Tillman's family. A letter from the president of the Board of Regents stated that an "administrative review" was under way to "explore whether anyone else at ASU was involved in what appears to be a blatant attempt to trade on the celebrity and patriotism of one of ASU's most honored and respected graduates" (Saidi 2004), and a letter from ASU President Michael Crow stated that the words on the poster were "offensive and insensitive to the Tillman family" (Saidi 2004).

Tillman became an object of study on campus. Students conducted various projects on the controversy, investigating the legal right to verify—and learn—how symbolic claims and statements are protected free speech. Many students expressed opinions that this was just wrong. On the one hand, the subtext was that we knew what Tillman stood for, what he believed in, and what he would have supported, while on the other, there was a claim that the image should not be used by the artist as though it was actually owned and operated by someone else. Indeed, it may have been copyrighted, but it was not. The constructed reality of Tillman was reified.

So people were very interested in protecting an image that had been constructed of Tillman, but so was his father, who expressed disgust at the role the military played in providing its self-serving scenario of heroics in order to cover up its blunders. When it became apparent the military covered up how Tillman died, Arizona Senator John McCain ordered an investigation. Over the next eighteen months, more details emerged about how his Ranger unit, split into two parts, suffered miscommunication, ultimately mistaking Tillman for an enemy, and fired repeatedly without verifying the target.

The soldiers in Afghanistan knew immediately that they had killed Tillman on April 22, 2004, and quickly began the cover-up, including burning his uniform and body armor. Army officials insisted that they did not know the truth, but later investigations revealed that a general was informed of this within the next ten days. Tillman's nationally televised memorial service on May 3, 2004, benefited the Army and other participants in the military–media complex. Tillman's parents did not learn how he died until weeks later, and even then many details were not disclosed (Staff 2005). Patrick Tillman Sr., an attorney, decried the "botched homicide investigation," adding,

> After it happened, all the people in positions of authority went out of their way to script this. They purposely interfered with the investigation, they covered it up. I think they thought they could control it, and they realized that their recruiting efforts were going to go to hell in a handbasket if the truth about his death got out. They blew up their poster boy. (Staff 2005)

The politics of fear shrouded Tillman as a subject and an object. The flesh and blood of Tillman was not relevant to the construction process. He was used for various purposes, and this use was constituted through mass-media coverage, publicity, and the entertainment format. He belonged to media worlds, very much of this world but certainly not a private, personal world. He became an agent of the politics of fear, a guardian of claims about legitimacy of war, and certainly a defender against those who might question the legitimacy of war.

HEROISM AND THE POLITICS OF FEAR

The construction of Tillman as a hero invites some reflection on the changing meanings and criteria of the "heroic," including such questions as whether heroism is a feature of an individual act or of general courage or its aftermath. Numerous scholars have explored the changing meanings of heroism throughout history, including how exceptional deeds were interpreted in view of political context, the legitimacy and utility of the act for the survival of the group or state, and the courage, suffering, and character of the individual (Klapp 1962). The criteria of hero vary a great deal. The development of writing and other representational media (e.g., folklore and mythology) that could capture accounts contributed to heroic development in terms of both sharing (while embellishing exploits) and creating fictional characters who may or not have had any resemblance to flesh-and-blood namesakes. An example of the latter is the host of "Wild West" heroes, noted for bravery and "taming the West" and standing for "law and order," while the information available suggests that they were often exploitative, cowards, gamblers, drunks, and "back shooters." Indeed, movie and television versions of the "Wild West" heroes often focused on constructing heroic horses and dogs and adding physical characteristics to help display their inner "emotions" and courage. For example, several movies were reported to add eyelashes to horses so that their emotions could be displayed, but the distortions also encompassed adding teeth to foals (http://pulprack.com/arch/2003/02/horses_in_the_w.html).

The changing forms of heroics in the United States accompanied industrial and occupational shifts, collective identities, and the rise of the politics of fear. Ironically, the politics of fear has changed and become more prevalent as everyday threats to physical health have diminished. As noted throughout this book, people do not fear "objective" threats, such as work-related injuries, driving accidents, or unhealthy air and water. People fear what they perceive to be threatening to lifestyle. Public attention has shifted from the numerous everyday struggles for survival as well as threats to life and limb that accompanied farming and extractive industries (mining and forestry work) and threats from other people, including crime and those who were perceived to threaten quality of life.

As society has become more affluent, public services have increased, public health has improved, and transportation and working conditions are safer, and with the exception of the large number of unemployed and dispossessed members of society—including numerous minority group members—the overall quality of life is vastly improved over the past fifty years. A key part of this improvement has been a dramatic increase in public service jobs that provide employment as well as public assistance for a more affluent citizenry. Such services include teachers at various levels, health inspectors, refuse service, building inspectors, alley and street maintenance, postal workers, fire departments, and police services. Public employees make up the largest single body of workers in the United States, but not all public employees are highly valued in terms of payment, benefits, notoriety, and prestige. The paltry salaries of schoolteachers in the United States are well known, as are the near-poverty-level wages of social workers, probation officers, and numerous public health employees.

Uniforms are increasingly associated with heroism in the United States. Those who wear military-like uniforms are different. Uniforms came to be associated with those who protected us and policed the many risks around us. Uniforms are the other half of the "other," the people, conditions, and circumstances that are regarded as threatening to our physical, moral, and symbolic order. Firefighters represent the threatened physical environment (e.g., fire), although in the past two decades, firefighters have moved into the front line of emergency health care by providing emergency medical services and acting as "first responders" to health

emergencies. The other threats include criminals, the poor, and the homeless. And uniformed people now capture most of the attention as heroes.
(One exception to the principle that uniforms count more today is correctional officers, who, like schoolteachers, caretakers in mental hospitals,
and day care workers, continue to be very poorly paid.) Even as society
was becoming more safe and less dangerous—in terms of everyday life
routines such as travel, work, and health—the public perception of fear
and danger was increasing. Numerous opinion polls document Americans' sense of danger. Despite the hyperbole, heroics were historically associated with an atypical act, usually by an individual, that was regarded
as being positive for the group or social unit (e.g., the state or society).
Simply being a member of an entity or conducting assigned work, no matter how dangerous—whether as a police officer, a fireman, a coal miner, a
nurse, or a lumberjack—would not qualify one as heroic. This changed
with the development of the mass media and the entertainment-oriented
popular culture, which celebrated heroes as extraordinary characters in
order to capture viewers or readers. The hero as audience bait became established. By the late twentieth century, hero and heroics became associated with the death of public employees (e.g., firefighters and police officers) even if their death was not caused by a specific feat (e.g., pulling
someone from a burning building). Numerous police officers who were
killed while driving to and from work were labeled heroes, as were their
colleagues who died in routine work (e.g., a weapon misfiring and accidentally killing them or even when they may have been shot by another
officer). The increase in heroics was fostered by entertainment, then, but
it was also supported by the expansion of civil servants in "uniforms,"
who, we argue, became key symbols in the politics of fear. The symbolic
designation of military and paramilitary uniforms dressed an increasing
public awareness and celebration of the role of these workers in keeping
us safe.

CONCLUSION

The politics of fear was reinforced by numerous symbolic acts in the days
following the 9/11 attacks. Leaders celebrated the resurrection by posing
with firefighters and police officers, wearing various insignia and markers,
including T-shirts emblazoned with "FDNY." They became our homeland
heroes, and the transition to the military forces was assisted with handing
off flags from the Twin Towers to be displayed on military vessels or to fly
over military outposts as well as writing revenge-laden messages on missiles and bombs destined for Afghanistan and Iraq. All uniforms stood out
in the United States. Pat Tillman wanted to belong. Prior to that time in his

young life, a professional football uniform—membership in the NFL—was the most cherished. He and other entertainers recognized the symbolic divide between mere sports heroes paid millions of dollars and the rekindled persona of uniform heroes, particularly the military. This realization, along with the public discourse about "being under attack," avenging the fallen uniformed forces, and making supreme sacrifices, would be appealing within the politics of fear, whereby individuals can join forces to defeat the latest threats to moral and symbolic order. Pat Tillman was constructed to stand for all of this.

10

Conclusion: Beyond the Politics of Fear

No one can terrorize a whole nation, unless we are all his accomplices.

—Edward R. Murrow

Power shows itself through fear in the modern world. This book began by discussing power. This is also the topic of the final chapter. Power is the ability to define a situation for self and others. The opening pages in chapter 1 told the story of Paula Zasadny, the mother of the young girl killed in Iraq, who thought that she and her daughter were being patriotic and serving their country because they were sacrificing in order to attack the object of fear: "terrorists" in Iraq. They were serving their country, but the foreign policy decisions that led to the death of her daughter, Holly McGeogh, were not based on solid military planning, coherent global trends, or a cogent analysis of U.S. interests; those policies were grounded in fear and sold to the American people through the politics of fear. It is a deadly game, usually paid for in blood and sacrifice by the weakest members of society. Powerful people assert their will in the modern world through the politics of fear by being part of the communication process that defines social issues and social problems. This usually involves the mass media. Poor people do not control any mass media in the world. Rather, they are the target for messages about fear.

The politics of fear is paradoxical. The complexities are illustrated in various crime control efforts as well as military interventions discussed in this book. On the one hand, the policies, programs, and changes that occur are perceived as beneficial in the short run because they keep us safe, solve problems, and prosecute—and kill—those who threaten us. On the

207

other hand, public perceptions change over time as more people come to regard such policies as reckless, destructive, and serving the interest of the manipulators. Recall that excesses and egregious civil rights violations by the FBI and the CIA were made public; these agencies were reined in by congressional action. However, the collective memory seems to last about as long as the next crisis, when entertainment-oriented news media fan the flames of "emergency" and shut out the soothing language of context and perspective. The problem, then, is that we are all increasingly implicated as being manipulators. More of us enjoy the alleged safety and security that is credited to the formal agents of social control with whom we have entrusted more of our lives. Part of the challenge, then, is to recognize how publics are cultivated through the mass media to accept the *ethic of control*: problems can and should be solved by more invasive control. After a brief overview of how citizens become involved in reducing their own citizenship rights, I will suggest some ways to offset, if not overcome, the pervasive politics of fear.

DEFINING THE POLITICS OF FEAR

As stressed in the previous chapters, social change and expansion of social control occur through acts of power. When social control changes are institutionalized, they become part of the fabric of social life. To the extent that formal social control efforts expand, we can see the growth in the politics of fear. To repeat, the politics of fear refers to decision makers' promotion and use of audience beliefs and assumptions about danger, risk, and fear in order to achieve certain goals. The politics of fear should correspond well with the amount of formal social control in any society. The source of fear may be an authority, God, or an internal or external enemy. Tracking the expanded control efforts over time can illustrate how the politics of fear has evolved in any social order. Moreover, behind most efforts to enact more control will be a series of events and accounts about "what should be done." Changes in public language and in the discourse of fear will also accompany social control changes. However, as emphasized here, once such changes are enacted, they symbolically enshrine the politics of fear even when public perceptions about the specific source of that fear process may diminish.

The politics of fear is exercised during times of conflict, but it accumulates and gradually informs policy and everyday-life behavior, even if there are occasional bouts of resistance. The politics of fear does not imply that citizens are constantly afraid of, say, a certain enemy day in and day out. The object of fear might change, but fear of threats to one's security is fairly constant. The context of control promotes this, as do numerous messages about menaces that justify general social control measures.

I argued in chapter 2 that force requires fear to be effective socially and politically. One aim of this book is to clarify the narrative of the politics of fear so that it may be read more clearly. Part of the story is that there is a temporal and cyclical nature to it. The capacity of human beings to adjust, normalize horrendous conditions, and eventually resist social control is the ultimate challenge to politicians of fear: The longer fear is promoted, the less effective it is. There is a temporal dimension of fear that must be regarded by the politics of fear: it cannot endure indefinitely; for it to be effective, there must be respites but not a predictable rhythm. This means that leaders cannot sustain a claim that they will forever be against fear or a source of fear—such as terrorism—by continually battling it in order to eradicate it. Paradoxically, the claim that the war will go on forever until the enemy is "eradicated" also serves to diminish its support and, ultimately will reduce support and effectively stop the most current war:

> This shift towards eradication politics is futile. An ongoing war against the causes of fear creates a condition of chronic fear. Unlike acute fear, which is expressed intensely and is over as quickly as the intense threat it responds to, chronic fear is a response to an enduring and persistent or growing threat to the subject. It encourages gnawing reflective worries to creep in, grinding away at the fearful one's integrity. Thus, the ongoing general condition of fearfulness produced by long-term war against the causes of fear eventually wears down the fear-ridden society, a process which is exacerbated by the fact that, while it endures, the fear-ridden society provides a fertile location for terrorist activity. (Sparks 2003, p. 204)

Of course, this does not mean that the politics of fear disappears; it is merely taken off the stage, so to speak, and awaits another opportunity for media-inspired propaganda efforts to promote the next crisis, drawing, as I have argued, on the context and nuances of the previous episodes of fear, including the policies and practices that have been institutionalized in everyday life, such as uniforms and surveillance.

This process of the politics of fear is also consistent with war programming discussed in chapter 8. I argue that even criticism of war making is included within the overall narrative of war; it has a place, but the script of "caution" and "opposition" is a feature of the entertaining news formats and popular culture. In this sense, I suggested that criticism is itself scripted and is part of the narrative of war programming that has emerged over the past thirty years or so. It is the context of meaning and experience that lends credibility to the most recent threat and crisis. Images and scenarios are drawn on and recycled as part of the continuing "battle" against threats to morality, civilization, and "our way of life."

Any response to the politics of fear must first recognize that it is a social construction that is linked to cultural meanings produced by the mass media. I have stressed that individual politicians are not to "blame" and should not be given credit for a country like the United States to wage war. There are numerous checks and balances in the U.S. system, and Congress, journalists, and the mass media, as well as public opinion, can—and ultimately will—stop reigns of terror that emerge from the politics of fear. It is not a "power grab" per se that enables conspirators like the members of the Project for a New American Century (chapter 8) to gain control of the reins of government and dominate foreign and domestic policy. This takes a lot of work, a lot of cooperation from many people of goodwill who, ironically, are just trying to do the right thing, to protect their families and country from harm. As I have tried to show in this book and in other work, it is what these social actors take into account about their past, how they draw on manipulated media images to understand their situation, and in turn what meanings they project into the future.

Fear promotes fear. Fear limits our intellectual and moral capacities, it turns us against others, it changes our behavior and perspective, and it makes us vulnerable to those who would control us in order to promote their own agendas. The politics of fear, as argued repeatedly in these pages, simply translates these "concerns" into preventive action; claims are made that the "bad situation" can be fixed through more control. This is true regardless of whether the hot issue is crime, illegal drugs, immigration, or international conflict. In most cases, the control is focused on regulating individuals rather than on broader social issues (e.g., poverty and oppressive foreign relations) that have contributed to the problem. More recently, however, the work linking fear to the politics of fear has become far more sophisticated; the recent "war on terrorism," for example, rests on important changes that have occurred in our culture and social institutions and owes less to cunning individuals who simply ride these cultural changes.

A truism in social science is that all social products reflect the process that made them. Fear is a product, and the politics of fear is part of the process. It is a process that includes the mass media because in the modern world we know very little beyond our immediate experience that is not mass mediated. I have argued in this book that the mass media, popular culture, and the process of media logic are the key to our strengths and weaknesses. We are an entertainment-oriented society, and virtually everything that is meaningful to us and taken for granted is part of a "program" that repeats, resonates, and reproduces our lives. Today, propaganda abounds; we just call it by different names. In Hitler's day, there was not a lot of propaganda, so he and one of his top henchmen, Josef Goebbels, created unique blends of glamorized falsehoods, refining the delivery of emotional symbols and slogans across radio, movies, and newspapers and building on a historical context of "Germany against the world." In our day, things are different; all major mass media are governed by propaganda, often in the guise of advertising and marketing, which rely on simplification, distortion, and emotional appeals to increase the "bottom line," the cultural culmination of profitability and success (Ewen 1976, 1999; Jackall 1994, 1999). Anything that brings in the market—that is, the people and their dollars—is permissible. The current generation—the age of my students—is the most marketed generation in history. Every aspect of their lives is fair game to commercial manipulators. This is critical because the most effective form of social control is when it is taken for granted as part of the normal course of things and is not even recognized as "control" but just as "what everyone knows." Social scientists refer to this as "normalization," and this occurs through a "socialization process" whereby individual members of society essentially acquire the expectations, assumptions, and patterns of everyday life. Soon, the way things are is the way things should be. This is the process that makes meaningful social change so difficult. This is also the process of the politics of fear.

Most of my students were born into the politics of fear and know nothing else. The pervasive surveillance that regulates more of our lives is part of their taken-for-granted baseline of experience (Marx 1988; Staples 2000). To some extent, this is true of each generation, but this one is different. For example, my generation (born in the mid-1940s) was taught about the dreaded superpower that challenged us: the Soviet Union, Russia, the communists, or the "commies." And the "other side" learned the same thing about us. We learned that there were many aspects of our lives that had to be regulated in order to "protect us," including foreign travel. And as the opening quote to this chapter from Edward R. Murrow indicates, there was a lot of concern about "internal" enemies and infiltration by the "commies." Senator Joseph McCarthy, eventually brought down by independent journalists like Murrow and others who dared to face him, raised havoc among American legislators, cultural creators, intellectuals, and activists. The Cold War chilled the culture. But unlike the present politics of fear, the technology of control did not penetrate our bodies. That is different today. Many of my students have had urinalysis and other drug screenings. They were born at a time of pervasive control, and for the most part they have normalized it; most see nothing wrong with being asked "to pee in a cup if you've got nothing to hide." They do not see the control. This is part of the politics of fear. Social routines and activities change to reflect the ethic of control: problems can and should be solved by more invasive control. This is especially the case when control is justified to contain threats to personal safety and national security. Few of my students are aware of a prior time when individual rights as citizens would not permit such bodily transgressions, where there were clear limits to how far surveillance could go.

Previous chapters addressed how crime and war are two sides of the politics of fear that have drastically changed our culture and paved the way to widespread acceptance of the latest justification known as the "war on terrorism." The politics of fear becomes part of culture, and it changes through the cultural process. One way to understand how this works is to monitor popular culture and the mass media (Surette 1998). While the politics of fear operates alongside cultural products, the cultural products demonstrate the results. We can examine some of these changes about crime, punishment, and the shifting focus from protecting the individual to protecting the state and the interests of the mass audience. This has important implications for citizenship.

Consider television programs about crime. Numerous scholars have noted how mass-media scenarios, narratives, and rhetoric have shifted since the 1960s from more concern with rights of the accused to the rights of the prosecution (Cavender 2004; Ericson 1995; Garland 2001; Surette 1998). Typically, popular-culture rhetoric does not celebrate both simultaneously. Moreover, the nature of rhetoric and cultural narratives entails treating individuals and the state in opposition; both cannot be promoted at the same time; rather, when one is promoted, the other is often disparaged and delegitimated or treated as morally contemptible. Many readers will recognize this in portrayals of the "rights of the accused" that are often presented in crime dramas. Also referred to as the Miranda rights (named after a famous legal case, *Miranda v. Arizona*), these are commonly depicted when an arresting officer informs an arrested person that they "have the right to remain silent . . . have the right to an attorney," and so on). Typically, the arresting officer will make a derogatory comment about the suspect, such as "you've heard it before . . . you probably know it better than we do." The message, as Surette (1998) argues, is that the courts and legal protections like the Bill of Rights are hampering law enforcement and are helping criminals, terrorists, and other merchants of fear.

Television crime shows shifted their emphasis between 1960 and 2000, from defense attorneys to the prosecution and from the deviant/outlaw to the law enforcer. Notwithstanding the seemingly constant fascination with the bravado of the Old West marshal, who outdueled desperadoes in taming the West, movies and television programs in the 1960s encouraged audiences to identify with the outlaw heroes (e.g., *Bonnie and Clyde*).

Cavender (2004) observes that widespread deviance from standard expectations of social control changed in the 1970s with a shift in crime policy. Popular-culture heroes emerged from their strong actions against violent fiends, hardly likable:

> Story lines began to change in the 1970s with films like *The French Connection* (1971) and *Dirty Harry* (1971). The Robin Hood-like crimes of Bonnie and Clyde or Butch and Sundance are replaced by serial murder, rape and the heroin trade. The depiction of the criminals who commit these crimes changes, too. They are psychopaths, rapists, terrorists and heroin traffickers, not the likable rogues of the 1960s films. These shifting depictions begin the process of "othering" the criminal. The films suggest that there is an evil side of human nature, and the villains personify it. These are not people with whom the audience might identify. (Cavender 2004, p. 344)

The portrayal of crime by popular culture and news accounts has influenced the way that the criminal justice system operates, including the work of judges who, according to Rudolph Gerber, a former member of the Arizona Court of Appeals, now are intent on dispensing "injustice":

> In the past twenty-five years, this state's lawmakers have linked political success to polishing a tough-on-crime image that translates, first and foremost, into the emphasis on unprincipled legal procedures and draconian severity of punishment that in turn translates into prison as the paradigm of severity. This penchant for severe prison sentences at all costs, including taxes and human lives, obstructs more realistic, less expensive, more effective, and more just crime policies. A companion folly of current crime policies is lawmakers' rampant ignorance of or indifference to empirical crime data. Lawmakers either cannot or will not respond to scholarly criminological research or even anecdotal reports from experienced workers in the trenches. (Gerber 2001, p. 173)

These studies, along with this book, represent an attempt to track some of the changes in symbolic representations of social order. The emphasis is on documenting changes that led to more acceptance of control, including the use of more membership criteria (us/them), more symbols and language of insiders/outsiders, as well as resistance that may be generated against this foundation, particularly by young people.

We become accustomed to more control, and it is gradually taken for granted. It becomes part of our cognitive and emotional baseline of experience, even how we structure our living conditions (Ellin 1997). It seems normal when it is expressed and somewhat different when it is challenged. The language of social control agencies pervades cultural experience. Each new step is a feature of the politics of fear and the cultural context of our age. And propaganda plays a large part in these efforts.

The politics of fear is a feature of the ecology of communication, which refers to the structure, organization, and accessibility of information technology, various forums, media, and channels of information (Altheide 1995). It provides a conceptualization and perspective that joins information technology and communication (media) formats with the time and place of activities. Routine activities and perspectives about everyday life reflect political decisions that have been made to increase social control activities that were justified to combat sources of fear. Political decisions have cumulative effects on social life as they "backwash," or flow over time, from their originating event and debates to seep into other aspects of everyday life. Crime control policies of the 1970s, for example, still inform everyday routines by police agencies and other social institutions. Numerous efforts to prevent crime that are taken for granted include "stop and frisk," "no-knock searches," "preventive detention," "presumptive arrest," and "police DUI checkpoints."

Technological changes promote the politics of fear as well. Fundamentally, the face of fear is expanded surveillance; it is ubiquitous and penetrating, ranging from satellite cameras to monitoring weather, troop movements, and terror suspects to invasive drug testing (e.g., urinalysis) and increasingly DNA surveillance to detect health risks. Surveillance is more pervasive because of technology that is less obtrusive and that can do more things for lower costs. More "miniaturization" of microchips, improved optics, and better wireless communication contribute to more communication devices like computers, cameras (including closed-circuit television), cell phones, personal digital assistants (PDAs or "Palm Pilots"), and iPods, but all these promote surveillance. Surveillance is virtually everywhere: work, home, school, stores and malls, sports stadiums, highways, airports, and even restrooms (Marx 1988; Staples 2000). For example, most cell phones come with a GPS locator that enables anyone with appropriate communication gear to find where you are at any time. Cameras abound in public, and they are becoming less expensive.

Controlling our borders is also about controlling us. I refer not just to the occasional capture of the "bad guy" but rather to how our expectations about everyday life become muted to numerous transgressions of basic civil rights as citizens. Recall that virtually no control movement put into effect is justified explicitly as "we want to control and regulate all citizens so that we can have more power over them." Rather, the case tends to be put in very apologetic if not painful terms, such as "unfortunately, we have to give up a few rights for our own protection" or, as more broadly stated after the 9/11 attacks, "the world changed that day," meaning that everything could justifiably be viewed as different from then on. This included control and surveillance.

Previous chapters referred to the massive changes in civil rights that occurred as a result of the USA Patriot Act and attendant legislation that accompanied the creation of the Department of Homeland Security. One of the big items was to increase surveillance along the U.S. borders, mainly in order to prevent terrorists from entering the United States. Tens of thousands of new jobs have been added to the Border Patrol, and several hundred million dollars have been spent for more technologically enhanced security along the borders. Very few—if any—bona fide terrorists have been captured as a result of this infusion of dollars and control along the border (although its proponents always argue the "negative," which is basically that these expanded efforts have deterred numerous attacks). (Yet, as the embarrassingly slow response by federal agencies to Hurricane Katrina's devastation of New Orleans in 2005 shows, there has been little attention paid to basic infrastructure repair and maintenance, emergency medical response, and systematic evacuation procedures.) But the security has had consequences. First, numerous foreign visitors, as well as U.S. citizens reentering the United States, have been checked and reminded again about the power of others over their bodies. Second, while drug arrests were common at the Mexican border for decades, the expanded surveillance approach did help nab people with criminal records. Thus, for all practical purposes, this portion of investment in Homeland Security—justified to keep us safe from terrorists—has provided us with more criminals. According to one report,

> About 30,000 of the 680,000 undocumented migrants who were arrested from May through December were identified as having criminal records, compared with about 2,600 during the same period in 2002, more than an elevenfold increase. Criminal undocumented immigrants are those with past arrests or convictions for crimes ranging from shoplifting to murder. Since its start as a pilot program in 2003, the system has identified about 24 people suspected of homicide, 55 of rape and 225 of assault, according to Border Patrol statistics. (Marosi 2005)

The report did not include severe limitations that had been noted several months earlier. One problem was that the technology being used along the borders relied on a system—IDENT—that used "two fingers" for identification rather than a far more accurate system that collected data on "ten fingers." The former was less expensive and more readily available but also much less accurate:

> The letter quotes Stanford researcher Lawrence M. Wein, who said his study found that at best, with a software fix, the two-finger system would properly identify only about three of four people. Two weeks ago, Wein told the Homeland Security Committee that the "implications of our findings are disturbing."

Turner accused homeland security officials of failing to be "more forth-coming" about the limitations of their approach. Turner asked Ridge to direct homeland security officials to "preserve all documents and electronic communications" relating to their decision on fingerprints.

"I understand your desire to deploy biometric screening at our borders as quickly as possible," Turner said in his letter. "But more than three years after the 9/11 attacks, we have invested more than $700 million in an entry-exit system that cannot reliably do what the Department so often said it would: Use a biometric watch-list to keep known terrorists out of the country." (O'Harrow and Higham 2004)

The borders are "tighter" since the infusion of dollars, technology, and agents, but are they fundamentally safer? Moreover, what has been the price of capturing a few dozen serious criminals who have fled to Mexico? Only a partial answer can be given at this time, but it is clear that surveillance has been expanded and more accepted by U.S. as well as Mexican citizens, and there is every indication that more illegal—and dangerous—crossings are being attempted across hostile deserts. It is also very likely that innovative modes of resistance to the new technologies will flourish.

The politics of fear exists and functions quite well even if each new control effort slips into "virtual irrelevance" for many members of society. The policies and procedures are still there, have symbolic clout, and become quickly reinforced when events—or skilled propagandists—call for them. Simply expanding the politics of fear via surveillance does not mean that all individuals are frightened to the point of inaction or that they tremble before those in power. To the contrary, like any negative reinforcement, surveillance and the tools of the politics of fear lose their effectiveness over time and with use. Children, prison inmates, students, and other creative citizens develop their own meanings about surveillance, most of which involve disrespect and combativeness. One of the ironies of expanded social control, then, is that efforts to regulate and protect at one point in time quickly become intrusions and obstacles to overcome at another point in time. This is particularly true when different audiences are involved at the different moments of control. Younger people, for example, may take for granted many of the original breaches of privacy by surveillance, but they are also likely to situationally disrespect the rules and the agents that enforce them. For example, many young people in the United States have violated rules (and sometimes state and federal laws) by taking contraband alcohol, drugs, weapon, or fireworks into protected places, such as stadiums, theaters, and commercial aircraft. Surveillance, then, does not always restrict activities; in some instances, it even promotes undesirable behavior. On the one hand, there are many instances where armed robbers "perform" before cameras. On the other hand, audiences, while aware of increased surveillance, may disregard it over time or develop various resistance strategies (e.g., covering faces while driving through intersections monitored by cameras, avoiding certain areas while driving drunk, or altering "body language" in retail stores).

These and other techniques of control that were examined in the previous chapters, including Internet surveillance, have social consequences even if individual actors adjust to them. It is the context of fear as the baseline, along with the expectation that authorities will constantly oppose it and protect us, that is important. This context involves an assumption of symbolic opposition to the sources of fear and other movements of change.

The discourse of fear permits widespread deviance from standard expectations of social control. Those who are really legitimate often believe that the rules really do not apply to them in the same way. Indeed, many U.S. citizens support profiling of likely suspects (e.g., minorities). For example, as noted previously, many law-abiding citizens routinely speed, smuggle alcohol and drugs into secured environments, and complain bitterly when they are subjected to "security checks," often amounting to semi–strip searches, pat downs, and shakedowns in airports. Many of these same people, particularly women, believe the extensive propaganda about the threat of terrorism to the United States and voted for a president who has pursued an imperial foreign policy. Few object to the profiling of Muslim and "Middle Eastern–looking" people in order to defeat the terrorists, yet they want to be treated with respect. Higher-status people are not accustomed to having their bodies treated as mere objects before a security agent who is perhaps a member of a minority group. The status quo is perceived by audiences accustomed to life framed as fear as protective and necessary in order to prevent the breakdown of social life. The fear shield that is erected becomes reified as the only reality possible rather than as an opaque shield covering possibilities.

The discourse of fear underlies modern propaganda. It comes from claims makers' construction of certain atypical events (e.g., the abduction of a child) as typical, common, and likely to happen to "you." These events are presented as symptomatic of all social life. These repeated propaganda messages are presented through mass-media entertainment formats to draw on audiences' emotions of fear on the one hand while providing a refreshed perspective for framing and interpreting subsequent events as further examples of the need for more control on the other. Thus, propaganda involving symbols of fear and threat contributes to how situations are defined and shaped by the expanding symbolic fear machinery. Public expectations about order accompany the new symbolic frameworks, but this leads to more examples of disorder, which in turn call for yet tighter controls to protect the moral foundations from the dark forces of fear. So strong are these symbolic parameters that anyone who questions the process or challenges the assumptions is likely to be the most visible and easily targeted threat to order.

The politics of fear quickly transforms many people into politicians of fear. We begin to self-monitor our language, behavior, and perspective. I have in mind the way in which everyday-life activities are monitored for compatibility with prevailing language, discourse, and assumptions underlying the politics of fear before they are carried out. One important consequence is that social actors become aware of this threat and begin to monitor their conduct through what Marx (1988) has referred to as "auto surveillance." This may be done by simply refraining from certain activities (e.g., not renting pornographic videos because someone will find out or writing letters to the editor of a repressive newspaper) or not going to certain places or participating in activities that challenge official rulings and programs (e.g., protest marches and demonstrations). A Canadian commented on the implications of this expanding surveillance gaze:

> "At some point, you start asking yourself, as you do in societies that aren't free, should I do this particular thing or not?" says Radwanski. "Not because it might be illegal or wrong, but because of how it might look to watchers of the state." (*Toronto Star*, May 12, 2003, p. A01)

Altering language is one of the most important ways that people display the politics of fear. The use of disclaimers or amending the meaning of our words prior to uttering them is increasingly common (Hewitt and Stokes 1975). For example, someone who opposes a foreign war might say to another whose views differ, "I support our troops, but I am not sure that this war was justified," or, "I am very patriotic and concerned about being attacked, but we need to plan our military action more carefully." Disclaimers enable us to maintain membership while skirting the edge of an issue that fundamentally challenges the very foundation and meaning of that membership. It is a covering device to protect us from outrage and scorn and, above all, from having our own legitimacy questioned by family, friends, peers, and fellows with whom we speak. Such caution is widespread in a world run on fear.

Citizenship is affected by the politics of fear. Successful politicians of fear obliterate the sanctity of citizenship, and they do this one case at a time. Bush administration officials engaged in numerous civil rights violations by arresting people and holding them without charge, denying access to attorneys, and conspiring with foreign governments to torture persons suspected of terrorism (Herbert 2005; Jehl and Johnston 2005).

The Bush administration's secret program to transfer suspected terrorists to foreign countries for interrogation has been carried out by the Central Intelligence Agency under broad authority that has allowed it to act without case-by-case approval from the White House or the State or Justice Departments, according to current and former government officials.

The unusually expansive authority for the C.I.A. to operate independently was provided by the White House under a still-classified directive signed by President Bush within days of the Sept. 11, 2001, attacks at the World Trade Center and the Pentagon, the officials said.

The process, known as rendition, has been central in the government's efforts to disrupt terrorism, but has been bitterly criticized by human rights groups on grounds that the practice has violated the Bush administration's public pledge to provide safeguards against torture. (Jehl and Johnston 2005)

They count on individual cases "blowing over" and not getting much attention, weakening the opposition, and, above all, silencing any news organizations that insist on publicizing such illegal conduct. These illegal acts are ensconced in a rhetoric of patriotism and moral justification, all wrapped up in the slogan "war on terrorism." Individual rights, we learn now (and learned in Hitler's Germany), are secondary to collective security; this means that citizenship becomes a matter of convenience, not a right that can be situationally lifted for a campaign of fear.

I have stressed throughout this book that citizenship all but disappears in a mass-media age, where the emphasis is on marketing and efficiency. Members of our society are far more likely to be regarded as audiences than as individual citizens with rights who are part of a collectivity that shares certain assumptions and indeed is represented by those who place citizen values above that of the market or control or power. After all, citizenship involves the theoretical relevance of the symbolic uses of fear with audiences' everyday life. Note that I am stressing audiences rather than citizens because in a mass-media age, all significant role relationships are governed by the market standard of justice by people in power. People simply make up the audiences for products and services. Politicians and corporate profits are turned on this basis, and even education and religion redefine students and congregations/parishioners/believers as clients and customers. Most of these relationships are shaped by mass-media and popular-culture discourse about membership and eligibility. For example, medical insurance is connected to jobs, and adequate housing is a feature of income, as is education. Minimal health care for the elderly, provided by Medicare, does not even include dental coverage. What people receive is a feature of markets rather than rights. And we exist in markets as audiences and consumers.

The context for the politics of fear that I am presenting is quite different from the classical notion of citizenship. T. H. Marshall (1965) and others

stressed that citizenship was constituted gradually by adding socially endowed rights to individuals, including civil rights (eighteenth century),
political rights (nineteenth century), and social rights (twentieth century).
Increasingly, citizen rights are subservient to market principles. This
means that individuals, organizations, and agencies that control markets
essentially control and regulate many aspects of everyday life. Conventional notions of inequality, freedom, and injustice fade in the dim neon
lights of markets and cast faint shadows in the glare of economic utility.
Increasingly, we regulate activities and attend to social problems insofar
as they are critical for markets rather than for human needs and suffering.
An exception is when natural disasters, disease, or conflict are amplified
by the mass media. Federal and state aid (e.g., food, shelter, and even low-
interest loans) will be given to all people if they are deemed to be victims
of natural disasters. But the notion of disaster is short-lived, and when
routine conditions return, the aid will be withdrawn no matter how bad
those conditions may be. What makes these situations different is partly a
collective sense that human suffering due to natural disasters should be
avoided. The message is amplified when mass-media images of suffering
are carried into homes throughout the country. However, routine suffering and deprivation related to poor housing, health, education, and dim
prospects for the future are by their very nature not sensational, are seldom stressed by the mass media, and therefore are tolerated (Newman
1999).

After completing a book like this, it would be immoral to not offer some
general guidelines for a way out. I cannot condone the politics of fear that
have dominated much of the modern world. I take a firm position on this
and offer the following modest comments. The politics of fear is relevant
for social life because it influences our activities, meanings, routines, and
perspectives. It is difficult to undo the policies and procedures that expand control and fear, partly because, as I noted previously, it becomes
taken for granted by the next generation. These effects can be reduced
through critical thinking and awareness of the social changes and the implications of blanket adjustments in security and policy. First, this requires
good investigation and clear language about the context, nature, and consequences of certain changes. Too often journalists and others who have
the public ear operate as though all these changes are unproblematic and
helpful. They are seldom reviewed, discussed, and examined critically, especially months or years following the event or events that helped launch
them. Previous chapters discussed drug policies, mandatory sentencing,
and foreign policy as examples. Second, very little of any consequence occurs in our society without popular culture. I expect that we will see more
investigative reports, movies, and television programs that dramatize the
injustice and oppression that result from this expansive control. Third, the

courts and aggressive attorneys—probably younger ones—should pursue both individual and class-action suits on behalf of those whose basic civil rights have been violated by specific policies and legislation. A fourth suggestion that I offer is partly informed by my doubts that the third point mentioned will be very successful in higher courts in the United States since it is our own government that is culpable and has been very reluctant to enforce court rulings against itself. The suggestion is that we continue to pursue international tribunals for redress against the illegal actions of the United States. Fifth, politicians and other decision makers should be held accountable for their actions. This may entail symbolic protests against their speaking engagements, writing letters, or simply stating their egregious sins in appropriate forums. Sixth, this is the time for educators—parents, teachers, religious leaders, and good neighbors— to show courage and speak truth to power. We should inform our students and citizens about war programming and the deadly role it plays in darkening our future. We must tell the young people about another way, about the implications of social control and bad decisions. Seventh, scholars and researchers of all persuasions should attend once again to the subtle forms of propaganda, deviance, and resistance. The relevance of these for all aspects of social life, symbolic communication, and moral conduct should be explored and promoted when morally justifiable. The foundation of this moral reasoning, in my opinion, must be citizenship and civil rights. In our endeavor, let us not become what we're trying to undo, let us not forget how moral absolutism and entertainment got us to this point. Above all, we must continue to tell our students and whoever will listen to be aware of the propaganda project but to not be afraid.

References

ABA Journal. 2004. "Another Close Call: George Bush and John Kerry Comment on Key Issues in the 2004 Presidential Election Race." *ABA Journal* 90:50–54, 75.

ABC News. 2003. "The Plan." *Nightline*, March 5.

Adams, William C. 1981. *Television Coverage of the Middle East*. Norwood, N.J.: Ablex.

———. 1982. *Television Coverage of International Affairs*. Norwood, N.J.: Ablex.

Advertising Research Foundation. 2001. "The ARF Supports Ad Council Coalition against Terrorism." *Informed*, December, www.arfsite.org/Webpages/informed/vol4-no6/page4.htm.

Alali, A. Odasuo, and Gary W. Byrd. 1994. *Terrorism and the News Media: A Selected, Annotated Bibliography*. Jefferson, N.C.: McFarland.

Aldridge, Meryl, and Nicholas Hewitt, eds. 1994. *Controlling Broadcasting: Access Policy and Practice in North America and Europe*. Manchester: Manchester University Press.

Altheide, David L. 1976. *Creating Reality: How TV News Distorts Events*. Beverly Hills, Calif.: Sage.

———. 1985. *Media Power*. Beverly Hills, Calif.: Sage.

———. 1987a. "Ethnographic Content Analysis." *Qualitative Sociology* 10:65–77.

———. 1987b. "Media Logic and Social Interaction." *Symbolic Interaction* 10:129–38.

———. 1992. "Gonzo Justice." *Symbolic Interaction* 15:69–86.

———. 1993. "Electronic Media and State Control: The Case of Azscam." *Sociological Quarterly* 34:53–69.

———. 1994. "Postjournalism: Journalism Is Dead, Long Live Journalism." In *Controlling Broadcasting: Access Policy and Practice in North America and Europe*, edited by Meryl and Nicholas Hewitt Aldridge, 134–70. Manchester: Manchester University Press.

———. 1995. *An Ecology of Communication: Cultural Formats of Control*. Hawthorne, N.Y.: Aldine de Gruyter.

———. 1996. *Qualitative Media Analysis*. Newbury Park, Calif.: Sage.

———. 1997. " The News Media, the Problem Frame, and the Production of Fear." *Sociological Quarterly* 38:646–68.

———. 1999. "The Military-Media Complex." *Newsletter of the Sociology of Culture* 13:1 ff.

———. 2000. "Identity and the Definition of the Situation in a Mass Mediated Context." *Symbolic Interaction* 23:1–27.

———. 2002a. "Children and the Discourse of Fear." *Symbolic Interaction* 25:229–50.

———. 2002b. *Creating Fear: News and the Construction of Crisis*. Hawthorne, N.Y.: Aldine de Gruyter.

———. 2002c. "Towards a Mapping of the 'E' Audience." In *Postmodern Existential Sociology*, edited by Joseph A. and John M. Johnson Kotarba, 41–62. Thousand Oaks, Calif.: Sage.

———. 2003. "The Mass Media as a Social Institution." In *Handbook of Symbolic Interactionism*, edited by Larry T. and Nancy J. Herman Reynolds, 657–84. Walnut Creek, Calif.: AltaMira Press.

———. 2004. "Consuming Terrorism." *Symbolic Interaction* 27:289–308.

———. In press, a. "Consuming Terrorism." *Symbolic Interaction* 27.

———. In press, b. "Towards a Mapping of the 'E' Audience." In *Postmodern Existential Sociology*, edited by Joseph A. and John M. Johnson Kotarba. Thousand Oaks, Calif.: Sage.

Altheide, David L., Barbara Gray, Roy Janisch, Lindsey Korbin, Ray Maratea, Debra Neill, Joseph Reaves, and Felicia VanDeman. 2001. "News Constructions of Fear and Victim: An Exploration through Triangulated Qualitative Document Analysis." *Qualitative Inquiry* 7:304–22.

Altheide, David L., and John M. Johnson. 1980. *Bureaucratic Propaganda*. Boston: Allyn and Bacon.

Altheide, David L., and R. Sam Michalowski. 1999. "Fear in the News: A Discourse of Control." *Sociological Quarterly* 40:475–503.

Altheide, David L., and Robert P. Snow. 1979. *Media Logic*. Beverly Hills, Calif.: Sage.

———. 1991. *Media Worlds in the Postjournalism Era*. Hawthorne, N.Y.: Aldine de Gruyter.

American Civil Liberties Union. 1995. "ACLU Asks U.S. Supreme Court to Extend Free Speech Protection to Vietnam Veteran Who Reveres the American Flag." November 7, http://archive.aclu.org/news/n110795.html.

Amis, Dave. 2002. "Internet Anxieties." Internet Freedom, www.netfreedom.org/news.asp?item=184.

Anderson, Walt. 1997. *The Future of the Self: Inventing the Postmodern Person*. New York: J. P. Tarcher.

Anglen, Robert, and Dawn Gilbertson. 2005. "Feds Look at Taser's Actions." *Arizona Republic*, AI, www.azcentral.com/news/articles/0107taser07.html, January 7, 2005.

Arendt, Hannah. 1966. *The Origins of Totalitarianism*. New York: Harcourt Brace & World.

Armstrong, David. 2002. "Dick Cheney's Song of America: Drafting a Plan for Global Dominance." *Harper's Magazine*, October, 76–83.

Ashwill, Mark A. 2003. "New American Century Group Abuses U.S. Power." *Buffalo News*, May 4, H5.

Associated Press. 2001. "Gun Industry Uses Sept 11 to Sell Weapons; Gun Industry Watch to Launch Counter-Campaign." *U.S. Newswire, Inc.*, December 6, Lexis/Nexis.

Atlas, James. 2003. "The Nation: Leo-Cons; A Classicist's Legacy: New Empire Builders." *New York Times*, May 4, sec. 4, p. 1, col. 3.

Baer, Justin, and William J. Chambliss. 1997. "Generating Fear: The Politics of Crime Reporting." *Crime, Law and Social Change* 27:87–107.

Bailey, Frankie Y., and Donna C. Hale. 1998. *Popular Culture, Crime, and Justice*. Belmont, Calif.: Wadsworth.

Baker, Al. 2001. "A Nation Challenged: Personal Security; Steep Rise in Gun Sales Reflects Post-Attack Fears." *New York Times*, December 16, p. 1, col. 3.

Baker, Kevin. 2001. "The Year in Ideas: A to Z.; American Imperialism, Embraced." *New York Times*, December 9, sec. 6, p. 53, col. 1.

Barnouw, Erik. 1990. *Tube of Plenty: The Evolution of American Television*. New York: Oxford University Press.

Barry, John, Michael Hirsh, and Michael Isikoff. 2004. "The Roots of Torture: The Road to Abu Ghraib Began after 9/11, When Washington Wrote New Rules to Fight a New Kind of War," www.msnbc.msn.com/id/4989422/site/newsweek, May 24.

Barson, Michael, and Steven Heller. 2001. *Red Scared! The Commie Menace in Propaganda and Popular Culture*. San Francisco: Chronicle Books.

Becker, Howard Saul. 1973. *Outsiders: Studies in the Sociology of Deviance*. New York: Free Press.

Beckett, Katherine. 1996. "Culture and the Politics of Signification: The Case of Child Sexual Abuse." *Social Problems* 43:57–76.

Beniger, James R. 1986. *The Control Revolution: Technological and Economic Origins of the Information Society*. Cambridge, Mass.: Harvard University Press.

Bennett, James. 2001. "Israel Wants Cease-Fire to Precede Truce Talks." *New York Times*, September 16, 1.

Bennett, W. Lance. 1988. *News: The Politics of Illusion*. New York: Longman.

Benson, Miles. 2002. "In the Name of Homeland Security, Telecom Firms Are Deluged with Subpoenas." Newhouse News Services. June 7, 2002, www.newhouse.com/archive/story1a041002.html.

Best, Joel, ed. 1995. *Images of Issues*. Hawthorne, N.Y.: Aldine de Gruyter.

———. 1999. *Random Violence: How We Talk about New Crimes and New Victims*. Berkeley: University of California Press.

Best, Joel, and J. Horiuchi. 1985. "The Razor Blade in the Apple: The Social Construction of Urban Legends." *Social Problems* 35:488–99.

Betin, Christophe, Emmanuel Martinais, and Marie-Christine Renard. 2003. "Security, Video Surveillance and the Construction of Deviance: The Example of the Center of Lyon." *Deviance et Societe* 27:3–24.

Bickley, Dan. 2004. "Memorial Adds to Legend." *Arizona Republic*, May 4, C1.

Biressi, Anita, and Heather Nunn. 2003. "Video Justice: Crimes of Violence in Social/Media Space." *Space and Culture* 6:276–91.

Blumer, Herbert. 1962. "Society as Symbolic Interaction." In *Human Behavior and Social Processes*, edited by A. M. Rose, 179–92. Boston: Houghton Mifflin.

———. 1969. *Symbolic Interactionism: Perspective and Method.* Englewood Cliffs, N.J.: Prentice Hall.

Brunsma, David L. 2004. *The School Uniform Movement and What It Tells Us about American Education: A Symbolic Crusade.* Lanham, Md.: Scarecrow Education.

Brunsma, David L., and Kerry A. Rockquemore. 1998. "The Effects of Student Uniforms on Attendance, Behavior Problems, Substance Use, and Academic Achievement." *Journal of Educational Research* 92:53–62.

Buchanan, Patrick J. 2001. "Whose War Is This?" *USA Today*, September 27, 15A.

Budzilowicz, Lisa M. 2002. "Framing Responsibility on Local Television News." Local TV News Media Project, University of Delaware.

Bumiller, Elisabeth. 2002. "U.S. Must Act First to Battle Terror, Bush Tells Cadets." *New York Times*, June 2, 1.

Burt, Tim, and Alexander Nicoll. 2002. "Action Stations: The US Defence Sector Is Attracting Renewed Interest from Investors as Contractors Race to Benefit from Sharp Increases in Pentagon Spending." *Financial Times*, February 27, 18.

Burton, Jason. 2002. "The People versus Larry Matthews." June 14, 2002. www .netfreedom.org/news.asp?item=22.

Calderon, Rodolfo Vera. 2003. "The United States Invasion of Panama: A Tri-Dimensional Analysis." *Entrecaminos*, www.georgetown.edu/sfs/programs/ clas/Pubs/entre2003/Panama.html.

Campbell, David. 1998. *Writing Security: United States Foreign Policy and the Politics of Identity.* Minneapolis: University of Minnesota Press.

Carey, James. 1989. *Communication as Culture: Essays on the Media and Society.* Boston: Unwin Hyman.

Carr, David. 2002. "The Media Business; Rolling Stone, Struggling for Readers, Names Briton as Editor." *New York Times*, January 13, 5C.

———. 2003. "White House Listens When Weekly Speaks." *New York Times*, March 11, 1.

Cavender, Gray. 2004. "Media and Crime Policy: A Reconsideration of David Garland's *The Culture of Control.*" *Punishment and Society* 6:335–48.

Cerulo, Karen. 1997. "Identity Construction: New Issues, New Directions." *Annual Review of Sociology* 23:385–409.

Cerulo, Karen A. 1998. *Deciphering Violence: The Cognitive Structure of Right and Wrong.* New York: Routledge.

———. 2002. "Individualism Pro Tem: Reconsidering U.S. Social Relations." In *Culture in Mind: Toward a Sociology of Culture and Cognition*, edited by Karen A. Cerulo, 135–71. New York: Routledge.

Cerulo, Karen, M. M. Ruane, and M. Chayko. 1992. "Technological Ties That Bind: Media Generated Primary Groups." *Communication Research* 19:109–29.

Chaptman, Dennis. 2002. "State High Court Case Tests Child Enticement Law in Internet 'Stings.'" *Milwaukee Journal Sentinel*, January 7, 1A.

Chen, David W. 2002a. "Lure of Millions Fuels 9/11 Families' Feuding." *New York Times*, June 17, A1.

———. 2002b. "Many Relatives, Wary and Anguished, Shun Sept. 11 Fund." *New York Times*, January 1, B1.

———. 2002c. "Struggling to Sort Out 9/11 Aid to Foreigners." *New York Times*, June 27, A1.

———. 2004. "New Study Puts Sept. 11 Payout at $38 Billion." *New York Times* November 9, www.nytimes.com/2004/11/09/nyregion/09victim.html?ex= 1101020832&ei=1&en=0aa7354723c0205e.

Chermak, Steven. 1995. *Victims in the News: Crime and the American News Media*. Boulder, Colo.: Westview Press.

Chiricos, Ted, Sarah Eschholz, and Marc Gertz. 1997. "Crime, News and Fear of Crime: Toward an Identification of Audience Effects." *Social Problems* 44:342–57.

Chiricos, Ted, Kathy Padgett, and Marc Gertz. 2000. "Fear, TV News, and the Reality of Crime." *Criminology* 38:755–85.

Chomsky, Noam, National Film Board of Canada, and Necessary Illusions. 1992. VHS. *Manufacturing Consent: Noam Chomsky and the Media*. Directed by Mark Achbar and Peter Wintonick. Montreal: Necessary Illusions.

Churchill, Ward, and Jim Vander Wall. 1990. *The Cointelpro Papers: Documents from the FBI's Secret Wars against Domestic Dissent*. Boston: South End Press.

Cicourel, Aaron Victor. 1974. *Cognitive Sociology: Language and Meaning in Social Interaction*. New York: Free Press.

CNN. 2001. *CNN Late Edition with Wolf Blitzer*, July 29, http://transcripts .cnn.com/TRANSCRIPTS/0107/29/le.00.html.

Coleman, Roy, and Joe Sim. 2000. "'You'll Never Walk Alone': CCTV Surveillance, Order and Neo-Liberal Rule in Liverpool City Centre." *British Journal of Sociology* 51:623–39.

Collom, Lindsey. 2004. "Tillman's Character Is Celebrated." *Arizona Republic*, May 9, A1.

Columbia Journalism Review Staff. 2004. "Brits vs. Yanks: Who Does Journalism Right." *Columbia Journalism Review*, May/June, 44–49, www.cjr.org/issues/ 2004/3/brits-yanks.asp.

Comstock, George. 1980. *Television in America*. Beverly Hills, Calif.: Sage.

———. 1991. *Television in America*. Newbury Park, Calif.: Sage.

Comstock, George A., and Erica Scharrer. 1999. *Television: What's On, Who's Watching, and What It Means*. San Diego: Academic Press.

Cooney, Daniel, and Omar Sinan. 2004. "More Than 5,500 Iraqis Killed during 1 Year." *Arizona Republic*, May 24, A4, www.azcentral.com/arizonarepublic/ news/articles/0524iraq-violent24.html.

Couch, Carl. 1995. "Oh, What Webs Those Phantoms Spin (SSSI Distinguished Lecture, 1994)." *Symbolic Interaction* 18:229–45.

Couch, Carl J. 1984. *Constructing Civilizations*. Greenwich, Conn.: JAI Press.

Couch, Carl J., David R. Maines, and Shing-Ling Chen. 1996. *Information Technologies and Social Orders*. New York: Aldine de Gruyter.

Couch, Carl J., Stanley L. Saxton, and Michael A. Katovich. 1986. *The Iowa School*. Greenwich, Conn.: JAI Press.

Cunningham, Brent. 2003. "Re-Thinking Objectivity." *Columbia Journalism Review*, July/August, 24–32.

Curl, Joseph. 2003. "Press Corps Doyenne Gets No Notice." *Common Dreams Newscenter*, October 7, 2005, www.commondreams.org/headlines03/0307-07.htm.

Curtis, Adam. 2004. "The Power of Nightmares: The Rise of the Politics of Fear."

Dahlgren, Peter, and Colin Sparks. 1992. *Journalism and Popular Culture*. London: Sage.

Davis, J. C. 1986. *Fear, Myth, and History: The Ranters and the Historians*. Cambridge: Cambridge University Press.

DeFleur, Melvin L., and Sandra Ball-Rokeach. 1982. *Theories of Mass Communication*. New York: Longman.

Denzin, Norman K. 1991. *Images of Postmodern Society: Social Theory and Contemporary Cinema*. London: Sage.

———. 1995. *The Cinematic Society: The Voyeur's Gaze*. London: Sage.

———. 2003. "Cultural Studies." In *Handbook of Symbolic Interactionism*, edited by Larry T. and Nancy J. Herman-Kinney Reynolds, 997–1019. Lanham, Md.: Rowman & Littlefield/AltaMira.

Der Derian, James. 2002. "The War of Networks." *Theory and Event* 5, http://muse.jhu.edu/journals/theory_and_event/v005/5.4derderian.html.

De Young, Mary. 2004. *The Day Care Ritual Abuse Moral Panic*. Jefferson, N.C.: McFarland.

Ditton, Jason. 2000. "Crime and the City: Public Attitudes towards Open-Street CCTV in Glasgow." *British Journal of Criminology* 40:692–709.

Doob, Leonard. 1966. *Public Opinion and Propaganda*. Hamden, Conn.: Archon Books.

Douglas, Jack D. 1970. *Deviance and Respectability: The Social Construction of Moral Meanings*. New York: Basic Books.

Doyle, Aaron. 2001. "How Television Influences Social Institutions: The Case of Policing and Criminal Justice." Doctoral diss., University of British Columbia.

Edelman, Murray J. 1985. *The Symbolic Uses of Politics*. Urbana: University of Illinois Press.

Editorial. 2004. "Spread the War Blame: The CIA Made Some Big Mistakes about Iraq, but It Should Not Be Made a Scapegoat for the Invasion." *Atlanta Journal-Constitution*, July 14, 10A.

Eggen, Dan. 2002. "Airports Screened Nine of Sept. 11 Hijackers, Officials Say: Kin of Victims Call for Inquiry into Revelation." *Washington Post*, March 2, A11.

Ekecrantz, J. 1998. "Modernity, Globalisation and Media." *Sociologisk Forskning* 35:33–60.

Electronic Frontier Foundation. 2001. "EFF Analysis of the Provisions of the USA PATRIOT Act That Relate to Online Activities (Oct 31, 2001)." Electronic Frontier Foundation. www.eff.org/Privacy/Surveillance/Terrorism_militias/20011031_eff_usa_patriot_analysis.html.

Electronic Privacy Information Center. 2002. "Public Opinion on Privacy." June 7, 2002. www.epic.org/privacy/survey.

Ellenius, Allan, and European Science Foundation. 1998. *Iconography, Propaganda, and Legitimation*. New York: Oxford University Press.

Ellin, Nan. 1997. *Architecture of Fear*. New York: Princeton Architectural Press.

Engel, Matthew. 2002. "War on Afghanistan: American Media Cowed by Patriotic Fever, Says Network News Veteran." *The Guardian*, May 17, 4.

Ericson, Richard V. 1993. "Is Anyone Responsible? How Television Frames Political Issues" (book review). *American Journal of Sociology* 98:1459–63.

———, ed. 1995. *Crime and the Media*. Brookfield, Vt.: Dartmouth University Press.

Ericson, Richard Victor, Patricia M. Baranek, and Janet B. L. Chan. 1987. *Visualizing Deviance: A Study of News Organization*. Toronto: University of Toronto Press.

———. 1989. *Negotiating Control: A Study of News Sources*. Toronto: University of Toronto Press.

———. 1991. *Representing Order: Crime, Law and Justice in the News Media*. Toronto: University of Toronto Press.

Ericson, Richard V., and Kevin D. Haggerty. 1997. *Policing the Risk Society*. Toronto: University of Toronto Press.

Espeland, Wendy Nelson. 2002. "Commensuration and Cognition." In *Toward a Sociology of Culture and Cognition*, edited by Karen A. Cerulo, 63–88. New York: Routledge.

Ewen, Stuart. 1976. *Captains of Consciousness: Advertising and the Social Roots of the Consumer culture*. New York: McGraw-Hill.

———. 1999. *All Consuming Images: The Politics of Style in Contemporary Culture*. New York: Basic Books.

Fairness and Accuracy in Reporting. 2003. "In Iraq Crisis, Networks Are Megaphones for Official Views," www.fair.org/reports/iraq-sources.html.

Ferraro, Kenneth F. 1995. *Fear of Crime: Interpreting Victimization Risk*. Albany: State University of New York Press.

Ferrarotti, Franco. 1988. *The End of Conversation: The Impact of Mass Media on Modern Society*. New York: Greenwood Press.

Ferrell, Jeff, and Clinton R. Sanders. 1995. *Cultural Criminology*. Boston: Northeastern University Press.

Fishman, Mark, and Gray Cavender. 1998. *Entertaining Crime: Television Reality Programs*. New York: Aldine de Gruyter.

Flannery, Pat. 2004. "Spirited Memorial for Athlete Turned Soldier." *Arizona Republic*, May 4, AI.

Flatten, Mark. 1993. "Policing for Profits." *Tribune Newspapers*, November 21–26.

Fowler, Roger. 1991. *Language in the News: Discourse and Ideology in the British Press*. London: Routledge.

Fox, Primm. 2001. "RSA Conference: Hackers, Threats and Security Concerns Dominate." *Computer World*, www.computerworld.com/securitytopics/security/story/0,10801,59469,00.html.

Fritz, Noah, and David L. Altheide. 1987. "The Mass Media and the Social Construction of the Missing Children Problem." *Sociological Quarterly* 28:473–92.

Frykholm, Amy Johnson. 2004. *Rapture Culture: Left Behind in Evangelical America*. Oxford: Oxford University Press.

Furedi, Frank. 1997. *Culture of Fear: Risk-Taking and the Morality of Low Expectation*. London: Cassell.

Gale, Peter M. 2002. "Hansonism, Howard and Representations: The Politics of Fear." Paper presented to the International Sociological Association, XV World Congress of Sociology, Brisbane, July 7–13, 2002.

Gamson, William A., David Croteau, William Hoynes, and Theodore Sasson. 1992. "Media Images and the Social Construction of Reality." *Annual Review of Sociology* 18:373–93.

Gans, Herbert J. 1979. *Deciding What's News: A Study of CBS Evening News, NBC Nightly News, Newsweek, and Time.* New York: Pantheon.

Garfinkel, Harold. 1967. *Studies in Ethnomethodology.* Englewood Cliffs, N.J.: Prentice Hall.

Garland, Catherine Ann. 1997. "The Context of Fear as an Indication of Healthy Community Investment: 80 Low-Income Neighborhoods in Los Angeles." Thesis, University of California, Irvine.

Garland, David. 2001. *The Culture of Control: Crime and Social Order in Contemporary Society.* Chicago: University of Chicago Press.

Gattiker, Urs E. 2001. *The Internet as a Diverse Community: Cultural, Organizational, and Political Issues.* Mahwah, N.J.: Lawrence Erlbaum Associates.

Gattone, Charles. 1996. "Media and Politics in the Information Age." *International Journal of Politics, Culture and Society* 10:193–202.

Gerber, Rudolph J. 2001. "On Dispensing Injustice." *Arizona Law Review* 43:135–72.

Gerbner, G., and L. Gross. 1976. " The Scary World of TV's Heavy Viewer." *Psychology Today,* April, 89–91.

Gerbner, G., L. Gross, M. Morgan, N. Signorelli, and M. Jackson-Beeck. 1978. "Cultural Indicators: Violence Profile No. 9." *Journal of Communication* 28:176–207.

Gerth, Hans H. 1992. "Crisis Management of Social Structures: Planning, Propaganda and Societal Morale." *International Journal of Politics, Culture and Society* 5:337–59.

Glassner, Barry. 1999. *The Culture of Fear: Why Americans Are Afraid of the Wrong Things.* New York: Basic Books.

Gold, Philip. 2002. "An Anti-War Movement of One." *Seattle Weekly,* September 11, 21.

Goodall, H. L., Jr. 2004. "Why We Must Win the War on Terror: Communication and the Future of National Security," http://hdshc.asu.edu/comweb/goodall/the_cold_war_and_the_war_on_terror/.

Goodykoontz, Bill. 2004. "Emotional Words Have TV Stations Scrambling." *Arizona Republic,* May 4, A10.

Gordon, Phillip. 2002. "Judge Leads Fight for Workplace Privacy." *Denver Post,* September 20, B7.

Goulden, Joseph C. 1988. *Fit to Print: A. M. Rosenthal and His Times.* Secaucus, N.J.: L. Stuart.

Gouldner, Alvin Ward. 1970. *The Coming Crisis of Western Sociology.* New York: Basic Books.

Graber, Doris S. 1984. *Processing the News: How People Tame the Information Tide.* New York: Longman.

Griffith, Robert. 1987. *The Politics of Fear: Joseph R. McCarthy and the Senate.* Amherst: University of Massachusetts Press.

Grimm, Matthew. 2003. "Good News, Bad News." *American Demographics,* July/August, 36–37.

Grimshaw, Allen Day, and Peter J. Burke. 1994. *What's Going on Here? Complementary Studies of Professional Talk.* Norwood, N.J.: Ablex.

Gronbeck, Bruce E., Thomas J. Farrell, and Paul A. Soukup. 1991. *Media, Consciousness, and Culture: Explorations of Walter Ong's Thought*. Newbury Park, Calif.: Sage.

Grossberg, Lawrence, Ellen Wartella, and D. Charles Whitney. 1998. *Mediamaking: Mass Media in a Popular Culture*. Thousand Oaks, Calif.: Sage.

Grossman, Lawrence K. 1997. "Why Local TV News Is So Awful." *Columbia Journalism Review*, November/December, 21.

Gunter, Barry. 1987. *Television and the Fear of Crime*. London: John Libbey.

Halberstam, David. 2000. *The Powers That Be*. Urbana: University of Illinois Press.

Hall, Peter. 1988. "Asymmetry, Information Control, and Information Technology." In *Communication and Social Structure*, edited by David Maines and Carl J. Couch, 341–56. Springfield, Ill.: Thomas.

Hall, Peter M. 2003. "Interactionism, Social Organization, and Social Processes: Looking Back and Moving Ahead." *Symbolic Interaction* 26:33–56.

Hancock, Lynnell. 2001. "The School Shootings: Why Context Counts." *Columbia Journalism Review*, May/June, 76–77.

Heath, Linda, and Kevin Gilbert. 1996. "Mass Media and Fear of Crime." *American Behavioral Scientist* 39:379–86.

Hendershot, Heather. 2004. *Shaking the World for Jesus: Media and Conservative Evangelical Culture*. Chicago: University of Chicago Press.

Herbert, Bob. 2004. "Death Comes Knocking." *New York Times*, November 12, www.nytimes.com/2004/11/12/opinion/12herbert.html?th.

———. 2005. "Our Friends, the Torturers." *New York Times* February 18, www.nytimes.com/2005/02/18/opinion/18herbert.html?ex=1109394000&en=a8465 1749cc4f1d5&ei=5070.

Herman, Edward S., and Noam Chomsky. 2002. *Manufacturing Consent: The Political Economy of the Mass Media*. New York: Pantheon.

Hersh, Seymour M. 2004. "The Gray Zone: How a Secret Pentagon Program Came to Abu Ghraib," www.newyorker.com/printable/?fact/040524fa_fact, May 24.

Hertog, James K., and David P. Fan. 1995. "The Impact of Press Coverage on Social Beliefs: The Case of HIV Transmission." *Communication Research* 22:545–77.

Hewitt, John P. 1991. *Self and Society: A Symbolic Interactionist Social Psychology*. Needham Heights, Mass.: Allyn and Bacon.

Hewitt, John P., and Randall Stokes. 1975. "Disclaimers." *American Sociological Review* 40:1–11.

Hibbert, Captain Monte. 2004. "PAO Offers Interview Tips." *Snakebite* 4:1.

Higgins, Alexander G. 2004. "Red Cross Report Reveals Abuse Widespread." *Daily Texan*, May 11, www.dailytexanonline.com/media/paper410/news/2004/05/11/WorldNation/Red-Cross.Report.Reveals.Abuse.Widespread-680390.shtml.

Hirsch, Paul. 1980. "The 'Scary World' of the Non-Viewer and Other Anomalies: A Reanalysis of Gerbner et al. Findings, Part 1." *Communication Research* 7:403–56.

Hoffman, Claire. 2004. "As Anxiety Grows, So Does Field of Terror Study." *New York Times*, September 1, www.nytimes.com/2004/09/01/nyregion/01disaster.html?ex=1095428710&ei=1&en=ed0be3c7892d98c9.

Holstein, James A., and Jaber F. Gubrium. 2000. *The Self We Live By: Narrative Identity in a Postmodern World*. New York: Oxford University Press.

House, Billy. 2002. "Bush Gives FBI New Domestic Surveillance Powers." *Arizona Republic*, May 31, 2002. www.arizonarepublic.com/news/articles/0531fbi-ashcroft.html.

———. 2004. "Tillman Killed by Friendly Fire." *Arizona Republic*, May 29, 1.

House, Billy, and Mark Shaffer. 2003. "Mom, Hopi, Hero: Piestewa an Icon." *Arizona Republic*, April 10, www.azcentral.com/news/specials/iraq/articles/retro-piestewa.html.

Hunt, Arnold. 1997. "'Moral Panic' and Moral Language in the Media." *British Journal of Sociology* 48:629–48.

Hunt, Darnell M. 1999. *O.J. Simpson Facts and Fictions: News Rituals in the Construction of Reality.* Cambridge: Cambridge University Press.

Iyengar, Shanto. 1991. *Is Anyone Responsible? How Television Frames Political Issues.* Chicago: University of Chicago Press.

Iyengar, Shanto, and Donald M. Kinder. 1987. *News That Matters.* Chicago: University of Chicago Press.

Jackall, Robert, ed. 1994. *Propaganda.* New York: New York University Press.

Jackall, Robert, and Janice M. Hirota. 1999. *Experts with Symbols: Advertising, Public Relations, and the Ethics of Advocacy.* Chicago: University of Chicago Press.

———. 2000. *Image Makers: Advertising, Public Relations, and the Ethos of Advocacy.* Chicago: University of Chicago Press.

Jackson, Robert. 1946. "One Hundred and Eighty-Seventh Day: Robert Jackson's Closing Speech." Pp. Part 6. Nuremberg, Germany, www.courttv.com/archive/casefiles/nuremberg/.

James, Barry. 1983. "Missile Jitters Threaten to Split Western Alliance: Will NATO Countries Waver on 'Zero Option'?" United Press International, January 26.

James, Daryl. 2004. "Tillman Fliers Spur E-Mail Backlash." *The Tribune*, October 9, www.abor.asu.edu/1_the_regents/clips/100904.htm#Tillman%20fliers%20spur%20e-mail%20backlash.

Janofsky, Michael. 1999. "Journalist Sentenced to 18 Months in Internet Pornography Case." *New York Times*, May 9, A17.

Jehl, Douglas, and David Johnston. 2005. "Rule Change Lets C.I.A. Freely Send Suspects Abroad to Jails." *New York Times*, March 6, 2005, www.nytimes.com/2005/03/06/politics/06intel.html?ex=1110776400&en=e36cc36fc5ef2f81&ei=5070.

Jenkins, Philip. 1998. *Moral Panic: Changing Concepts of the Child Molester in Modern America.* New Haven, Conn.: Yale University Press.

———. 1999. *The Cold War at Home: The Red Scare in Pennsylvania, 1945–1960.* Chapel Hill: University of North Carolina Press.

Johnson, J. M. 1995. "Horror Stories and the Construction of Child Abuse." In *Images of Issues*, edited by Joel Best, 17–31. Hawthorne, N.Y.: Aldine de Gruyter.

Joseph, Nathan. 1986. *Uniforms and Nonuniforms: Communication through Clothing.* New York: Greenwood Press.

———. 1990. "Fashions in Uniform." Presented at the Brisbane International Sociological Association.

Joseph, Nathan, and Alex Nicholas. 1972. "The Uniform: A Sociological Perspective." *American Journal of Sociology* 77:719–30.

Kappeler, Victor E., Mark Blumberg, and Gary W. Potter. 1999. *The Mythology of Crime and Criminal Justice.* Prospect Heights, Ill.: Waveland Press.

Katz, Jack. 1987. "What Makes Crime 'News'?" *Media, Culture and Society* 9:47–75.

Kellner, Douglas. 1992. *The Persian Gulf TV War.* Boulder, Colo.: Westview Press.

———. 2003. *From 9/11 to Terror War: The Dangers of the Bush Legacy.* Lanham, Md.: Rowman & Littlefield.

Kerr, Donald M. 2000. "Internet and Data Interception Capabilities Developed by FBI." Federal Bureau of Investigation, www.fbi.gov/congress/congress00/kerr072400.htm.

Kimball, George. 2004. "Bitter Twist to the True Story of a Hero's End." *Irish Times,* May 31, 24.

Kimmelman, Michael. 2002. "In New York, Art Is Crime, and Crime Becomes Art." *New York Times,* December 18, www.nytimes.com/2002/12/18/arts/design/18FEAR.html?ex=1041231425&ei=1&en=14502da3abfe7b7f.

Kingston, Anne. 2002. "You're a Goof. Buy Our Beer: What the Canadian Ad Awards Reveal about Us." *Saturday Post,* April 20, SP 1.

Klapp, Orrin Edgar. 1962. *Heroes, Villains, and Fools: The Changing American Character.* Englewood Cliffs, N.J.: Prentice Hall.

Knickerbocker, Brad. 2002. "Return of the 'Military-Industrial Complex'?" *Christian Science Monitor,* February 13, 2.

Krugman, Paul. 2003. "Who's Accountable?" *New York Times,* June 10, www.nytimes.com/2003/06/10/opinion/10KRUG.html?ex=1056269380&ei=1&en=3e9d471867a5e53e.

Langford, Duncan. 2000. *Internet Ethics.* Houndmills: Macmillan.

Lauderdale, Pat, and Annamarie Oliverio. 2005. *Terrorism: A New Testament.* Whitby, ON: de Sitter Publications.

Leonard, Jack, and Monte Morin. 2002. "Stalking the Web Predator: A Colorado Homemaker Has Won Praise—and Arrests—for Her Efforts against Kiddie Porn. But Critics of Such Online Crusaders Call It a Form of Vigilantism." *Los Angeles Times,* January 17, A1.

Levy, Leonard Williams. 1996. *A License to Steal: The Forfeiture of Property.* Chapel Hill: University of North Carolina Press.

Lewis, Neil A. 2001. "Rebels in Black Robes Recoil at Surveillance of Computers." *New York Times,* August 8, 1, www.nytimes.com/2001/08/08/national/08COUR.html.

Leyden, John. 2001. "AV Vendors Split over FBI Trojan Snoops." *The Register,* November 27, www.theregister.co.uk/content/55/23057.html.

Lobe, Jim. 2003. "Politics-U.S.: Neo-Cons Quick to Turn Their Sights on Iran." Inter Press Service, May 26.

Lopez, George A., and Michael Stohl. 1984. *The State as Terrorist: The Dynamics of Governmental Violence and Repression.* Westport, Conn.: Greenwood Press.

Lyon, David. 2001. *Surveillance Society: Monitoring Everyday Life.* Philadelphia: Open University.

———. 2003. "Technology vs. 'Terrorism': Circuits of City Surveillance since September 11th." *International Journal of Urban and Regional Research* 27:666–78.

MacArthur, John R. 2003. "The Lies We Bought: The Unchallenged 'Evidence' for War." *Columbia Journalism Review,* May/June, 62–63, www.cjr.org/year/03/3/macarthur.asp (accessed May 31, 2003).

MacKuen, M., and S. L. Coombs. 1981. *More Than News: Media Power in Public Affairs.* Beverly Hills, Calif.: Sage.

Maines, David R. 2001. *The Faultline of Consciousness: A View of Interactionism in Sociology.* Hawthorne, N.Y.: Aldine de Gruyter.

Maines, David R., and Carl J. Couch. 1988. *Communication and Social Structure.* Springfield, Ill.: Charles C. Thomas.

Malec, Michael A. 1993. "Patriotic Symbols in Intercollegiate Sports during the Gulf War: A Research Note." *Sociology of Sport Journal* 10:98–106.

Mann, Jonathan, and Walter Rodgers. 2003. "A Look at the Failure to Find Any Weapons of Mass Destruction in Iraq." *CNN Insight,* June 3.

Manning, Peter K. 1998. "Media Loops." In *Popular Culture, Crime, and Justice,* edited by Frankie and Donna Hale Bailey, 25–39. Belmont, Calif.: West/Wadsworth.

Manning, Peter K., and Betsy Cullum-Swan. 1994. "Narrative, Content and Semiotic Analysis." In *Handbook of Qualitative Research,* edited by Norman K. Denzin and Yvonna S. Lincoln, 463–78. Newbury Park, Calif.: Sage.

Margolis, Howard. 1996. *Dealing with Risk: Why the Public and the Experts Disagree on Environmental Issues.* Chicago: University of Chicago Press.

Markham, Annette N. 1998. *Life Online: Researching Real Experience in Virtual Space.* Walnut Creek, Calif.: AltaMira Press.

Marosi, Richard. 2005. "Print System Nabs Migrant Criminals." *Arizona Republic,* February 20, A12, www.azcentral.com/arizonarepublic/news/articles/0220border20.html.

Marshall, T. H. 1965. *Class, Citizenship, and Social Development: Essays.* Garden City, N.Y.: Doubleday.

Marx, Gary T. 1988. *Undercover: Police Surveillance in America.* Berkeley: University of California Press.

Massing, Michael. 2003. "The Unseen War." *New York Review of Books,* 16–19, www.nybooks.com/articles/16293.

Massumi, Brian. 1993. *The Politics of Everyday Fear.* Minneapolis: University of Minnesota Press.

McDonald, James H. 1994. "Te(k)nowledge: Technology, Education, and the New Student Subject." *Science as Culture* 4:537–64.

McLuhan, Marshall. 1962. *The Gutenberg Galaxy: The Making of Typographic Man.* Toronto: University of Toronto Press.

———. 1964. *Understanding Media: The Extensions of Man.* New York: McGraw-Hill.

McLuhan, Marshall, and Quentin Fiore. 1967. *The Medium Is the Massage: An Inventory of Effects.* New York: Bantam.

McLuhan, Marshall, and Bruce R. Powers. 1989. *The Global Village: Transformations in World Life and Media in the 21st Century.* New York: Oxford University Press.

Mead, George Herbert, and Charles W. Morris. 1962. *Mind, Self, and Society from the Standpoint of a Social Behaviorist.* Chicago: University of Chicago Press.

Meyrowitz, Joshua. 1985. *No Sense of Place.* New York: Oxford University Press.

Miller, Greg. 1999. "Online Chat Is Sting of Choice in Illicit-Sex Cases." *Los Angeles Times,* September 25, AI.

Mills, C. Wright. 1940. "Situated Actions and Vocabularies of Motive." *American Sociological Review* 5:904–13.

———. 1959. *The Sociological Imagination*. New York: Grove Press.

Moehle, Kurt A., and Eugene E. Levitt. 1991. "The History of the Concepts of Fear and Anxiety." In *Clinical Psychology: Historical and Research Foundations*, edited by Clarence Eugene Walker et al., 159–82. New York: Plenum.

Monaco, James. 1978. *Media Culture: Television, Radio, Records, Books, Magazines, Newspapers, Movies*. New York: Dell.

Morin, Richard, and Dana Wilbank. 2004. "Most Think Truth Was Stretched to Justify Iraq War." *Washington Post*, February 13, A01.

Morrison, David E., and Howard Tumber. 1988. *Journalists at War: The Dynamics of News Reporting during the Falklands Conflict*. London: Sage.

MSNBC. 2001. "FBI Confirms 'Magic Lantern' Exists." MSNBC. June 7, 2002, www.msnbc.com/news/671981.asp?0si=-&cp1=1.

Musheno, Michael C., James P. Levine, and Denis J. Palumbo. 1978. "Television Surveillance and Crime Prevention: Evaluating an Attempt to Create Defensible Space in Public Housing." *Social Science Quarterly* 58:647–56.

Naphy, William G., and Penny Roberts. 1997. *Fear in Early Modern Society*. Manchester: Manchester University Press; distributed exclusively in the United States by St. Martin's Press.

Nash, Jeffrey E., and James M. Calonico. 2003. "The Economic Institution." In *Handbook of Symbolic Interactionism*, edited by Larry T. and Nancy J. Herman-Kinney Reynolds, 445–69. Lanham, Md: Rowman & Littlefield/AltaMira.

Natsis, James J. 2003. "Electoral Valuation: Did W.Va. Get Value for Electoral Votes Cast in 2000?" *Charleston Gazette*, June 26, P5A.

Newman, Katherine S. 1999. *No Shame in My Game: The Working Poor in the Inner City*. New York: Knopf and the Russell Sage Foundation.

Newman, Rachel. 2001. "The Day the World Changed, I Did, Too." *Newsweek*, October 1, 9.

Offe, Claus. 2002. "Political Liberalism, Group Rights and the Politics of Fear and Trust." *Hagar: International Social Science Review* 3:5–17.

O'Harrow, Robert, Jr., and Scott Higham. 2004. "2-Fingerprint Border ID System Called Inadequate." *Washington Post*, October 19, A08.

Oliverio, Annamarie. 1998. *The State of Terror*. Albany: State University of New York Press.

Pearson, Geoffrey. 1983. *Hooligan: A History of Respectable Fears*. London: Macmillan.

Perinbanayagam, Robert S. 1974. "The Definition of the Situation: An Analysis of the Ethnomethodological and Dramaturgical View." *Sociological Quarterly* 14:521–41.

———. 1986. "The Meaning of Uncertainty and the Uncertainty of Meaning." *Symbolic Interaction* 9:105–26.

Pew Charitable Trusts. 2002. "Internet and American Life." Pew Charitable Trusts, www.pewinternet.org/reports/reports.asp?Report=32&Section=ReportLevel1&Field=Level1ID&ID=119.

Pfuhl, Erdwin H., and Stuart Henry. 1993. *The Deviance Process*. New York: Aldine de Gruyter.

Pilger, John. 2002. "Axis of Evil: John Pilger Exposes the Frightening Agenda in Washington That Is Behind the United States Threat to World Peace." *Morning Star*, December 14, 19.

———. 2003. "What Now? Civil Disobedience Is the Sole Path Left for Those Who Cannot Support the Bush-Blair Pact of Aggression. Only Then Will Politicians on Both Sides of the Atlantic Be Forced to Recognise the Folly of Their Ways." *New Statesman*, March 17, www.newstatesman.com/200303170002.

Porter, David. 1997. *Internet Culture*. New York: Routledge.

Potter, J., and M. Wetherell. 1987. *Discourse and Social Psychology*. Thousand Oaks, Calif.: Sage.

Powell, Michael. 1999. "How to Bomb in Selling a War." *Washington Post*, May 27, C01.

Project for Excellence in Journalism. 2001. "The Look of Local News," www.journalism.org/resources/research/reports/localTV/2001/look.asp.

———. 2005. "The State of the News Media," www.stateofthemedia.org/2005/narrative_localtv_intro.asp?cat=1&media=6.

Prothero, Stephen. 2004. "Marketing the Messiah: Two Books Examine the Popular Appeal and Agendas of Evangelical Christians." *Washington Post*, April 18, BW09, www.washingtonpost.com/ac2/wp-dyn?pagename=article&contentId=A16231-2004Apr15&notFound=true.

Pyszczynski, Thomas A., Jeff Greenberg, and Sheldon Solomon. 2003. *In the Wake of 9/11: The Psychology of Terror*. Washington, D.C.: American Psychological Association.

Rand, Jonathan. 2004. *Fields of Honor: The Pat Tillman Story*. New York: Chamberlain Bros.

Reilly, Rick. 2004. "The Hero and the Unknown Soldier." *Sports Illustrated*, May 3, 80.

Remore, Ellen. 2003. "Your Views." *The Record*, March 2, 3.

Ricks, Thomas E. 2001. "Empire or Not? A Quiet Debate over U.S. Role." *Washington Post*, August 21, A01.

Robin, Corey. 2002. "Primal Fear." *Theory and Event* 5, http://muse.jhu.edu/journals/theory_and_event/v005/5.4robin.html.

———. 2004. *Fear: The History of a Political Idea*. Oxford: Oxford University Press.

Rosenzweig, David. 2000. "Internet Sex Probe Was a Trap, Court Says; Appeal: Federal Judges Free a Convicted Air Force Veteran and Criticize an E-Mail Sting Operation." *Los Angeles Times*, June 30, B1.

Roy, Arundhati. 2003. "Seize the Time." *In These Times*, July 7, 14.

Russell, Katheryn K. 1998. *The Color of Crime: Racial Hoaxes, White Fear, Black Protectionism, Police Harassment, and Other Macroaggressions*. New York: New York University Press.

Rutenberg, Jim, and Bill Carter. 2001. "Draping Newscasts with the Flag." *New York Times*, September 20, C8.

Ryan, Joan. 2002. "Media Feeding the Fear." *San Francisco Chronicle*, October 15, A23.

Saidi, Nicole. 2004. "Professor under Investigation for Posters." *The State Press*, www.abor.asu.edu/1_the_regents/clips/110104.htm#Professor's%20art%20sparks%20public%20outcry.

Savage, David G. 2002a. "Response to Terror; Courts Likely to Endorse FBI Policy, Experts Say; The Law: A Government Spying on Its People in Public Is Not Seen as a Violation of the 4th Amendment." *Los Angeles Times*, May 31, 22.

———. 2002b. "Ruling Halts Internet Limits; Computers: A U.S. Court Rejects a Law Forcing Public Libraries to Block Sexually Explicit Sites. The Government May Appeal the Case." *Los Angeles Times*, June 1, 12.

Schlesinger, Philip, Howard Tumber, and Graham Murdock. 1991. "The Media Politics of Crime and Criminal Justice." *British Journal of Sociology* 42:397–420.

Schneider, Jeffrey. 1997. "'The Pleasure of the Uniform': Masculinity, Transvestism, and Militarism in Heinrich Mann's *der Untertan* and Magnus Hirschfeld's *die Transvestiten.*" *Germanic Review* 72:183–200.

Schutz, Alfred. 1967. *The Phenomenology of the Social World.* Evanston, Ill.: Northwestern University Press.

Schwalbe, Michael, Sandra Godwin, Daphne Holden, Douglas Schrock, Shealy Thompson, and Michele Wolkomir. 2000. "Generic Processes in the Reproduction of Inequality: An Interactionist Analysis." *Social Forces* 79:419–52.

Scott, Marvin, and Stanford M. Lyman. 1968. "Accounts." *American Sociological Review* 33:46–62.

Shales, Tom. 2001. "Patriotism Advertising." *Washington Post*, December 30, 2, www.washingtonpost.com/ac2/wp-dyn?pagename=article&node=& contentId=A35030-2001Dec28.

Shapiro, Michael J. 1992. *Reading the Postmodern Polity: Political Theory as Textual Practice.* Minneapolis: University of Minnesota Press.

———. 1997. *Violent Cartographies: Mapping Cultures of War.* Minneapolis: University of Minnesota Press.

———. 2002. "Wanted, Dead or Alive." *Theory and Event* 5, http://muse.jhu.edu/ journals/theory_and_event/v005/shapiro.html.

Shaw, D. L., and M. E. McCombs. 1977. *The Agenda-Setting Function of the Press.* St. Paul, Minn.: West.

Shirlow, Peter, and Rachel Pain. 2003. "The Geographies and Politics of Fear." *Capital and Class* 80:15–26.

Sieber, Gary, and Michael J. Schmiedeler. 1996. *Cyberspace Virtual Unreality?* Princeton, N.J.: Film for the Humanities.

Signorelli, Nancy, and George Gerbner, eds. 1988. *Violence and Terror in the Mass Media: An Annotated Bibliography.* New York: Greenwood Press.

Signorelli, Nancy, George Gerbner, and Michael Morgan. 1995. "Violence on Television: The Cultural Indicators Project." *Journal of Broadcasting and Electronic Media* 39 (spring): 278–82.

Skogan, W., and M. Maxfield. 1981. *Coping with Crime.* London: Sage.

Slevin, James. 2000. *The Internet and Society.* Cambridge: Polity Press; Malden, Mass.: Blackwell.

Smith, Charles R. 2001. "F.B.I. vs. C.I.A.: Battle in Cyberspace." Newsmax.com, www.newsmax.com/archives/articles/2001/11/28/142513.shtml.

Smith, Gary. 2004. "Code of Honor: Pat Tillman 1976–2004." *Sports Illustrated*, May 3, 40–46.

Snow, Robert P. 1983. *Creating Media Culture.* Beverly Hills, Calif.: Sage.

Solomon, Sheldon, Jeff Greenberg, and Thomas A. Pyszczynski. 2004. "Fatal Attraction." *American Psychological Society* 17:13–15.

Soothill, Keith, and Sylvia Walby. 1991. *Sex Crime in the News.* London: Routledge.

Sparks, Chris. 2003. "Liberalism, Terrorism and the Politics of Fear." *Politics* 23:200–206.

Sparks, Richard. 1992. *Television and the Drama of Crime: Moral Tales and the Place of Crime in Public Life.* Milton Keynes: Open University Press.

Spector, Malcolm, and John I. Kitsuse. 1977. *Constructing Social Problems*. Menlo Park, Calif.: Cummings.

———. 1987. *Constructing Social Problems*. New York: Aldine de Gruyter.

Speier, Hans. 1969. *Social Order and the Risks of War: Papers in Political Sociology*. Cambridge, Mass.: MIT Press.

Staff of the *Washington Post*. 2005. "Tillman's Parents Lash Out at Army." *Washington Post*. May 23, 2005. http:www.eastvalleytribune.com/index.php?sty=41825.

Staff of the *New York Times*. 2003. "Fighting the War at Home." *New York Times*, October 15, 18, www.nytimes.com/2003/10/15/opinion/15WED2.html?ex=1067243348&ei=1&en=73a32367e2369883.

Staples, William G. 1997. *The Culture of Surveillance: Discipline and Social Control in the United States*. New York: St. Martin's Press.

———. 2000. *Everyday Surveillance: Vigilance and Visibility in Postmodern Life*. Lanham, Md.: Rowman & Littlefield.

Stepanek, Marcia. 2000. "Now, Companies Can Track Down Their Cyber-Critics: A New Service Allows Corporate Spinmeisters to Retaliate against Outspoken Citizens with 'Reeducation Efforts'—or Worse," www.businessweek.com/bwdaily/dnflash/july2000/nf00707g.htm?scriptFramed.

Stern, Ray. 2002. "Sex Tour Sting in Arizona Nabs 10: Law Enforcement Uses Web to Battle Child Molestation." *Tribune*, May 11, 1.

Stone, Gregory Prentice, and Harvey A. Farberman. 1970. *Social Psychology through Symbolic Interaction*. Waltham, Mass.: Ginn-Blaisdell.

Strom, Stephanie. 2002. "Families Fret as Charities Hold a Billion Dollars in 9/11 Aid." *New York Times*, June 23, 29.

Sullivan, Dan. 2001. "Washington Is Calling. Will Anyone Answer? Antimilitary Elitism at Top Universities Dissuades Our Brightest Young People from Serving Their Country." *Newsweek*, October 22, 12.

Sullivan, Tim. 2004. "Patriotism at Its Best Instinctive, Not Forced." *San Diego Union-Tribune*, www.signonsandiego.com/sports/sullivan/20040723-9999-1s23sullivan.html.

Surette, Ray. 1992. *Media, Crime, and Criminal Justice: Images and Realities*. Pacific Grove, Calif.: Brooks/Cole.

———. 1998. *Media, Crime and Criminal Justice: Images and Realities*. Belmont, Calif.: West/Wadsworth.

Surratt, Carla B. 2001. *The Internet and Social Change*. Jefferson, N.C.: McFarland.

Thiele, Leslie Paul. 1993. "Making Democracy Safe for the World: Social Movements and Global Politics." *Alternatives* 18:273–305.

Thomaz, Omar Ribeiro. 1997. "Bosnia-Herzegovina: The Victory of the Politics of Fear." *Novos Estudos CEBRAP* 47:3–18.

Tillman, Pat, Sr. 2004. "Pat Tillman Sr. Thanks the Valley." *Arizona Republic*, May 31, B6.

Toohey, Paul. 1999. "Ice-Cream Santa on US Child Sex Charges." *The Weekend Australian*, June 26, 7.

Traub, James. 2003. "The Next Resolution." *New York Times*, April 13, sec. 6, p. 50, col. 1.

Tunstall, Jeremy. 1994. *The Media Are American: Anglo-American Media in the World*. London: Constable.

Tunstall, Jeremy, and Michael Palmer. 1991. *Media Moguls*. London: Routledge.

Unsworth, Barry. 1995. *Morality Play*. London: Hamish Hamilton.

USA Today. 2001. "E-Monitoring of Workers Sparks Concerns." June 6, 2002, www.usatoday.com/life/cyber/tech/2001-05-29-worker-privacy.htm.

Uslaner, Eric M. 2000. "Trust, Civic Engagement, and the Internet." Pew Charitable Trusts. June 13, 2002, www.pewtrusts.com/pdf/vf_pew_interest_trust_paper.pdf.

van Dijk, Teun A. 1988. *News as Discourse*. Hillsdale, N.J.: Lawrence Erlbaum Associates.

Vidich, Arthur J. 1991. "Social Theory and the Substantive Problems of Sociology." *International Journal of Politics, Culture and Society* 4: 517–534.

Vogel, Steven. 1998. "Military Trains a Special Corps of Public Relations Troops; 3,500 Journalists a Year Are Schooled at Brand-New Center at Fort Meade." *Milwaukee Journal Sentinel*, October 25, 6.

Walker, Jesse. 2002. "Panic Attacks." *Reason*, March, 36–42.

Warr, Mark. 1980. "The Accuracy of Public Beliefs about Crime." *Social Forces* 59:456–70.

———. 1983. "Fear of Victimization: A Look at the Proximate Causes." *Social Forces* 61:1033–43.

———. 1985. "Fear of Rape among Urban Women." *Social Problems* 32:238–50.

———. 1987. "Fear of Victimization and Sensitivity to Risk." *Journal of Quantitative Criminology* 3:29–46.

———. 1990. "Dangerous Situations: Social Context and Fear of Victimization." *Social Forces* 68:891–907.

———. 1992. "Altruistic Fear of Victimization in Households." *Social Science Quarterly* 73:723–36.

Wasburn, Philo C. 2002. *The Social Construction of International News: We're Talking about Them, They're Talking about Us*. Westport, Conn.: Praeger.

Weiler, M., and W. B. Pearce. 1992. *Reagan and Public Discourse in America*. Tuscaloosa: University of Alabama Press.

Weisman, Robert. 2001. "FBI Waves 'Magic Lantern.'" News Factor Network. December 13, 2001, www.newsfactor.com/perl/story/15301.html.

Welsh, Brandon C., and David P. Farrington. 2003. "Effects of Closed-Circuit Television on Crime." *Annals of the American Academy of Political and Social Science* 587:110–35.

Westfeldt, Wallace, and Tom Wicker. 1998. *Indictment: The News Media and the Criminal Justice System*. Nashville: First Amendment Center.

Westphal, David. 2001. "Buildup Quickly Erasing Post-Cold War Peace Dividend: As the United States Mounts Its Campaign against Terrorism, Defense Spending Will Increase Rapidly." *Star Tribune*, October 8, 5A.

Willis, William James, and Albert Adelowo Okunade. 1997. *Reporting on Risks: The Practice and Ethics of Health and Safety Communication*. Westport, Conn.: Praeger.

Wilton, Mark. 2002. "A Paedophile's Story." *Centralian Advocate*, April 23, 5.

Wire Services. 2002. "Web-Based Child Porn Sting Leads to Raids on 200 Homes." *The Record*, May 9, A4.

Wojtusiak, Erward. 1982. "On the Problem of the Social Uniform: A Sociological Essay." *Kultura i Spoleczenstwo* 26:107–32.

Wu, Denis H. 2000. "Systematic Determinants of International News Coverage: A Comparison of 38 Countries." *Journal of Communication* 50:110–30.

Wuthnow, Robert., ed. 1992. *Vocabularies of Public Life: Empirical Essays in Symbolic Structure*. New York: Routledge.

Yavuz, M. Hakan. 2002. "The Politics of Fear: The Rise of the Nationalist Action Party (MHP) in Turkey." *Middle East Journal* 56:200–221.

Zagorin, Adam, and Timothy J. Burger. 2004. "Beyond the Call of Duty." *Time*, October, www.truthout.org/docs_04/102504V.shtml.

Zakaria, Fareed. 2002. "The Answer? A Domestic CIA." *Newsweek*, May 27, 39.

Zerubavel, Eviatar. 1985. *Hidden Rhythms: Schedules and Calendars in Social Life*. Berkeley: University of California Press.

Zhondang, P., and G. Kosicki. 1993. "Framing Analysis: An Approach to News Discourse." *Political Communication* 10:55–69.

Zillman, D., and J. Wakshlag. 1987. "Fear of Victimization and the Appeal of Crime Drama." In *Selective Exposure to Communication*, edited by D. Zillman and J. Bryant, 141–56. Hillsdale, N.J.: Lawrence Erlbaum Associates.

Zulaika, Joseba, and William A. Douglass. 1996. *Terror and Taboo: The Follies, Fables, and Faces of Terrorism*. New York: Routledge.

Index

Abu Ghraib prison, 68, 70
accounts, 15, 38, 40, 62, 65, 69, 70, 80, 81, 92, 114, 115, 126, 157, 164, 169, 187, 188, 189, 192, 196, 202, 208, 213; disclaimers, 218
Aljazeera, 51
Al Qaeda, 112, 162, 165
Amber Alert, 77; children and fear, 77
America's Most Wanted, 65
American Red Cross, 99
Annan, Kofi, 23
Ashcroft, John, 105, 132, 134, 144, 145; blaming critics, 105
audience, 1, 9, 23, 29–47; control narrative, 135; discourse of fear, 127; everyday life, 116; heroes and athletes, 186; postjournalism news, 182; target, 52; vocabulary of motives, 187; war programming, 159
Azscam, 25, 67

Balkans, 22
bank accounts, 99
baseball, 2, 3, 87, 190
bin Laden, Osama, 4, 19, 96, 97, 101, 106, 107, 111, 162, 166
breaking the news format, 183

Broadmor Elementary School, 31, 33, 34
bureaucratic trends, 88
Bush, George W., 3–13; crime control, 30; evil ones, 92; "first strike," 110; playing aviator, 5; terrorism and election, 7; torture, 69
Byrd, Robert, 176

Carnivore (computer program), 145–47
Cheney, Richard (Dick), 4, 5, 7, 105, 109, 161, 162, 168, 169, 171
CIA, 24, 26, 28, 70, 101, 103, 104, 145, 147, 162, 164, 181, 197, 208, 219
citizenship, 217. *See also* Patriot Act
claims makers, 74, 117, 123, 126, 183, 215
Clarke, Richard, 164, 165
COINTELPRO, 101, 145
collective memory, 17
communicating control, 16
communicating order and power, 88
communication, 8, 9, 10, 11, 12, 26, 40, 48–51, 52–56, 57, 59, 62, 65, 67, 72, 73, 74, 79, 88, 90, 91, 94, 95, 116, 134–37, 138, 140, 142, 145, 147, 149, 150, 154, 155, 156, 158, 183, 193, 205, 212, 219; broadcasting/narrowcasting, 52; computer-mediated, 138; control,

183; deceptive communication, 138; environment, 53; format of the Internet, 134; hierarchies, 55; identity, 49–54; international relations, 91; Internet and visual, 134–37, 138; power, 72; process, 137; resistance, 72; risk communication, 135, 149; social change, 72; surveillance, 136. *See also* mass media
control narrative, 134, 135, 154, 156; defined, 12
Conyers, John, Jr., 101–2
crime, 2, 203, 205, 208, 210–12; crises, 94; distorted media coverage, 75; drugs, 111; frames, 117; myths, 115; politics, 115; "terror story," 119; terrorism, 107; victimization, 114; why it is entertaining, 74
crime news, 65, 75, 76, 84; KVUE criteria, 84
critical criminology, 36
cultural logics, 71

Delgado, Carlos, 3
discourse of fear, 5, 12, 15, 16, 64, 73, 77, 79–84, 114, 115, 116, 117, 119, 120, 123, 126, 127, 128, 130, 150, 215; crime, 115; defined, 11
dispensing injustice, 211
Doyle, Leonard, 179
drug war, 10, 16, 21, 25, 30, 85, 97, 106, 113, 131; linked to terrorism, 106
drugs, 25, 28, 29, 30, 31, 36, 41, 62, 77, 79, 82, 83, 85, 94, 106, 107, 111, 119, 120, 149, 150, 208, 214, 215

E-audience, 54–55; defined, 196; information technology persona, 55
ecology of communication, 50
entertainment formats, 10, 38, 73, 74, 83, 193, 215
everyday life, 8, 10, 11, 12, 15, 16, 23, 34, 37, 49, 51, 52, 54, 58, 60, 72, 73, 74, 79, 84, 90, 94, 95, 110, 113, 114, 116, 123, 150, 154, 204, 209, 211, 214, 219, 220

Fairness and Accuracy in Reporting (FAIR), 118, 177
Falklands War, 29
FBI, 5, 26, 58, 70, 101, 103, 104, 132, 139, 141, 143, 144, 145, 146, 147, 148, 149, 150, 151, 152, 153, 206
fear and crime: emphasize children and innocence, 77; media trends and discourse, 76
fear and entertainment, 72; chronic and acute fear, 207; hoaxes, 81; lens of fear, 85; meaningful side of force, 21; political uses, 21; psychology, 5; symbolic environment, 84; tsunami, 17
"Five O'Clock Follies," 178
formal agents of social control, 66, 67, 83, 85, 115, 140, 148, 149, 150, 152, 153, 154, 206
formats, illustrated, 90
Fox news, 5, 32, 139, 166
framing, 36, 68, 79, 184, 215

gangs, 29, 31, 62, 76, 77, 79, 94, 120
Getler, Michael, 179
Gitlin, Todd, 106
Givens, Jess, 4
"God Bless America," 39
Goebbels, Josef, 47
"Golden Age of Wiretapping," 145
gonzo justice, 65, 66
Goodman, Ellen, 175
Grenada, 16, 27, 28, 167; Operation Urgent Fury, 27
Guantanamo Bay, 68, 69
gun industry, 96
Gunsmoke. See Strauss, Leo

Halliburton, 5
heroism, 14, 44, 182, 186, 188, 196, 202–3; hero as audience, 204; politics of fear, 202; propaganda, 186
Homeland Security, Department of, 70; airports, 102; media support, 104; promoting fear, 102; university benefits, 34, 37
Hurricane Katrina, 213

Hussein, Saddam, 5, 13, 27, 29, 157, 158, 159, 160, 161, 162, 164, 169, 175, 179, 181

ideal norms, 177
IDENT (computer system), 213
identity, 11, 14, 17, 21, 37, 40, 42, 49, 51, 52, 54, 55, 74, 81, 82, 83, 88, 89, 91, 93, 94, 98, 102, 111, 119, 123, 128, 129, 132, 137, 148, 150, 153, 186, 187, 189, 196, 197, 198, 199, 200–201; commensuration, 88; national, 88
ideology, 17, 18, 50, 100, 117; promotes mythology of evil, 29
immigrants, 94, 103, 105, 213
information technology, 9, 49, 50, 51, 52, 59, 62, 72, 136, 141, 183
infotainment, 84, 166, 169
Innocent Images, 150, 152; cyberpatrol, 152
Internet, 12, 34, 52, 53, 54, 63, 91, 101, 103, 131–56, 176, 183, 188, 190, 191, 196–205, 207–17; computer technology, 135; hackers and national security, 139; mediated interaction perspective, 156; microtechnology of surveillance, 136; monitoring communication, 138; paradox, 138; social control, 134; superpanoptic, 135; visible communication, 138
Internet stings and surveillance, 148; Cyberarmy Pedophilia Fighters, 154; Innocent Images, 150; Julie Posey, 154; Larry Matthews, 152; law, 141; Mark Poehlman, 153; Operation Candyland, 151
Iran-Contra scandal, 26; Oliver North, 26
Iraq War, 28, 52, 118, 157–58, 159, 161–63, 169, 176, 178, 180–84

Jackson, Robert. *See* Nuremberg trials
journalism, 29, 74, 76, 85, 118, 121, 152, 158, 171, 177, 178, 183, 184
journalists, 4, 21, 29, 59, 62, 67, 68, 69, 76, 101, 109, 118, 127, 150–60,

168–85, 196, 210, 211, 220; intimidation, 177; Rather's confession, 100

Kefauver Committee, 25
Kerry, John, 4, 181
Koppel, Ted, 103, 168
Kristol, William, 4, 19, 20, 168, 169, 170, 171, 173
KVUE, 83–85

Leahy, Patrick, 5
Leanos, John, 200
lens of fear, 84
Lynch, Jessica, 188

Magic Lantern, 132, 146, 147, 155
Marshall, T. H., 217
mass media, 1, 2, 8, 10, 20, 32, 34, 40, 45, 47, 48, 49, 54, 55, 57, 61, 62, 63, 66, 70, 74, 78, 79, 82, 91, 93, 104, 105, 110, 113, 115, 116, 130, 159, 182, 186, 200, 204, 206, 208, 209, 210, 218; defined, 48; formats, 10, 47, 67
McCain, John, 190
McCarthy hearings, 17
McGeogh, Holly, 1, 205
media logic, 38, 47, 50–67, 90, 91, 113, 116, 158, 182, 193, 197, 210; defined, 9, 116; propaganda, 158
mediated interaction, 136
Middle East, 4, 22, 38, 104, 121, 166, 172, 174
military–industrial complex: Bush administration and Carlyle Group, 109; defense budget, 109
military–media complex, 11, 91, 92, 100, 110, 167, 201
Miranda v. Arizona, 210
missing children problem, 65
morality plays, 14, 60, 186
moral panic, 30; process (ideology), 29
Murrow, Edward R., 205
Musa, Said, 23

narrative, 12, 134, 160. *See* accounts
nationalism, 14, 39, 90, 186

National Rifle Association (NRA), 96–97

national security, 26, 138, 139, 165, 210; Nixon abuse and propaganda, 26

Nazi Germany, 26

neoconservatism, 20

net logic, 135

news sources, 50, 83, 93, 110, 114, 115, 117, 127, 131, 146, 161, 169, 170, 171, 176, 178, 179, 184, 185; coverage of PNAC, 169; defining the situation for war, 165; Fairness and Accuracy in Reporting (FAIR), 118, 177; key stories ignored, 118; McChesney comparison to *Pravda*, 118; news management, 118; and the politics of fear, 117

9/11, 4, 6, 7, 9, 11, 12, 18, 19, 24, 27, 32, 34, 36, 37, 44, 45, 67, 68, 70, 82, 85, 88, 89, 92–96, 97, 102, 110, 111, 116, 119, 120–24, 126, 128, 141, 142, 143, 161, 162, 165, 166, 170, 173–76, 178, 181, 182, 183, 190, 204, 212, 214

Nixon, Richard, 5, 21, 26

Noriega, Manuel, 159. *See* Panama

Nuremberg trials, 180

O'Neill, Paul, 164

"othering," 115

Panama, 16, 27, 28, 167; Operation Just Cause, 27

panoptic governance, 23

paradox of Internet security, 155

Patriot Act, 4, 17, 21, 27, 101, 143, 144, 145, 213; Ashcroft, John, 145; civil liberties, 143; President George W. Bush, 144

patriotic packaging, 3

Piestewa, Lori: compared with Tillman, 188–89

PNAC, 4, 12, 157; *Harper's Magazine* coverage, 167; lack of news coverage, 167; *Mein Kampf*, 164; news sources, 169; some members, 169,

PNAC discourse, 169; imperialism and empire, 172

politics of fear, 1–47, 68, 110, 113, 114, 117, 119, 120, 123, 126, 127, 129, 130, 131, 132, 185, 199–205, 207–20; citizenship, 211; combating, 220; context, 29; context and citizenship, 219; cultural narratives, 212; defined, 15, 208; fearmongering, 35; marketing rights, 220; media and schools, 32; news coverage, 120; popular culture, 117, 130; religion, 39; Tasers at school, 31; universities benefit, 35; university courses, 37

popular culture, 2, 8, 10, 11, 14, 21, 34, 38, 40, 50, 51, 54, 55, 61, 62, 70, 72, 74, 79, 85, 88, 91, 95, 102, 110, 113, 115, 123, 125, 130, 150, 177, 186, 204, 209, 212, 213, 220

postjournalism, 59, 182; portjournalism era defined, 181

Powell, Colin, 4, 69, 105, 118, 161, 168, 175, 177, 181

power, 1, 17, 18, 22, 24, 25, 26, 27, 48, 49, 50, 59, 66, 72, 86, 88, 90, 102, 110, 117, 128, 134, 136, 140, 161, 168, 169, 171, 172, 173, 174, 183, 185, 194, 207, 208, 210, 214, 215, 216, 219, 221; defined, 15, 72

prisoners, 69, 70, 188

problem frame, 60, 61, 84, 116, 130

profiling, 110, 217

programming, 61, 183, 184

Project for a New American Century. *See* PNAC

Project for Excellence in Journalism, 75

propaganda, 1–40, 45, 56, 68, 74, 88–95, 101–31, 157ff; Clark and Knowlton promote Gulf War, 29; consuming for victory, 88; mimetic war, 90; Nazis in WWII, 90 (*see also* Goebbels, Josef); news sources, 113; Ogilvy and Mather, 112; Pentagon controls visuals of dead soldiers, 29; political context, 164

public opinion: Iraq War, 162; monitoring citizens, 140; public opinion polls, 78, 140, 162, 204

punishment, 75, 115, 140, 212, 213

qualitative content analysis, 12
qualitative document analysis, 9, 119
Quayle, Dan, 4, 170
Qutb, Sayeed, 18

Racketeer Influenced and Corrupt
Organizations Act (RICO), 25. *See
also* Azscam
Rather, Dan, 17, 21, 37, 55, 77, 100, 101,
166, 207, 214
Reagan, Ronald, 5, 20, 26, 28, 68, 164,
187; acting and audience, 187;
Reagan Doctrine, 20
rendition, 70, 195, 219
resistance strategies, 217
retrospective interpretation, 189
Rice, Condoleezza, 171, 175, 181
risk and risk society, 1, 11, 15, 62, 73,
77, 79, 82, 84, 94, 104, 111, 114, 116,
128, 129, 134, 136, 140, 143, 149,
150, 154, 155, 208; "policing the
risk society," 135; politics of fear,
202
Rome, Jim, 185, 191
Rwanda, 22

Schmitt, Gary, 169, 170
Schroeder, Mary (judge, Ninth
Circuit): rejects surveillance, 142
security industry, 35. *See also* uniforms
September 11. *See* 9/11
social construction of reality, 72, 116
social control, 1, 9, 12, 15, 16, 17, 27, 30,
33, 36, 38, 42, 47, 56, 64, 65, 82, 113,
123, 134, 136, 138, 140, 141, 153, 155,
208, 209, 214, 217, 221; irony, 216;
language, 213; rituals of control,
131; socialization, 211; sociology
and the university, 34
social policy, 73, 160
social sciences, 36
sport and propaganda, 185
stenography journalism, 184
Strauss, Leo, 18–20; *Gunsmoke*, 19;
Perry Mason, 19
Super Bowl, 85, 106, 107; Ogilvy and
Mather drug message, 107

surveillance, 4, 12, 16, 26, 31, 33, 64, 66,
67, 83, 85, 94, 101ff; auto, 218;
biometric screening, 216; borders,
215; cameras and safety, 33; FBI and
CIA spying on citizens, 26;
institutionalized, 21; Schroeder,
Mary, 142; of students, 33;
technology, 214; unintended
consequences, 33, 156
Sutherland, Kiefer, 70
symbolic boundaries, 59, 72, 80
symbolic dominance, 18
symbolic interaction, 49, 186
symbols, 6, 8, 39, 40, 45, 51, 95, 113,
114, 115, 117, 127, 158, 159, 187,
204–5, 211, 213, 217; manipulating
meanings, 22

Tasers, 31
terrorism, 2; advertising industry, 95;
art project, 116; countries against,
107; critics attacked, 103; defined,
23; gun industry, 97; hoaxes, 116;
identity, 89; Kyl's bill, 95; military
spending, 108; 9/11 and, 1–16;
opposition perceived as terrorist
behavior, 107; propaganda and
drugs, 85; state sponsored, 24
terrorism discourse, 129
terrorism of abject poverty, 23
"three strikes law," 75
Tillman, Pat, 14, 185ff; hero
construction, 191; mainstream
press, 197; memorial services,
195–96; military lies and
propaganda, 192; poster
controversy, 200–201; retrospective
interpretation, 189
torture, 23, 24, 69, 70, 103, 188, 218,
219; Dershowitz, Alan, 103
tough talk, 5
tracking discourse, 11
Triangle Boy, 147, 148; could benefit
terrorism, 147

uniforms, 10, 16, 31, 35, 39, 40, 41, 42,
43, 44, 45, 180, 203–4, 205, 209;

appearance of order, 41; contrary
   evidence, 41; Dieter Troster case, 43;
   flags and nationalism, 43; identity
   and the other, 41; students protest,
   42

victim/victimization, 7, 12, 23, 60;
   collective identity, 111; identity, 73;
   popular culture, 74
Vietnam War, 96, 178
voyeurs, 135, 155

Walsh, John, 65
war programming, 14, 157, 158, 159,
   160, 165, 171, 179, 180, 181, 182, 183,
   184, 209, 221; sequence, 158
Watergate, 21, 26, 27
Wein, Lawrence, 215
Wolfowitz, Paul, 4, 19, 168, 169
words of fear, 119; in news coverage,
   120
World Trade Center, 95, 111, 219; relief
   funds, 98, 99. *See also* 9/11

About the Author

David L. Altheide is Regents' Professor in the School of Justice and Social Inquiry at Arizona State University, where he has taught for thirty-one years. A sociologist who uses qualitative methods, his work has focused on the role of mass media and information technology for social control. His theoretical and methodological statements on the relevance of the mass media for sociological analysis include *An Ecology of Communication: Cultural Formats of Control* (1995) and *Qualitative Media Analysis* (1996). Another recent book, *Creating Fear: News and the Construction of Crisis* (2002), focuses on the news media's constructions of a discourse of fear and the social consequences of this. This book received the 2004 Cooley Award as the best book for the year in the tradition of symbolic interaction from the Society for the Study of Symbolic Interaction. Dr. Altheide also won this award in 1986 for his book *Media Power*. He has also applied qualitative research designs to investigate the nature and process of educational reform, with particular emphasis on school context and culture. Dr. Altheide's contributions to social science were recognized when he received the 2005 George Herbert Mead Award from the Society for the Study of Symbolic Interaction.